Heavenl

From Darkness Into Light

By

Shaykh Nazim Adil Al-Haqqani

Foreword By

Shaykh Muhammad Hisham Kabbani

INSTITUTE FOR SPIRITUAL AND CULTURAL ADVANCEMENT

Library of Congress Cataloging-in-Publication Data

Published and Distributed by:
Institute for Spiritual and Cultural Advancement

17195 Silver Parkway, #401
Fenton, MI 48430 USA
Tel: (888) 278-6624
Fax:(810) 815-0518
Email: staff@naqshbandi.org
Web:
http://www.naqshbandi.org

First Edition June 2013
ISBN: 978-1-938058-20-2

Shaykh Nazim Adil al-Haqqani (right) with his disciple of fifty years, Shaykh Muhammad Hisham Kabbani. Head of the world's largest Naqshbandi Sufi spiritual order, Shaykh Nazim is known for his life-altering lessons in how to discipline the ego, reach a state of spiritual surrender, and achieve true liberation from the bondage of worldly distraction and pursuit. Shaykh Hisham Kabbani, Shaykh Nazim's deputy, has accompanied the venerable shaykh on his many visits to various regions of the world, where they have met with political and religious leaders, media, and throngs of common folk.

CONTENTS

FOREWORD

Bismillahi-r-Rahmani-r-Rahim
In the Name of God, the Most Beneficent, the Most Merciful

All praise is due to God Almighty, Allah the Exalted and Boun-
teous and the most fluent, abundant and sweet praise and blessings
be upon His perfect servant, the mercy to all creation and exemplar
of perfect character, ethics and morality Prophet Muhammad 鑾,[1]
and upon his family and Companions.

This book is a compendium of *sohbets* or spiritual discourses by
our master—chief of saints and reviver of the Prophetic path to divine enlightenment, teacher of millions and worldwide leader of the
Naqshbandi-Haqqani Sufi Order, Mawlana Shaykh Muhammad
Nazim Adil al-Haqqani, may God grant him health and long life.

In this particular selection of discourses, Mawlana Shaykh
Nazim emphasizes the importance of spiritual development and the
need for a disciplined practice in order to achieve any progress on
the Path. Without discipline, he illustrates, our soul is left to the
hands of its enemies, from within and without, and is defenseless to
prevent its own destruction. Therefore, throughout these discourses,
Mawlana Shaykh emphasizes the need to develop the spiritual
strength and capabilities to defend one's spiritual side from the un-
ceasing attacks of its "natural enemies", the four negative elements in
every human being: the selfish ego, desire for the world, carnal de-
sires and Satan.

---

[1] 鑾 stands for *"Salla-Llahu 'alayhi wa sallam,"* meaning, "Allah's peace and blessings be
upon him," the Islamic invocation for Prophet Muhammad 鑾.

Attending an interfaith conference recently, Mawlana Shaykh was asked the question by the Orthodox Pope: "Why are troubles increasing in our time?" In his famously pithy manner, Shaykh Nazim replied, "did Satan take a vacation?" In a similar vein, in this book, Mawlana Shaykh dwells on the interference of Satan in the lives of mankind today and the many remedies available to those who seek spiritual solutions. Utterly pragmatic, Mawlana Shaykh does not suffer fools who refuse to do the spiritual work needed to prevent their lives from sliding down the slippery slope of negativity, into spiritual affliction, depression and possibly even self-destruction. Rather he demands they face their problems head on and seek the spiritual remedies needed to pick themselves up, reverse self-loathing and self-pity and to raise the bar of spiritual gamesmanship to seek not only normalcy but further themselves to attain championship status in the spiritual realm.

May God bless you as you pick up this volume and read some of the holy teachings my master has brought to light. It is well known in the Naqshbandi Sufi tradition, that pure words of guidance are able to elevate the reader to the stations and states described simply through the blessed character, *baraka*, of the one authorized to teach them. Further, these teachings will remain with you and part of you in this life and on, into the hereafter.

I am only a student yet I have been learning from my teacher Mawlana Shaykh Nazim, who, despite his 93 years of age—may God grant him long life—is still incredibly active spreading the teachings that come to his heart from the spiritual "central headquarters." What I saw and learned from my master I cannot express because those fountains are always pouring forth, continuously flowing. The hearts of such saints are like waterfalls: giving always and they are not asking anything from their students but only asking to give.

As the world around us seems to slide further into disarray, in a time when negativity and doubt plague the hearts of even the sincerest seekers, the faithful of all beliefs seek a beacon to lead them to a divine shelter of peace and protection. Presented in this volume are essential aspects of a spiritual discipline which dates back to the time when Prophet Muhammad delivered the divine message—a message preserved by Sufi masters over forty generations.

In these times when Islam is more and more visible on the world stage, it is hoped through this humble work that readers will come to better understand the true teachings of Islam, namely, the universal endorsement to practice moderation and follow the middle course, to hold patience, to uphold tolerance and respect for others, to approach conflict resolution via peaceful means, to condemn all forms of terrorism, and above all, to love God, appreciate His Divine favors, and strive in His Divine service. The greatest Islamic teaching is that there is no higher station than to serve the Lord Almighty.

Shaykh Muhammad Hisham Kabbani
Fenton, Michigan
May 8, 2013

INTRODUCTION

Endless praise and thanks be to God Most High, who guides His servants to His light by means of other servants of His whose hearts He illuminates with His Divine love.

Since the beginning of human history, God Most High has conveyed His revealed guidance to mankind through His prophets and messengers, beginning with the first man, Adam ﷾. The prophetic line includes such well-known names as Noah, Abraham, Ishmael, Isaac, Jacob, Joseph, Lot, Moses, David, Solomon, and Jesus, peace be upon them all, ending and culminating in Muhammad, the Seal of the Prophets ﷺ, a descendant of Abraham ﷾, ﷾who brought the final revelation from God to all mankind.

But although there are no longer prophets upon the earth, the Most Merciful Lord has not left His servants without inspired teachers and guides. *Awliya*—holy people or saints—are the inheritors of the prophets. Up to the Last Day, these "friends of God," the radiant beacons of truth, righteousness and the highest spirituality, will continue in the footsteps of the prophets, calling people to their Lord and guiding seekers to His glorious Divine Presence.

One such inspired teacher, a shaykh or *murshid* of the Naqshbandi Sufi Order, is Shaykh Nazim Adil al-Qubrusi al-Haqqani. A descendant not only of the Holy Prophet Muhammad ﷺ but also of the great Sufi masters 'Abul Qadir Gilani and Jalaluddin Rumi, Shaykh Nazim was born in Larnaca, Cyprus, in 1922 during the period of British rule of the island. Gifted from earliest childhood with an extraordinarily spiritual personality, Shaykh Nazim received his spiritual training in Damascus at the hands of Maulana Shaykh 'Abdullah ad-Daghestani (fondly referred to as "Grandshaykh"), the mentor of such well-known figures as Gurjieff and J. G. Bennett, over a period of forty years.

Before leaving this life in 1973, Grandshaykh designated Shaykh Nazim as his successor. In 1974, Shaykh Nazim went to London for the first time, thus initiating what was to become a yearly practice during the month of Ramadan up to 1990s. A small circle of followers began to grow around him, eagerly taking their training in the ways of Islam and *tariqah* at his hands.

From this humble beginning, the circle has grown to include thousands of *murids* or disciples in various countries of the world, among whom are to be found many eminent individuals, both religious and secular. Shaykh Nazim is a luminous, tremendously impressive spiritual personality, radiating love, compassion and goodness. He is regarded by many of his *murids* as the *qutub* or chief saint of this time.

The shaykh teaches through a subtle interweaving of personal example and talks ("Associations" or *sohbets*), invariably delivered extempore according to the inspirations that are given to him. He does not lecture, but rather pours out from his heart into the hearts of his listeners such knowledge and wisdoms as may change their innermost beings and bring them toward their Lord as His humble, willing, loving servants.

Shaykh Nazim's language and style are unique, so eloquent, moving and flavorful that not only do his teachings seem inspired but also his extraordinary use of words. His *sohbets* represent the teachings of a twentieth century Sufi master, firmly grounded in Islamic orthodoxy, speaking to the hearts of the seekers of God of any faith tradition from his own great, wide heart, in a tremendous outpouring of truth, wisdom and divine knowledge which is surely unparalleled in the English language, guiding the seeker toward the Divine Presence.

The sum total of Shaykh Nazim's message is that of hope, love, mercy and reassurance. In a troubled and uncertain world in which old, time-honored values have given place to new ones of confused origins and unclear prospects, in which a feeling heart and thinking mind is constantly troubled by a sense of things being terribly disordered and out of control, in which the future seems forebodingly dark and uncertain for humanity, he proclaims God's love and care for His servants, and invites them to give their hearts to Him.

Shaykh Nazim holds out to seekers the assurance that even their smallest steps toward their Lord will not go unnoticed and unresponded to. Rather than threatening sinners with the prospect of eternal Hell, he offers hope of salvation from the Most Merciful Lord, and heart-warming encouragement and incentive for inner change and growth. As one who has traversed every step of the seeker's path and reached its pinnacle, he offers both inner and practical guidelines for attaining the highest spiritual goals.

This book consists of Shaykh Nazim's talks from the February of 2002 through April. Each of these talks is entirely extempore, as Shaykh Nazim never prepares his words but invariably speaks according to inspirations coming to his heart.

In keeping with the shaykh's methodology—the methodology of the prophets, particularly of the Last Prophet, Muhammad, peace be upon him and upon them all, and of the Qur'an itself—of reinforcing vital lessons by repetition and reiteration, the same themes and anecdotes recur again and again. The talks seem to come in unannounced clusters, centering around a primary theme, which develops and evolves according to the spiritual state of the listeners. Thus, Shaykh Nazim may cite the same verse or *hadith*, or tell the same tale on different occasions, each time reinforcing a slightly different aspect of the eternal message of love and light which is Islam.

The shaykh's talks are interspersed with words and phrases from Arabic and other Islamic languages. These are translated either in the text itself, in footnotes the first time they occur, or, for general and recurrent terms, in the Glossary at the end of this volume. Qur'anic verses quoted in the text have been referenced for easy access.

Every attempt has been made to retain the shaykh's original language with minimal editing. However, some inadvertent errors may have found their way into the text. For these, we ask Allah's forgiveness and your kind indulgence. May He fill your heart with light and love as you read and reflect upon these inspired words, and guide you safely to His Exalted Divine Presence.

PUBLISHER'S NOTE

Shaykh Nazim is fluent in Arabic, Turkish and Greek, and semi-fluent in Engish. Over three decades, his lectures have been transated into twenty or more languages, and to date have reached the furthest corners of the globe. We sincerely hope the reader will appreciate the author's unique language style, which has been painstakingly preserved in this work.

As some of the terms in this book may be foreign, to assist the reader we have provided transliterations, as well as a detailed glossary.

NOTES

The following symbols are universally recognized and have been respectfully included in this work:

The symbol ﷺ represents *sall-Allahu 'alayhi wa sallam* (Allah's blessings and greetings of peace be upon him), which is customarily recited after reading or pronouncing the holy name of Prophet Muhammad ﷺ.

The symbol ؑ represents *'alayhi 's-salam* (peace be upon him/her), which is customarily recited after reading or pronouncing the holy names of the other prophets, family members of Prophet Muhammad ﷺ, the pure and virtuous women in Islam, and the angels.

The symbol ؆/؇ represents *radi-Allahu 'anhu/ 'anha* (may Allah be pleased with him/her), which is customarily recited after reading or pronouncing the holy names of Companions of the Prophet ﷺ.

1

In the Name of Allah, The Beneficent and The Munificent

This, my English, is strange English. Not everyone can understand because, *subhanallah*, meanings are coming to my heart, and when running in my heart to give to you, I am using any means – from here, from there - bringing any word which may be useful.

I am like a person waiting for water to run out from the faucet. Then, when suddenly it comes, and he knows the water is going to be turned off, stop running, he may take any container – with a no-good shape, broken on one side, or anything he may find there – quickly bringing them to take that water and store it. Therefore, when meanings are coming to my heart, I am trying to explain with any word, which you may understand or not. But you must understand, because we have a saying, "Listeners must be more wise than speakers." Therefore, when inspiration comes, we must explain.

They are living words, not plastic – bananas, plastic; apples, plastic, and grapes. Even if the shapes are not much, they are living, real. When you are going to arrange them in measures, good system; when you are going to be engaged by outside forms, you are losing meanings.

1

CONCERNING CHRISTMAS AND NEW YEAR CELEBRATIONS

Bismillahi-r-Rahmani-r-Rahim.

As salamu 'alaikum![2]

For about one week I have not been strong enough to speak to you, and people are rushing at me. *Alhamdulillah,*[3] today my Lord granted me a little bit of power to address you. May Allah bless His most beloved servant, most glorious servant, Sayyidina Muhammad ﷺ,[4] through whom we are in existence.[5]

---

[2]"Peace be upon you," the Islamic greeting.

[3]Praise be to Allah.

[4]*"Sayyidina"* means "Sir," or, in this context, "Our master," a title used for prophets and other holy people.

[5]The above symbol stands for *"Sallallahu 'alayhi wa sallam,"* meaning, "May Allah's peace and blessings be upon him." The words, "through whom we are in existence" relate to the following *hadith,* reported by 'Abdullah ibn 'Abbas:

> Allah revealed to the prophet Jesus ﷺ , "O Jesus, believe in Muhammad and order your community to do so. If Muhammad were not in existence, I would not have created Adam, nor would I have made Heaven or Hell." (Hakim, Abu ash-Shaykh)

A'udhu bil-Lahi min ash-Shaytan-i-rajim. Bismillahi-r-Rahmani-r-Rahim.[6] Allah Almighty is first of all warning, "O people, O My servants, beware of Shaytan,[7] beware of Shaytan!"

Up to today, I have never seen a sign saying, "O people, beware of Shaytan," but in so many houses you may find a sign, "Beware of the dog." That means dogs are more, much more important than Shaytan.

They are saying, "Beware of the dog!" Why are not those who are leaders or guides warning, saying to people, "Beware of Shaytan"? Therefore, we are asking to follow and listen and obey our Lord's advice. He created us and is warning us, "Beware of Shaytan!"

Now, we are saying *"Bismillahi-r-Rahmani-r-Rahim."* The first, first *tawaqudh*, awakening, is to say *"Bismillahi-r-Rahmani-r-Rahim."* That prevents Shaytan from reaching you.

We are weak people, coming here. Among billions of people, a handful of people are coming here. But the sound of *Haqq*, Truth, can be heard throughout East and West, that the Lord is saying, "O My servants, beware of Shaytan!"

If they are not hearing it today, tomorrow they must hear it, or after tomorrow or after that. Today, we are here, a handful of people from different places of this world, from different countries, different races, different colours, different languages; we are here. And today is a holy day.[8]

---

[6] I take refuge with Allah from Satan the accursed. In the name of Allah, the Beneficent, the Merciful.

[7] Satan.

[8] January 1, 2008.

"Holy day"—it is not good to say a "holy day" [for New Year's Day], yet this is, for all people, when they are not working, a holy day. "Holy day" means to give yourself that day to holy things, to make Allah Almighty happy with you. *That* is a holy day, not the day when people are disobedient to their Lord but they say, "This is a holiday." No, that is Shaytan's holiday!

Now, today, there is a speciality throughout East and West, including the Islamic world, including Muslims. [9] What is that? They are saying, "Today is the first of a new year."

What is New Year, a new-born year, 2008? They are inventing this. Today is simply the first of January of 2008. Just before today, last night, it was the last night, they are saying, of 2007. I don't know from where people are making up such a thing.

Perhaps it was something in Christianity. Even Christians, they are coming to each other with wrong ideas about the birthdate of Jesus. Some of them are saying, "It was the twenty-fifth of December"; some others saying another, another, another thing. And all historians, they know that no one was expecting that there would come such a person and he would be a prophet, surrounded by *khawariq, mu'jizat*, miraculous powers, miracles. No one was expecting him.

And no one knew that Sittna Maryam ﷺ[10] was carrying a baby—no, because it was well-known that she was unmarried and she had been given to the Lord's service.[11] Therefore, it was impossible

---

[9]The Shaykh is reflecting on the situation in the Muslim world where a number of people, including Muslims, have begun to celebrate Christmas and New Year, in imitation of western nations, without reflecting on the meaning of what they are doing.

[10]Our lady Mary, peace be upon her.

[11]See Holy Qur'an, 3:35, 37, 42-43.

4

for anyone to follow her to where she went to give birth to that ba-by[12]—no, the contrary. When people heard that, they were so an-gry.[13] Their nation, Banu Isra'il, the Children of Israel, was very an-gry, and they accused Sayyidina Zakariya[14] 🕮 of adultery, *astagh-firullah!*[15]

Therefore, it was never written in any history book that Jesus Christ was born on this night or that night. No *dalil,* no proof for them! Therefore, it is, from the base, nonsense. Such a thing can't be believed! And historians, they never write such things if they do not have close to one hundred per cent certainty in their hearts. All of them were written afterwards, but yet they are saying, "This night or that night."

Yes, if they accept that in earlier times it *was* a holy night—a ho-ly night, not a dancing night, not for doing every bad thing that Heavens prohibits and curses. It is not such a night! If it really *was* that night, it is a holy night, and Christians must come to their churches or their monasteries and everywhere that they are praying. They must come, they must give their thanks to Allah Almighty and ask for forgiveness.

That is suitable for such a heavenly event—to say, "O our Lord, thanks to You that You sent us a guide to reach Your Divine Pres-ence." *That* is suitable. But now, what are they doing? What are they doing?

They are doing every cursed action and they are saying, "This is a free night for us to do everything!" Everywhere, people are drunk.

---

[12]This is clear from the Qur'anic statement that Mary *"conceived him and she retired with him to a remote place"* (19:22) to give birth.

[13]Holy Qur'an, 19:27-28.

[14]The prophet Zechariah.

[15]I seek Allah's forgiveness.

They are saying, "This night is free to do everything. We can do everything!" Okay, *you* can do, but what about Muslims?

[Here, Maulana speaks in Turkish, addressing Turks.] "Eh! We celebrated it in our house. We prepared a turkey, laid the table, dressed in new clothes. We danced, we congratulated each other for the New Year; we did everything. No money is left in our pockets. We woke up in the dirt next morning."

What about the Muslim world? They are following the Christian world. On a page in the Turkish prayer calendar, the meaning of a *hadithi sharif*[16] is written:

> *Bismillahi-r-Rahmani-r-Rahim. Qal an-Nabi, 'alayhi-s-salat wa-s-salam, la tatba'una sunan man kana qablakum shibran shibran wa dhira'a dhira'a hatta, lau dakhalu juhra dab, ta-bi'tumuhum.'*[17]

That is a *mu'jizah*, miracle, that the Prophet ﷺ was warning his nation about future days that it would reach. Rasul-Allah[18] was saying ﷺ, "O my nation and O my Companions, you are going to follow the ways of those people—first, the Jewish people, second, the Christians. Both of them, they passed away before you." The Old Testament of the Jewish people, they left it. The New Testament, Christians, they are changing it every time, and they are doing every bad thing and saying, "Our nation's way, that is the true way."

---

[16]A noble *hadith.*

[17]In the Name of Allah, the Beneficent, the Merciful. The Prophet, Allah's peace and blessings be on him, said, "You will surely follow the practice of those before you span by span, cubit by cubit, until, if they enter a lizard's hole, you will follow." The remainder of the *hadith,* not quoted above, reads, "We [the Companions who were present] said, 'O Messenger of Allah, [do you mean] the Jews and Christians?' He said, "Who, then?" (Bukhari, 9:422)

[18]The Messenger of Allah.

"O my nation," [Rasul-Allah continued], "I am seeing that you you will run after Jewish and Christian ways that are *haram*, prohibited. Allah Almighty never likes it, never accepts it, but you are going to do as they do, following in their footsteps. Where they put their feet, there you will put *your* feet.

There is a creature with small feet but you can't see any bones. It makes its holes, to be in safety from other creatures, so narrow. Only it can enter there because it has no bones. "If they do this, among those people who have been given holy books, you are going to follow them. Step by step, you are going to do as they do." And you see people's clothing; particularly young girls, what they are wearing; it is so narrow, so tight, because it is a new fashion. And Jews and Christians, they are sending this to the Islamic world, to do and to dress in such a way, and saying, "This is a new, new fashion, modern. Modern life, this!"

This is what Prophet was informing us about. Correct or not? The Prophet was saying in powerful words that you are going to do that. *Muhaqqaq, muhaqqaq!*[19] You understand? *"No doubt, you are going to do that!"* Fifteen centuries ago he was informing the world about what we are now doing!

This morning I was asking, "What news? Any news?" And first, the TV was opening from Baghdad—Baghdad, where people are living but there is killing and bombing. And they were all of them in the streets, shouting, drinking, doing every forbidden thing. Look!

---

[19]Unquestionably, definitely, certainly.

If I were to say to them, "Go! There is Sultan Gilani, 'Abdul-Qadir Gilani, *qaddas Allahu sirruhu 'aliya*.[20] Go there and ask him! He is *sultan*.[21] He may send away every *mujrim*, criminal—may send them away in one night!" they would say, "For what would we go there? You still believe in such things?" And they will be punished! The Arab world will be punished! The Islamic world will be punished!

Just now, trees are shedding their leaves. The Islamic world is going to be like this. Beware, beware! O our Lord, don't write our names with such people. Keep us on Your right path!

This is a warning. If anyone is listening, it is for himself. If not listening, there will be a punishment for him or for her.

May Allah forgive us! There are forty powerful people on earth, whose power may be like the power of Sayydina Gilani, Allah bless him. If you can find one of them, he may do as Gilani Hazretleri[22] can do. But they are not looking for them, saying, "This is *khorafa*, this is *asatir*, tales."[23]

Therefore, today, *alhamdulillah*, I am just warning my ego and all of you, also, here: Beware! When a heavenly punishment comes, it is so difficult for it to be taken away. If it reaches, it will finish them.

May Allah forgive us! For the honour of the Seal of Prophets, Sayyidina Muhammad, *sallallahu 'alaihi wa 'ala ahlihi wa sahbihi wa sallam—Fateha!*[24]

---

[20]'Abdul-Qadir Jilani (b. 1077-d. 1166), one of the greatest Islamic saints *(awliya)*, who is buried in Baghdad. The invocation for *awliya*, *"Qaddas Allahu sirruhu 'aliyya,"* following his name means "May Allah sanctify his lofty secret."

[21]*Sultan*: King or a saint of very high rank.

[22]*Hazretleri*: an honorific Turkish title for Islamic saints.

[23]Fairy tales, fables, myths, legends.

[24]May Allah's peace and blessings be on him and on his family and his Companions—*Fateha!* [the opening *surah* (chapter) of the Qur'an].

2

ALLAH'S FIRST WARNING AGAINST SHAYTAN

Welcome! Welcome to you! *A'udhu bil-Lahi min ash-Shaytani-r-rajim. Bismillahi-r-Rahmani-r-Rahim. La haula wa la quwwata illa bil-Lahi-l-'Aliyi-l-'Adhim.*[25]

We are asking forgiveness from Allah Almighty because all of mankind, they are on the wrong way. The wrong way, it is Shaytan's, Satan's, way.

Allah Almighty was warning Adam when he was in Paradise. The first warning was to Sayyidina Adam. He was the first man, Sayyidina Adam, in Paradise, our first father, with Hawa, Eve, *'alayhima salam.*[26]

He created! That is our Lord's biggest blessing, the biggest *ikram*, grant, from Allah. We were not in existence and He created us! And the first man and first woman, for them He prepared Paradise, *subhanallah*, granting them from His divine grants, *ikram*, and never asking anything in return, free. And Allah Almighty, He said to Adam and Eve, "This *Jannatu-l-'Adn*, Eden, it is for you! You are free; you are free. Eat from its fruits, drink from its rivers, enjoy yourselves, and

---

[25]There is no power or might except with Allah, the Most High, the Almighty.
[26]Peace be on the two of them.

you will be here. Only, as your Lord, the Creator, I am asking from you to hear and listen to Me and obey Me.

"All Paradise is for you. Enjoy yourself as you like. Only there is one tree on which I am putting a ban, a banned tree. As I am the Lord and Creator, I am ordering to you: you must not approach that tree and you must not taste from its fruits. I am not asking anything from you. Enjoy!"[27]

And at the same time, Allah Almighty was warning them, saying, "O Adam, when I created you and gave to you from My holy Spirit and dressed you in an honorable dress in which I never dressed any other creature, dressed you and put on your head the crown of being My *khalifa*,[28] you were shining with My divine lights, and I said to the angels, 'Prostrate to Adam, make *sajdah*[29] to him,' you remember that all the angels prostrated to you except one.

"You know that that one is your most terrible and dangerous enemy. Beware of that one! I am putting every protection for you, but that enemy is such a dangerous enemy, wanting to reach you and make you fall in a dark area; to be taken from you lights, heavenly lights; to be taken from you the crown of being My deputy and the glorious, honorable clothes that I am putting on you. His aim is to take this from you and make you like himself. Beware!"

The first warning from Allah Almighty was to Adam. He was addressing Adam, not addressing Eve; no—Adam, because man's

---

[27]The story of Adam's creation and Satan's rebellion, and the fall, repentance and descent to earth of the first pair is told in the following verses of the Qur'an: 2:30-39, 4:117-120, 7:11-27, 15:26-43, 17:61-65, 18:50, 20:115-126, 38:71-85, 55:14-15.

[28]Deputy, vice-gerent.

[29]Prostration.

nature is powerful, and woman's is weak. Therefore, you must, everyone must take their lessons from the first warning. Allah Almighty was addressing Adam, not Eve, and that was the first warning from Allah Almighty. Then *that* happened, or so many things happened, because Sayyidina Adam, peace be upon him, listened to Shaytan, not directly, but through Eve.[30]

That is a big lesson. How are people falling into such a terrible situation now—what is the reason, what was the seed of these troubles? That Shaytan reached to Adam not directly, but through his wife, our first mother.

[Eve was saying (parodies):] "We can taste, we can taste!"

Adam ﷺ: "How can we taste?

"You can do it!" Coming from this side. "O Adam!"

"O my darling!"

"How would it be? What is going to happen if . . .? We must try. O my darling!" Coming from that side. "O my darling, only a taste!" *Tauba, astaghfirullah!*[31]

Adam ﷺ, he was sixty yards tall, not like you; like *this*. "I see that you are not so happy."

"Only one *ısır,* bite! If anything happens, then you don't eat." Eating a bite, a little bit, one bite, Eve doing like this and giving to Adam.

---

[30]The meaning here is that Allah warned Adam not to listen to Shaytan. But Eve, to whom the warning had not been addressed, cajoled Adam into disobedience to the divine command.

[31]Repentance, I seek Allah's forgiveness.

'Wa 'asa Adamu Rabbahu faghawa.'[32] *Astaghfirullah!* Then Allah was saying, "*Ya Adam*, what did you do, not obeying My order, putting My order under your feet? And now you can't be here! You and all of you,[33] quickly get out!" That honourable dress fell off; they were naked, running like this, running like that, to cover themselves. No tree of Paradise [except one] would give them anything of its leaves to cover themselves. Only the fig tree was clothing them.

"Out, quickly! O angels, land them on earth," and in Paradise, they were in lights, heavenly lights. Oh-h-h! "Land them, all of them!"

Adam landed in one place and Eve in another place. "Shaytan, also! Land Shaytan down, not to go around Paradise!" And the one who had made a way for Shaytan to get into Paradise was an angel, the guardian of Paradise, and Allah ordered it to be a snake. "All of them, throw all of them on the earth, to be enemies to each other— all of them!" and the door closed. And that first warning, you can't name a price for what Adam and Eve lost.

Subhanallah, glory be to Allah! Glory be to Allah, He is Allah and we are servants! The first lesson that Allah Almighty gave to Adam and Eve was, "You and your wife are My servants. I am your Lord. You must listen and obey Me! I am the Lord of Heavens! No one can say something and his saying goes over My Will and order. I

---

[32] *"And Adam disobeyed his Lord and erred."* (Qur'an, 20:121)

[33] That is, Adam, Eve, Satan and the snake, through whose mouth Satan had entered into Paradise and addressed Adam.

don't like it! Go down!" *Allahu Akbar! Astaghfirullah! Astaghfirullah, ya Rabbi!*[34]

Then Adam and Eve, when they came together, they had gotten their lessons, 'graduated.' Adam and Eve had graduated, and they were saying to their children, "O our children, beware of Shaytan! We were in Paradise but we did not obey the warning of our Lord, and then, as a punishment, we were thrown out."

And Allah Almighty addressed Adam and Eve: "O Adam, I have sent you out of Paradise and you are mourning." Adam stood on one foot for three hundred years, crying. In Ceylon, Sri Lanka, in that area; he was standing and asking forgiveness from Allah Almighty, for three hundred years crying, crying, and Allah Almighty created those precious stones [of that country] from his teardrops.

Then Almighty accepted their repentance, *tauba*, and gave His blessing to them and said, "O Adam, I have not thrown you out of Paradise forever, no. But I will send to you and to your sons, up to the Last Day, My warning through some of your sons whom I am going to dress in the heavenly dress of being My prophets and deputies. My warning will continue up to the Last Day so that whoever hears My warning and obeys, they will find a way to My Paradise. You will come there. But if they do not take care, to where I will send Shaytan, Hells, I will send them there, also."

That is what happened with the warning, the first warning from Allah Almighty. Up to today, there are still coming some people who are warning about Shaytan. Yet even religious people who are dressing in religious clothes, they aren't able to say to people, "O

---

[34]Allah is Most Great! I seek Allah's forgiveness! I seek Allah's forgiveness, O my Lord!

13

people, beware of Shaytan!" because Shaytan is now in power every-where. If holding an election, Shaytan is one hundred per cent the winner, in power. Now in power on earth, it is shaytanic power, nothing else! If you say anything [against it]—ooh-h, finished; they will take you away. Only those who have been dressed in heavenly protection, never mind for them, but other people, they should be taken away.

Now in power, the Party of Devils—in power everywhere! If you say this, they will be very angry. I am saying, "You are not giv-ing me money, no. I am free to say [what I please]. And I am saying it."

The most important party, most powerful party, winning a hun-dred per cent in every election, it is the shaytanic party, everywhere! But they are saying, "No, we are not a shaytanic party, we are just such-and-such a party." But they are, everywhere, in power, the shaytanic party, graduated by Shaytan! We reject Shaytan and his party. True? If not true, you are going with his party, also! [Laugh-ter.] *Tauba, astaghfirullah, ya Allah*!

That is so! May Allah change it! Are you understanding my English? I am okay!

Shaytan just delivered a declaration two days ago, saying, "I am ordering all mankind who are living on earth—I am your emperor—that you must be prepared for New Year's night! [Mimics:] I am ordering you to prepare yourselves for the celebration of 2008!"

"Huh?"

"If anyone goes in oppositon to my order, they should find themselves in a very bad situation. I am going to cut everything from them that I am granting to you, O mankind!"

Therefore, people are saying, "What is your order, O our Lord?"

"Therefore, you must use my urine. That night, it is free, to make you drunk! All of you must be drunk! I am not accepting anyone on earth, East and West, North to South, not to be drunk! And the secret power of being drunk is because I am putting my urine in it!" *Tauba, astaghfirullah!* [Laughter.]

Allah Allah! I was tired, I was lying down up to *Dhuhr,*[35] but now I am getting power. [Laughter.]

Yes, sir! That is our situation. And then, if we are going to continue, if They[36] give permission, I may speak on that subject because I have graduated on that subject, the first one on earth. I may continue up to next New Year for them. Another urine from Shaytan to them!

May Allah forgive us! O people, beware of Shaytan, beware of Shaytan! *Astaghfirullah, astaghfirullah! Rabbana, dhalamna anfusana wa in lam taghfir lana wa tarhamna, la-nakunanna mina-l-khasirin. Aman, ya Rabb! Aman, ya Rabb!*[37] We are weak, we are weak servants. *Adrikna, ya Rabbana! Adrikna, ya Rabbana!*[38] All shepherds of flocks, they are wolves. *Ya Rabbi, Anta-l-Mubaddil, Anta-l-Mumakkin! "Wa'da Allahu-l-ladhina amanu minkum wa amilu-s-salihati la-*

---

[35]The second prayer of the day, observed in the early afternoon.

[36]Referring to the Naqshbandi *awliya* who have left this life and are the source of Shaykh Nazim's inspirations.

[37]I Allah's forgiveness, I seek Allah's forgiveness! Our Lord, we have wronged ourselves, and if You do not forgive us and have mercy on us, we will be among the lost. Safety, O Lord! Safety, O Lord!

[38]Reach us, O our Lord! (two times).

yastakhlifannahum. . . Wa man kafara ba'da dhalika, fa ulaika humu-l-fasiqun.[39]

That is a holy verse, holy *ayah*, giving to my heart a fresh power because that is the Lord of Heavens' good tidings. "Even now, what is happening, and people are thinking that everything is in their hands through shaytanic powers, I am promising believers that once again before the Day of Resurrection, I will give all power to believers, Muslims."

That must come! That gives me power. Otherwise, I would like to die instantly. But I am asking to reach those days and all of you to reach those bright days, with heavenly powers everywhere covering people, giving pleasure to them, giving honour to them, because Shaytan is making men to be under other people's feet, and *dhulm*, oppression, has covered the whole world. May Allah take it away quickly!

Therefore, as I am seeing now, our Islamic New Year is coming on the tenth of January, 2008. Next week, a week from today, it is going to be the first of our new year, Muharram, and before Muharram, the last day of Dhul-Hijjah should be Tuesday and the first day of Muharrram, Wednesday. Fourteen twenty-eight is finishing, 1429 beginning on Wednesday, and we are hoping that some power will come to Islam, to true ones.

And you must try to be defenders of truth, *haqqani*. *Haqqani* ones should be happy through this year—we hope this—and their *batil*, false, regimes will fall down, and the truth castle should rise up and the flags of truth, flags of the skies, will be put there. It is from

---

[39]You are the Changer, You are the Strengthener! *"Allah has promised those who believe among you and do righteous deeds that He will surely grant them succession [to authority on earth]. . . . But whoever disbelieves after that—then those are the defiantly disobedient."* (24:55)

Sunnah[40] to fast the last day of the passing year and at the beginning of the new year, and the Prophet was giving good tidings that if anyone fasts the last day and first day, he or she is going to be like a person fasting the whole year.

May Allah forgive us and send us what we are hoping for. *Fateha,* for the honour of the Seal of Prophets ﷺ!

I was not thinking to say anything, I was so weak, but They are making me to address you in such a way. It is not something from my thinking, no. Directly, that is a channel from Heavens to our Grandshaykh,[41] and he is granting to me.

Shaykh Adnan Efendi is sending his *salams.* I was a little bit late today, but just as I was coming, he was phoning to me. He is a *qutub*[42] and Shaykh Hisham Efendi is also a *qutub.* He said to me that he is with me.

Shaykh Adnan Efendi was in *Hajj;* everyone running and kissing his hands and saying, "O Shaykh Nazim!"

"No Shaykh Nazim!"

"No, you are Shaykh, grandshaykh!" kissing him, asking something from him.

He was saying, "What am I going to give to you? If I give you small, small bits from my clothes, I am going to be naked!" Thou-

---

[40] The Prophet's practice.

[41] "Grandshaykh" refers to Maulana Shaykh 'Abdullah ad-Daghestani, Shaykh Nazim's shaykh, who passed away in 1973.

[42] A spiritual 'pole,' one of the highest ranking *awliya* (saints) in the spiritual hierarchy.

sands of people were coming to him because he was dressed in more greatness, Adnan Efendi, *masha'Allah!*[43]

There are seven big ones,[44] the first, Shaykh Adnan Efendi, may Allah bless him. *Aman, ya Rabbi!*[45] *Fateha!*

In Lebanon, oh-h-h, rain and snow and blowing, ooh-h-h-h! Trablus [Tripoli]—I like that place, a holy place, powerful place, by the *barakat*[46] of Shamu-sh-Sharif.[47] I was first there in 1944. I was at that time twenty-two years old.

For the appearance of the Sahibu-z-Zaman[48] and Sayyidina 'Isa,[49] *'alayhima as-salam*, peace be upon them; for the fall of the tyrants, the victory of *Ahlu-l-Islam*[50] and opening the world for Islam— *Fateha! Allah Allah!*

---

[43] As Allah willed.

[44] Radiant, illuminated ones.

[45] Safety/security, O my Lord!

[46] Blessing.

[47] Holy Damascus, whose sanctity derives from it being the place of resurrection, the resting place of thousands of Companions of the Prophet (s) and saints, the place which the Prophet (s) described as the sanctified land of God, and its connection with the prophecies concerning the Mahdi, the divinely-appointed spiritual leader whose coming at the End-Time of this world, preceding the second coming of Jesus, is mentioned in many *ahadith*.

[48] The Master of the Time, the Mehdi.

[49] Our master, Jesus.

[50] The People of Islam.

3

ABOUT BEING TRUTH DEFENDERS

As-salamu 'alaikum! Dastur, ya Sayyidi, ya Sultanu-l-Awliya. Madad, ya Rijal-Allah! Madad, ya Rijal-Allah![51]

A'udhu bil-Lahi min as-Shaytani-r-rajim. Bismillahi-r-Rahmani-r-Rahim. La haula wa la quwwata illa bi-Lahi-l-'Aliyi-l-'Adhim. Madad, ya Sultanu-l-Awliya!

This is the last Sunday of the passing *Hijri* calender.[52] One thousand four hundred twenty-eight years are just going to finish, and we hope that Tuesday will be the last day and Wednesday will be the first day of the holy month of Muharram for the new *Hijri* calendar, beginning. May Allah forgive us!

Allah Almighty is asking His servants for servanthood to Him, Almight. But now among the people who are living on earth—maybe six billion people—if, among six billion people, if we can find even sixty million who are trying to be servants to the Lord of Heavens, to our Creator, we will be happy. But, including me, also, we are not trying to be good servant to our Lord.

---

[51]Support, O men of Allah!

[52]The Islamic lunar calendar.

Everyone now is trying to be a servant of Shaytan, and Shaytan, he is our most terrible and dangerous enemy. But people are saying, "No, no! Perhaps that is our first, best friend. We will be with him. In what he is calling us to do, we are finding refreshment, we are finding pleasure. Therefore, we are trying to follow him."

Turks are in such a way, Arabs are in such a way; Pakistan is in such a way, Iran in such a way, Iraq in such a way, Syria in such a way, Egypt in such a way. The whole Islamic world's people, they are saying, "We must follow the shaytanic way and we must try to be the best followers of Shaytan" (not saying "Shaytan" but "Our king, our most important leader").

Every leader who is leading people now in the twenty-first century, all leaders have just been graduated by Shaytan. They should be unhappy that I am saying this. Yes, it is true! *La'nat Allah 'ala-l-kadhibin,* Allah curses those who are lying!

We are not lying. *Insha'Allah,*[53] I am not cheating you, I am not calling you to a dark way. I am only, every time, asking, "O our Lord, keep us on Your lighted way."

Two ways—a lighted way leading to Paradise, a dark way leading people to Hells. And up to today, these problems are mounting, mounting. But I am seeing that they have reached the limit of this period, this period that is mentioned in our Prophet's holy *hadith.*

There is a limit for every period. This is the period of tyrants that is just mentioned in the Holy Qur'an and in the sayings, *hadith,* of Rasul-Allah, peace be upon him. The Prophet was saying ﷺ, "I am walking on a way. I am seeing what is in front of me, where my way is reaching. And also I am leading or I am guiding my followers on a lighted way, leading you to Paradise." And anyone who is fol-

---

[53]God willing.

lowing the Seal of Prophets, he or she is on the lighted way here, leading them to Paradise.

Everywhere there are elections; everywhere you are finding them. [Parodies:] elections in Kenya, elections in Argentina, elections in Pakistan, elections in Turkey. Eh! Somalia, internal wars; yes.

Everywhere, some people are in power, some people are in opposition. That is a shaytanic scenario that people are making. "You are in power, we are in opposition. Today they are in power, but we must not be silent. When they are in power, we must run in the streets, saying, 'Oh, you are the wrong people! You must come down, we must come to power!'" Then when they are coming to power, those people who are now the opposition, they are beginning, "Eh, you are all wrong!"

Allah's curse will come on them. *Hasha*![54] Therefore, no rest for people. When the opposition comes to power, the people who were in power before them get to be against them, coming in the streets. The streets are never going to be empty! This is the time of tyrants because they never listen to heavenly orders, they never take care about the commands of the Lord of Heavens![55]

---

[54]Never! God forbid!

[55]Referring to a *hadith* stating that at the beginning of the Islamic era, the rule of the Islamic *ummah* (nation) would first be in the hands of caliphs, then of kings, then of princes, and finally of tyrants.

The Prophet of Allāh ﷺ said:

After me come caliphs, and after the caliphs come princes, and after princes there will be kings and after the kings, there will be tyrants. And after the tyrants a man from My House will fill the earth with justice, and after him is al-Qahtani. By the One who sent me with the Truth! Not a word less. Na'im bin Hammad in "Fitan"

Footnote continued…

21

When there were *sultans* or kings or emperors, there was no opposition. The beasts, the violent animals, they were in Bastille Castle in France. When that opened, the opposition came. Up to today, their descendants have never ended. But the Lord of Heavens has put a limit for them, also, not to be forever going on that way, no. And we hope that the beginning of this new year, *Hijri* year, is going to be their last limit and they can't put one more step on their way. Now they are going to come, coming, coming, coming down.

You may imagine a circle. Bad people, they have reached the top point, and good people, they are at the lowest point of this situation, under the dirty feet of those tyrants. But this circle is always turning, not like a line going straight, but going around, like this. Some of them, it is taking up, some of them are coming from up to down. Now they have reached the topmost point.

You are drivers; all of you drive cars. There is a meter registering and showing your speed. If it is 100 kilometers, as much as you push this [accelerator], 100 can't be 101; 200 is 200, no more. Now their period is not going to be more, but they are doing this [pushing the pedal], uh-h, trying to make it move. Finished; no more! The top point has just moved now. We are beginning to go up, they are beginning to come down. And this circle, its way can't be changed. No, this is it!

Therefore, I hope that this new year, the Islamic year 1429, is going to be the beginning of tyrants finishing, beginning to come down. Their power is going to be less, less, less, less, and our power, true ones', will begin to go up. Therefore, my advice to you is to be truth-defenders—truth-defenders. You must ask for what is true. Truth comes from Heavens; Shaytan is on earth, shaytanic rules for

---

from ‘Abd ar-Rahman bin Qays bin Jabir al-Sadafi, *Kanz al-‘ummāl*, hadith #38704, related by at-Tabarani.

tyrants. Don't be defenders of shaytanic ways or regimes! Try to be defenders of Heavens, heavenly truth. If you are doing that, you should be in safety here and Hereafter. If you are not doing that, then your final station should be in Hells. May Allah forgive us!

O people, now it is wintertime. All trees, they have dropped their leaves and they are sleeping, sleeping, sleeping till springtime. In springtime, a holy command will come to nature, "Wake up! Winter has just passed. Wake up!" And this water, by its Lord's command, will begin to move through the trees about which you were saying, "These trees, they are now dried."

They were thinking that they were dry and they were intending to cut them, but at that time the holy command will come from Heavens to nature, "Flow through the veins of trees by your Lord's command," and that will begin, and buds will begin to be seen. People are saying, "You must not leave this! We must take those buds away." Can't be! Can't be! The holy command has just arrived. They are awakening. No one can make them sleep again.

Now we are in those days. I hope that the beginning of the Islamic year, *Hijri* year, is going to be a command from Heavens to nature, "Wake up! By your Lord's command, wake up!" and what people were thinking had died will begin to awaken. *Masha'Allah!* It should be in such a way that people will think they are living in Paradise.

That will be for a short time, but there should be the appearance of Paradise on earth. That Dajjal,[56] Antichrist, and his group should be taken away and there should remain only believers. Those

---

[56] The arch-deceiver whose coming at the end-time of this world is foretold in numerous *ahadith*.

who are sincere believers, they should remain and the majority should be taken away. Guard yourself!

I am nothing, but, as our Holy Prophet and heavenly orders are saying to make people wake up, this is an *intibah*, warning—a warning to stand up. That means, Don't lie on the railroad tracks because the train is coming, and whomever it finds in its way, it will cut. Wake up!

They are saying, "No, nothing! We are resting here," and the train is coming. Ooh-h, finished! The time is over.

May Allah forgive us! And use your minds and think about your position. Think, "What am I doing?" Think, "For whom am I working? For my Lord, His pleasure, or am I working to make Shaytan pleased with me?" Look! Keep that balance; you should be safe. If not, you are going to finish.

Maybe a handful of people will remain. Doesn't matter! Allah Almighty sent the flood at the time of Noah, peace be upon him, saving from the flood only a handful of people. Their number did not reach one hundred. Only they landed in the Ark.

From that, look! Billions of people have come from those people. Therefore, now Allah Almighty is sending not a flood of water but sending fire. Every nation is preparing more power, more fire, to destroy, inside and outside. No mercy in their hearts; finished! No justice, no mercy!

They are going to finish. Finishing, and then Allah Almighty will send new ones, new ones. In a handful of years, you should find this world full of believers who will say, *"La ilaha illa-Llah. . . ."*

[Maulana makes a short *dhikr*.] *La ilaha illa-Lah, sayyiduna wa nabiyyuna Muhammadu-r-Rasul-Allah.*[57]

May Allah guide us to His lighted way to Paradise. Be patient! Don't run in the streets, don't join those people, or you will bring your punishment on yourself. Curses are coming on those people who are running in the streets—I am sorry to say, like Pakistani people. They are Muslims but they are running in the streets and shouting.

I am saying, "Why? You are Muslims. Why are you running in the streets? Why not going to mosques, to say, *"Ya Rabbi, ya Rabbana,*[58] save us!' What for are you running in the streets? How are you Muslims?" And people with turbans, long beards—for what is this? What is this politics? Politics are shaytanic; everywhere destroying. People are running in the streets, while there are mosques! Go and say, "O our Lord, save us!" *Tauba, ya Rabbi! Bi-hurmati-l-Fateha!*[59]

---

[57]There is no deity except Allah. . . There is no deity except Allah, our master and prophet Muhammad is the Messenger of Allah.

[58]My Lord, our Lord.

[59]Repentance, O my Lord! By the sacredness of *[Surat al-]Fateha!*

4

CARRYING OUT OUR HEAVENLY SERVICE IN THE BEST WAY

A'udhu bil-Lahi min ash-Shaytani-r-rajim. *Bismillahi-r-Rahmani-r-Rahim.* Welcome to you! For what are you coming? For what are you coming?

It is an Association.[60] We are trying to follow the ways of Seal of the Prophets, peace be upon him. We are trying to follow the ways of followers of *Sahabah*, the Companions of Rasul-Allah ﷺ. We are trying to follow the good footsteps of *awliya*. Where they have put their steps, it is a safe, safe step. If not doing that, you should be in a dangerous position.

This is a world, *dunya*. Sometimes we are seeing some operations of armies. They are, for their defense, putting mines under the earth. Can't be seen, can't be known—terrible! If stepping on it, *boom!*—going away! No joking from mines. They are not looking or distinguishing who is stepping on them, a general or an ordinary person from the army. No, anyone. If a king steps, the king goes up; if an emperor, the emperor goes up. Therefore, armies use a *muta-khassis*, a prepared person, an expert, one who knows.

---

[60] *Sohbet* (Arabic, *suhbah*): the gathering of a shaykh with his *murids*, followers.

Now, prophets are the first level people who know that there is danger for mankind, to kill them. A holy order from Heavens is saying, "O My beloved ones, O My messengers, look and try to protect My servants on earth because their most dangerous enemy, Shaytan, is putting so many mines or traps in various places, or bringing hundreds of thousands of tricks to take people to that trap, to that mine." The first order from the Lord of Heavens for all messengers, prophets, peace be upon them, is, "Take care to protect My servants from falling into the trap of Shaytan."

Shaytan is going freely from East to West, West to East, North to South, South to North. He is not in need to carry a passport, no need to use a visa. He is saying, "I am free. Sometimes I am making myself clear for some of my best friends, but mostly I am camouflaging myself among people and they think that I am their first class *nasih*, advisor."

Shaytan is free to go anywhere, even in the K'abah. Yes, even in the K'abah, even in the Prophet's holy *masjid*,[61] yes. 'Arafat,[62] also; everywhere he is free, like newspaper people, when they are showing this newspaper identification card.

[Parodies:] "I have very important work with some V.I.P. people. V.I.P. people are coming here today, and I will look after them to make them to drink more, and they are going to be drunk and they will say, 'Come and make a speech.' I will come and say, 'I am Number One here now. I see that there are so many V.I.P. people, but I think that I am the chief of the V.I.Ps.'

"Yes, O my servants, I was thinking that I would make a good speech for you, but I am not prepared and I do not remember any-

---

[61] The Prophet's Mosque in Medina.

[62] The plain of 'Arafat is the site of the principal rites of *Hajj*, the Pilgrimage.

thing. Bring me another champagne so that I may speak to those donkeys!"

Everywhere, Shaytan is going, making inspection. The chief inspector for mankind, for whomever does not believe in heavenly knowledge and tidings, is Shaytan, looking everywhere. Anywhere there is something about heavenly knowledge or positions, he is saying, "Take that away!" Therefore, Allah Almighty is saying, "You must run away from Shaytan! You must ask for protection."

You must ask for protection. If not, carrying you away, also, like a person looking for a station but not knowing how to read where he is going; getting in the train and going to another place, losing his chance. *Ya Rabbi*, we are running to You from that one! Don't leave us in front of that dangerous enemy. We are weak ones. Therefore, we are saying, *"A'udhu bil-Lahi min ash-Shaytani-r-rajim. Bismillahi-r-Rahmani-r-Rahim."*

What is the title of our Association? That all prophets are calling people to be servants of their Lord, and that is the main point for which men are created. And men must know for what they are in existence, for what they are created.

Now, millions or billions of people believe this, but they do not give enough time or energy for heavenly service. Most people, they do not think about it [at all]; they do not acknowledge anything related to heavenly service. Then, so many people accept that they have been ordered to do heavenly service but they do not give enough care for that service, no. Their most important goal is to reach more, as much as possible of *dunya*. They are doing *some* heavenly service but it is not their main goal. And heavenly service is our most important goal. We have been created for heavenly service. Any doubt?

"Wa ma khalaqtu-l-jinna wal-insa illa li-y'abuduni.[63] I did not create men or jinn for any other purpose than My service—*'ubudiya*, to be workers, servants for My Divine service." Yes. So many people, they are doing this heavenly service. But what was the main purpose of *Sahabah*[64] when they were coming around the holy circle of the holy one, the most holy one? What was their aim, always running and listening?

Although they knew that they had been created for heavenly service, still they were every time coming, running to the Prophet, peace be upon him. Why? They were asking for more, more urging power for themselves for heavenly service. They were thinking to learn, to know what is the best worshipping to our Lord. "How can we do our heavenly service in the best way, to be the best ones?" That is important!

Yes, you may pray five times a day, but five times is not your main goal because, outside of prayer times, you are working, working, giving your full energy for what? For those five times? No!

[Parodies:] "Enough, enough! We have so many things to do. We are directors, we are businessmen, we are this, we are that, important, V.I.P.s. We must look after that. This five times, doesn't matter! We may also pray quickly but running there."

Allah is looking or not looking at what he is saying? "My servant is running to another service, not giving full attention to My heavenly service in which I dressed him, to be an honour for him in *dunya* and in *akhirah*.[65] Look, O angels, at these My servants! Mostly

---

[63]51:56.

[64]The Prophet's Companions—that is, the first generation of Muslims who were physically present with him.

[65]The Hereafter.

29

they are never thinking about heavenly service. Who are they considering?

"And look, some servants are doing heavenly service, but they are giving a very short time." Sometimes they are saying, "*Sunnah*, it is not needed,"[66] like *Salafi*[67] people, not taking much care for *Sunnah* or *zawa'id*[68] that the Prophet, peace be upon him, did, saying, "I am only doing the obligatory prayers. Pray this and go, go and work."

When you leave the work that is for Allah, to where are you running? Who is the foreman of mankind in their service? Foreman Number One, Shaytan, is calling, "U-u-hh!" East and West, they are looking and saying, "What is the order of our boss?"

"Look after my servants, not to give too much time for their prayers. No, try to make them leave prayers completely. If you can't, you must grant them a very short time for heavenly service." They are finishing like this [hurriedly], *"As-salamu 'alaikum! As-salamu 'alaikum wa rahmat-Allah,"* taking their shoes and running away. To where?

Allah is looking and saying, "For whom are they running, for whose service are they running? Did I create them for My heavenly service or did I create them to follow their dangerous enemy and *dunya?*"

You know, O our Lord, You know best. You created them for Your divine service, but mostly they are not giving any time for that service, and those who are giving time, they are giving a very short

---

[66] That is, the prayers that the Prophet used to pray regularly but which are not obligatory.

[67] Wahhabism, an approach to the Islamic teachings that stresses externals while rejecting spiritual aspects, rejecting the many narrations from the Prophet (s) on the importance of purification of character and morals.

[68] *Sunnah:* the Prophet's practice; *zawa'id* additional, extra.

time, taking their shoes, quickly running. For what? For Shaytan's way! They are workers for shaytanic service. How are people going to be happy in this *dunya?*

Therefore, I am happy. Those of you who are coming here, *alhamdulillah,* you are sitting, not thinking about any other service. You are sitting; no one is thinking about their work, no. And your main target—this is the title of our Association that our Grand-shaykh, may Allah bless him, is granting us. "Say to our brothers, sisters, sons, grandsons, granddaughters, that we are doing this Association to learn how we can do our service for our Lord in the best way."

That is what They are 'translating.'[69] Your goal is how you can do your heavenly service in the best way.

That must be in your heart always, how I can give my best service to the Lord of Heavens. Therefore, we are saying, "Welcome to you," as prophets they were welcoming people who were coming in such a way. Some people were coming [to him], taking something and running away. They are not on the same rank of heavenly service as other people sitting in front of the Prophet ﷺ. They were asking for more knowledge to practice their heavenly service in the best way. That must be.

Therefore, here is a handful people who are asking to do their best service for the Lord of Heavens. *Aferin,* capital, for those people, but for others, dangerous days are coming. Dangerous days are coming, and I am asking forgiveness from Allah Almighty and asking Him to keep us on the lighted way, not to let us fall into dark ways. Darkness is the worst for people to see.

---

[69]The holy people, saints, of 'Spiritual Headquarters' are sending to Shaykh Nazim's heart.

May Allah forgive us! More than enough! This Association may be for the whole world's people, to be like a sun shining in their hearts. May Allah forgive me, and give much more power and authority through the coming Muharram to take away the ways of *ghaflah*, heedlessness, so that people may run from *dunya* to *Akhirah*. *Fateha*, for the honour of the most honoured one in Your Divine Presence!

5

ABOUT FIGHTING AGAINST SHAYTAN

May Allah forgive us! *As-asalamu 'alaikum!*

Today, from last night, Shaykh Hisham Efendi Hazretleri, *Madadu-l-Haqq*,[70] has honoured us, giving honour to our *dergâh*.[71] We have been honoured, and also I am happy that, as long as he is here, he is going to address to you whatever Allah Almighty gives to him. Before, I was speaking and people were listening, but it was a heavy burden to speak to people. To be an *imam*,[72] to be a *khatib*,[73] it is not what you are saying, like a formality, but really an *imam* must have something of spirituality to give to people.

Wood to wood or candle to candle can't give anything, but if the candle is lighted, if there is fire on it, one may reach one thousand, even one million or one billion people. One candle is enough to wake up our candles in our hearts. But now it is so difficult to reach such people[74] because they, all of them, are hidden, hidden, and you are not asking. If you do not give your whole energy to asking for such a person, it is difficult to find him. So many people,

---

[70]Supporter of Truth.

[71]*Dergah.* Lodging and gathering place for *murids* (followers) of a Sufi shaykh.

[72]Leader; specifically, leader of Islamic prayers.

[73]One who gives the *khutbah* (Friday sermon).

[74]People who are able to light hearts, *awliya.*

they know so many things, but yet their candles are not awakened. If not awakened, they can't make you to wake up. And that is the sign of the Last Days.

A'udhu bil-Lahi min as-Shaytani-r-rajim. *Bismillahi-r-Rahmani-r-Rahim.* We are beginning by running to Allah, running to Allah from Shaytan, because Shaytan, any time he sees a lighted candle, comes and extinguishes that. Therefore, we are saying, *"A'udhu bil-Lahi min as-Shaytani-r-rajim, bismillahi-r-Rahmani-r-Rahim,"* to keep Shaytan away from our meetings. Don't give a way to Shaytan!

How can you *not* give a way? When you say, *"A'udhu bil-Lahi min as-Shaytani-r-rajim, bismillahi-r-Rahmani-r-Rahim,"* Shaytan runs away, but after a while he comes, comes, not leaving you. Therefore, the most important, most important *wird*[75] now is to say *"A'udhu bil-Lahi min ash-Shaytani-r-rajim."*

A'udhu bil-Lahi min ash-Shaytani-r-rajim! For every purpose, say, *"A'udhu bil-Lahi min ash-Shaytani-r-rajim,"* because our egos are asking to run after Shaytan. And after that, our egos are asking to dive, to dive. Where? Into sewage channels,[76] quickly asking to run into them because their pleasure, egos' pleasure, is to run into sewage channels. Therefore, when you are looking and seeing that your ego wants to run, say, *"A'udhu bil-Lahi min ash-Shaytani-r-rajim!"*

Beware, or you will find yourself in sewage channels! People they are like rats, *lup lup lup lup lup!* "This is modern life that we must

---

[75]The daily *tariqah* litany, assigned by a shaykh to his *murid.*

[76]Actions or states of filth and degradation, metaphorically what one would experience if falling into a sewer or open drainage channel found in many less-developed parts of the world.

reach, like Europeans and Americans, Western people! Look how high their life is, high life!"

"Where?"

"Come, come, come, come! Come with me. Sewage channels—try it!"

"Can I do it?"

"Yes, free, free! Jump in it!" *Lup!*

Then saying, "*Yahu,*[77] come out!"

"No, no! Here, there is modernized life, Western life, high life!" *Tauba, astaghfirullah! Tauba, astaghfirullaha-l-'Adhim!*[78]

Therefore, a *mu'min*, believer, must be an awakened person. If not, Shaytan will quickly take you to fall into sewage channels. *Aman, ya Rabb!*[79] All people are running, running, running after this!

"A'udhu bil-Lahi min ash-Shaytani-r-rajim"—at at least forty times daily you must use it to be powerful for *hajamati-sh-Shaytan,*[80] if Shaytan rushes at you. And then, *subhanallah*, Maulana Shaykh, Sultan ul-Awliya,[81] may Allah raise his rank, was saying, "Now there is no way for *murids* to reach from one level to a higher station. The only important *wird* is to say, for every occasion, *"Bismillahi-r-Rahmani-r-Rahim! Bismillahi-r-Rahmani-r-Rahim! Bismillahi-r-Rahmani-r-Rahim!"* *La yatumu-l-'amal*[82]—it is not going to be perfect obedience without

---

[77]A Turkish expression, meaning "See here!" or "My goodness!"

[78]Repentance, I seek forgiveness of Allah! Repentance, I seek forgiveness of Allah the Almighty!

[79]Safety/security, O Lord!

[80]Satan's pouncing, assault, attack.

[81]Grandshaykh 'Abdullah.

[82]Not a complete, perfected action.

"Bismillahi-r-Rahmani-r-Rahim." If you do not say *"Bismillahi-r-Rahmani-r-Rahim,"* it is never going to be a perfect, acceptable service for the Lord of Heavens. And also, it is mentioned in holy *hadith* that whoever does not say the beginning of anything, any action, *"Al-hamdu lil-Lahi Rabbi-l-'Alamin,"*[83] it is not going to be perfect.

Therefore, say, *"Bismillahi-r-Rahmani-r-Rahim, al-hamdu lil-lahi Rabbi-l-'Alamin,"* that we can come here, we can sit and listen, we can to force our egos to follow us. That gives this spiritual power, pumping, pumping, because you can use it once. For the second action, you must again pump power and enough *"Bismillahi-r-Rahmani-r-Rahim, alhamdulillahi Rabbi-l-'Alamins."* But one time we must say, *"A'udhu bil-Lahi min ash-Shaytani-r-rajim."* Then you may say, *"Bismillahi-r-Rahmani-r-Rahim, al-hamdu lil-Lahi Rabbi-l-'Alamin."*

When a person says this, he may be able to conquer his ego and defeat Shaytan from himself. It is not something for which you need to read hundreds of books, no. Such a simple thing, it gives power, power! We are beginning and Allah is finishing it. If you begin with His Holy Name and praise Him, you should be granted a dress of honour.

That is *nur*, that is heavenly lights with which your real being is honoured and lighted. For every action for which you are saying, *"Bismillahi-r-Rahmani-r-Rahim, al-hamdu lil-Lahi Rabbi-l-'Alamin,"* you are dressed in a dress of honour that gives you more glory, preparing you to be in the Divine Presence with such *nur*, lights.

When Shaykh Hisham Efendi Hazretleri is ready to address you, each *wali*, he has another channel. That Shaytan-box, TV, has so many channels, and *awliya*, saints, they have common channels and

---

[83]"Praise be to Allah, Lord of the worlds," the opening verse of the Qur'an.

also they have special channels for themselves. Therefore, when he speaks to you, addressing you, his channel is something else.

There are never going to be, on this earth, any two happenings that are the same, exactly one hundred per cent the same. No, always change is coming. Therefore, when one *wali*, saint, is speaking and giving new news from heavenly stations, there may be a billion people and they may take a billion special channels. Your channels are going to be forty, fifty, sixty, hundred, never reaching five hundred, but channels that *awliya* are reaching may be millons, billions, trillions, quadrillions; pentrillions—may be. *Subhanallah, subhana-l-Mutiyi-l-Wahhab!*[84]

Therefore, now I am making an introduction for Shaykh Hisham Efendi. If I do not speak, he may speak. He is not happy to speak when I am here, but I am nothing. What he is saying, [he may] say it! His channel is special; I may hear from him something that I am not hearing from my channel. Therefore, it is not something that belongs to our egos, and I am going to be happy. Such people Allah Almighty is sending from His selected *awliya*, who are carrying from me, also. He may speak.

Eh! Welcome to you, welcome, Shaykh Hisham Hazretleri! I think that he needs a little bit of rest because he arrived after midnight and perhaps was sitting early for *salatu-l-Fajr.*[85]

We are like an old car. What to do? Therefore, I am leaving here today; it is enough. Tomorrow, he may speak to you from his special channel. *Masha'Allah*, he is going around East and West—so many people, high level people, the level of presidents, level of

---

[84]Glory be to Allah, glory be to the Giver, the Granter!

[85]*Fajr*, the dawn prayer.

crown princes, level of tyrants, level of shaytans, bombarding them. Therefore, he has a speciality, in such a way, among *awliya, mashhurun wa ma'rufun,*[86] Shaykh Hisham Efendi.

May Allah forgive us, and *mubarak* [Islamic] New Year! May Allah make it *mubarak*, blest—to be a blest year. I hope it will be a new beginning for the history of Islam, beginning from today, the first of Muharram, 1429—to be a good, new beginning, that Islam is going to appear, appear, appear and *kufr*[87] will come down, come down, and Shaytan's sultanate is going to finish and vanish, and Islam is going to appear, to appear, to get up, to get up throughout East and West, from North to South, everywhere, to say, "*La ilaha illa-Lah! La ilaha illa-Lah! La ilaha illa-Lah. Sayyidina wa nabiyuna Muhammadu-r-Rasul-Allah* ﷺ.'[88]

Sheikh Hisham Efendi, he is going to be with us *insha'Allah* five or six days. May Allah give him much more power, much more *nur*, for the Muslims, for the *barakah* of this blessed month, *shahru Muharramu-l-Haram, bi jahi Nabiyi-l-Karim, Sayyidi-l-Awwalin wa-Akhirin—Fateha!*[89]

---

[86]*Mashhur:* well-known, famous, renowned; *ma'ruf:* known, well-known, recognized.

[87]Unbelief.

[88]There is no deity except Allah [three times]. Our master and prophet is Muhammad, may Allah's peace and blessings be upon him.

[89]The month of Muharram the sacred, for the glory of the noble prophet Muhammad, Master of the First and the Last—*Fateha!*

6

REVERTING TO THE INNOCENCE OF LITTLE CHILDREN

A'udhu bil-Lahi min ash-Shaytani-r-rajim. Bismillahi-r-Rahmani-r-Rahim. Dastur, ya Sayydi, ya Sultanu-l-Awliya! Madad! Madad, ya Rijal-Allah! Madad!

Look! That baby, that child, with one bonbon, he is getting happy, so happy! If I gave you a sackful, you would say, "What am I going to do with this?" He is happy, very happy, but people they are not happy with a sack of bonbons.

Yes, a baby, he is happy with one bonbon. We are not happy. Till our characteristics become like a little one's, we are not going to be acceptable in the Divine Presence. Little ones never do anything to be guilty, no; no guilt for children. And children, they do not think about doing some evil. No, they do not think about it.

Children, they are not envious; no jealousy, no, no. Never do they quarrel with their parents, little ones, to say, "I must have like what that boy has." Whatever you are dressing them in, they are happy. And they are not occupying their minds or their hearts with something that Allah Almighty is not happy with. They are not running after buildings, they are not running to have a Mercedes car or a garbage truck, no. They are not getting angry or sorry if anyone asks from them a precious ring, "Give it to me and take this red-colored bonbon." Quickly they give it. Yes?

39

Makarima-l-akhlaq,[90] good manners! You can do this? No, we can't, we can't do it! We think that everything must be for ourselves. Yes, you may reach so many things from this life and you may save billions or trillions in banks; you may keep and save so many precious stones, gems, and you are happy. If someone asks, "Give for the sake of Allah," giving one disliked stone, ring or very cheap bracelet. And we think that what we are saving, it is for ourselves. But no one takes what they saved when they pass away. Yes!

In Egypt, in olden times, the ancient period when there were pharaohs, they were saving treasures, and also they were preparing themselves for when they would pass away from this life. They believed "one day we will come back and these treasures must be under our control, must be for us."

They saved like hills of treasures. And people who were specialists in keeping the bodies of pharaohs from being decayed, they did that. But after thousands of years, one day, even though their treasures were just hidden, hidden, Allah Almighty sent some servants to their treasures, to their tombs, to find a way and to reach their decayed bodies. And perhaps you have seen their mummies.

If you look at their decayed bodies from thousands of years ago, you may run away. Perhaps for a long time you won't be able to eat anything, or you are scared at nighttime and in the daytime you don't want to eat. How were they, and, after thousands of years, how are their bodies? They tried to be here forever, which is impossible, and they saved treasures for themselves, but treasures couldn't be for them. Finished!

Now, therefore, for this boy, nothing is important, what he is wearing or what he has been given to eat, never asking for the best

---

[90]A noble characteristic or quality.

car, never asking for a castle or a palace. No, they are happy! And when you come back to that state, that is *safa*,[91] purity.

They are pure. We are not pure. Therefore, we are living in trouble, in miseries, and people are running in the streets everywhere, asking for something but they do not know for what they are asking, no. You saw little ones running in the streets and shouting? No. They are happy with their lives. Why would they shout or destroy or burn or kill people—for what? They are happy!

Men, when they grow up or when they learn something, they must think about it, what are the goals to which they are running. That boy is happy. Millions or billions of people now, they are not happy—*un*happy. *Safa*, purity; purity must be in our hearts. Prophets never came to people to call them to *dunya*, to treasures or *mata'a-d-dunya*, the materials of this life. You must take your lesson from those little ones. Look! Very happy, very happy, very happy.

And *dunya gharrara*,[92] is cheating. And Shaytan is every day coming and shouting to people. [Parodies:] "I have a very beautiful girl, daughter. I would like to marry her to someone. Who can give me her *mahr*, her dower, O people?" Running from East to West, from West to East, from North to South, showing her and saying, "Oh, look—look how beautiful she is! Who is coming?" And people are beginning to quarrel, to fight, to reach that Shaytan's daughter. Every day those who are quarrelling for Shaytan's daughter, for *dunya*, the next day they are going to disappear, finished.

O people, all prophets came and brought heavenly messages. Heavenly messages, you must read, you must keep, and you must

---

[91]Clear, limpid, pure, undisturbed, serene.
[92]This world is deceptive.

believe in them to be happy here and Hereafter. But people, they are doing the contrary, opposite.

We must follow prophets' footsteps. As long as you are following the footsteps of Shaytan, you are never going to reach anything to be pleased and to reach pleasure here or Hereafter.

Subhanallah! Mankind, they are killing each other, as the Prophet was saying, peace be upon him, Sayyidina Rasul-Allah ﷺ: "When the Last Days approach, people will get more angry and affected by shaytanic ideas, and friends are going to be enemies, relatives are going to be enemies." And we are living now in that. *Subhanallah!*

A big *'alim*, scholar, an authority in Islamic knowledge who did a big *tafsir*, [Qur'anic] commentary, he was saying that one day he heard a seller shouting in the marketplace. What was he selling?

Kar, snow, taking from a mountain and bringing to the city, and calling people, "O people, reach me quickly because my capital is going to melt! Quickly run to me! My capital is finishing. Take!" And that is, *subhanallah*, *"Wal 'asri, inna-l-insana lafi khusr,"*[93] *Surat al-'Asr*, a holy *surah*, saying that man is like that person, losing, because our capital, day by day, is going to melt and finish.

You must save your capital, at least! Take your capital or it is going to finish. And so many people, at the last moment, they are looking and—*uff!*—no profit and no capital. The capital finished, melted, and no profit, also. "Daily we are running, but our capital is going to melt, going." He was even calling people, "O people, come and take because my capital is going to finish!"

---

[93] *Surah al-'Asr* (Time): *"By Time, indeed, mankind is in loss, except for those who believe and do righteous deeds, and advise one other of truth and advise one other of patience."* (103:1-3)

Angels are looking at people. And in that *ayatu-l-karima* in which Allah Jalla Jalaluhu[94] says, *"Bismillahi-r-Rahmani-r-Rahim. Wal 'asr! Innna-l-insana lafi khusr*, men are losing," how are they losing?

Their capital is going to finish. That is *zarar*, harm, loss. So many people are losing, nothing remaining to them of capital and not reaching any profit. Millions of people now, their capital is finishing and they are not taking even a quarter or a tenth or one out of one hundred parts. They are never taking any benefit. *Subhan-allah!*

It is a good lesson for people to understand that point because daily their capital is melting, each day going away and not bringing any profit. O people, may Allah forgive us! Try not to lose; try to take a profit. What Allah has granted us, this life that is *muwaqqat*,[95] a temporary life, when finishing, if you have reached a benefit or profit, you are happy; if you can reach even one part, you must be happy. If never taking anything, you have lost completely, finished!

May Allah forgive us! *Allah, ya Rabbi*—O our Lord, You are our Lord! Keep us on Your true way, not to be cheated by the enemy of mankind, Shaytan. Keep us in Your Divine Presence, dressed in a dress of honor, dressed in a heavenly dress. Try for that purpose! If not, you will have lost a hundred per cent, and what should be for you from the Divine Presence, what is going to be granted to you, whether something or not, think about it. May Allah forgive us! *Fateha!*

---

[94]Allah, may His Glory be exalted.

[95]Appointed, fixed, *scheduled* time.

7

WALKING IN THE STEPS OF THE MOST PRAISED AND GLORIFIED ONE IN THE DIVINE PRESENCE

As-salamu 'alaikum wa rahmatullah wa barakatuhu![96] *A'udhu bil-Lahi min ash-Shaytani-r-rajim. Bismillahi-r-rahmani-r-Rahim.*

This is a *nasihah*, advice. Our Grandshaykh is ordering me to make Association with believers, with *mu'mins*. It is an order.

When They are ordering, that means They are supporting and controlling what we are saying. *Ijazah*, that permission, is just granted from our Grandshaykh for advising throughout East and West, from North to South. And Their *ijazah*, Their permission, it is all right. Anyone may come. Each one of mankind is in need of hearing advice from the beloved ones—I mean to say, firstly prophets, and then after them, those who are following the footsteps of prophets.[97] And now there are no other footsteps, only the footsteps of Sayyidina Muhammad, peace be upon him.

Madad, ya Sayyidi, dastur! If you are asking, "Who is that one?" you must know, you must know: Sayyidina Muhammad, peace be upon him.

---

[96]Peace be upon you, and Allah's mercy and His blessings.
[97]That is, *awliya*, Muslim saints.

44

When the Seal of the Prophets, Sayyidina Muhammad ﷺ, was invited during the Night Journey, *Me'raj*, coming from Makkah [Mecca], may Allah make its honor more, he was taken from Makka-tu-l-Mukarramah[98] and coming to Quds ush-Sharif, Jerusalem, the third most praised place on earth.

When he arrived in Jerusalem from Makkatu-l-Mukarramah, all the [earlier] prophets welcomed him. They were awaiting his coming and they were, all of them, expecting to reach much more honor and glory by being with him. They welcomed him, and the Seal of the Prophets, he prayed two *rak'ats*[99] to thank Allah Almighty that He had granted him such a glory. With that glory, he came from the House of the Lord in Makkatu-l-Mukarramah to Jerusalem and prayed two *rak'ats,* and all the prophets prayed behind him, his *ja-ma'at.*[100]

One hundred and twenty-four thousand prophets, they were making their rows behind him and praying two *rak'ats* for the honor that had been granted to the Seal of Prophets, Sayyidina Muhammad, peace be upon him. Therefore, we are saying, "Who is that one that is most glorified and praised in Divine Presence?" You must know the answer.

That one was and is now, from pre-eternity up to eternity, Say-yidina Muhammad, peace be upon him. He is that one, the most glorified servant in the Divine Presence, Sayyidina Muhammad ﷺ! Yes. We have been ordered to follow in his footsteps.

---

[98]Mecca the Honored. According to the Prophet's own narrative, one night, while he was asleep in his bed in Mecca, he was miraculously transported to Jerusalem, where, as described here, he led all the earlier prophets in prayer. He was then taken to the seven Heavens and, alone and unaccompanied, admitted to his Lord's Divine Presence. (Bukhari, 5:227, 1.345, 4:462, 4:647, and others)

[99]Cycles or units of *salat.*

[100]Congregation.

When the first prophet, the father of mankind, Sayyidina Adam, was taken out of Paradise and landed on earth, he was crying and asking forgiveness and asking to be back in Paradise.

He was told, "O Adam, you and each one of your children who may walk in the footsteps of My most glorious servant, Sayyidina Muhammad, peace be upon him—whoever follows his footsteps, he is going to be in Paradise. If not walking in his footsteps, no one can enter My Paradise."

You must understand this. It is an important point to be told to mankind now in our days. *Subhanallah!* Now mankind, the whole world, is in the biggest troubles, biggest problems, endless sufferings, endless miseries. Mankind is in it now!

Someone may ask how mankind can save themselves from problems, from miseries, and what is the reason for them. How are they falling into those bad conditions, the worst situation, most terrible situation, terrible troubles, sufferings, and terrible miseries? What is the reason that mankind has fallen into it now?

I don't think that anyone in East and West or from North to South can reject what we are saying here. I am an ordinary servant, making this declaration from East to West, from North to South, if they are asking to save themselves here and Hereafter. And the cause of mankind's falling into such a terrible condition, endless troubles and problems, sufferings, is because they are walking in the footsteps of Shaytan, about whom Allah Almighty says, "O mankind, your most terrible enemy, that is Shaytan, who refused My order to make *sajdah* to Adam."[101]

---

[101]See 6:142, 7:22, 12:5, 17:53, 28:15, 35:6, 36:60, 43:62.

Yes; it is clear, I think, what we are saying. No pope, no bishop, no patriarch, no rabbi, no one can say this is not true. If they reject this clear truth, then they have no right to object to what Allah may do. Yes, that is the reason. It is well-known. Now, what is the way that all mankind can be saved from this terrible situation?

The answer is that till these people who are living now on earth walk in the footsteps of the most glorious servant and holy representative of Allah Almighty, Sayyidina Muhammad, they won't be able to save themselves. That is the reason, and that is the way to save themselves. You are not in need of any other knowledge, only this.

May Allah forgive us! *As-salamu 'alaikum! Fateha!*

Take this! If anyone asks, give this cassette to him to understand who is speaking and what we are saying, what we are doing. We are not following any politician, no. Our way is from Allah to Allah. If they are accepting, accepting. If not accepting and wanting to give trouble to any of our people, they should beware that Allah is Watcher over everything. *Fateha!*

We may speak up to morning, up to evening, up to next week, up to next month, up to next year, but we are speaking in summary so that you may keep it, so no one may forget it. It is the real information, a real warning from Heavens. If opposes this clear warning they should beware of the Lord's Divine retribution. *Tauba, ya Rabbi! Tauba, ya Rabbi! Tauba, astaghfirullah!* May Allah forgive us!

Give a way for the nation of Muhammad ﷺ, O our Lord, particularly for Pakistani people, who are just falling into bottomless troubles and miseries. O our Lord, send them someone to save them—to make them, on the one hand, be with Your beloved servant, Your glorious prophet, Sayyidina Muhammad, for his honour;

and to take away bad people; to make Muslims in Pakistan and Hindistan [India] be at rest and turn back to their real beliefs, to be *mu'mins*, to be servants of their Lord, Allah Almighty, not to run after Shaytan, not to follow Shaytan, that they may leave Shaytan and become Muslims, *mu'mins*, real ones. Give them that honour, O our Lord, O Allah Almighty, our Creator and our Lord! *Fateha!*

8

THE EXISTENCE OF CREATURES IS PROOF OF THE CREATOR

Dastur, ya Sayyidi, ya Sultanu-l-Awliya! Madad, ya Rijal-Allah!

A'udhu bil-Lahi min ash-Shaytani-r-rajim. Bismillahi-r-Rahmani-r-Rahim. O our attenders, welcome to you! May Allah bless you! And we are saying, *"A'udhu bil-Lahi min ash-Shaytani-r-rajim."* That means we are running to Allah, asking for a shelter, and saying, *"Bismillahi-r-Rahmani-r-Rahim,* by the name of our Creator, Allah, who granted us life."

Yesterday we were not in existence. Today we are seeing ourselves in existence but tomorrow we are not going to be in existence. And we have been ordered to say His most honoured Name and Names, which are *"Bismillahi-r-Rahmani-r-Rahim,* by the Name of Allah, who has endless Mercy Oceans."

No one knows the limits of His Existence, no one knows His Mercy Oceans' limits, from where beginning or to where reaching. Yes; therefore, we are saying, *"A'udhu bil-Lahi min ash-Shaytani-r-rajim.* I am running from the worst and most terrible enemy to Allah. We are running to Him." *Madad, ya Rijal-Allah!* And we are asking for our Association a spiritual support or heavenly support.

If They give support, I may speak, you may speak; but from one person to another, our speech is going to be different. As our mentalities are different, people may add, up to a limit, various kinds of mentalities, but no limits for [individual] mentalities.[102] And glory be to the Lord of Heavens, who created. Yes, One! What we are saying now is that there is a creation. That is a never-changed or an unchangeable reality. Mankind must know this.

I am a weak servant, perhaps the weakest servant. And I may ask anyone if there is a creation. No one can say "No" because there are creatures in existence. If creatures are in existence, that means you are admitting, recognizing, that there must be a Creator.

If creation and creatures are in existence, everyone's intellect must say that they need a Creator. No one can deny this. If denying, that means he is a no-mind person. His head may be a head of donkey, yes; a donkey can't think but men can think. Men can think, but do you think that any other creatures can think? Who can say that a dog can think? Who can say a rabbit can think? Who can say that an elephant thinks, who can say a panther thinks, who can say a cat thinks, who can say a mouse can think? Can anyone say that? I don't think so.

If anyone says so, that saying, also, it is a fruit of thinking. Without thinking, no one can say that a mouse can think. Yes? I am nothing, I am only a weak creature and my branch, species, among creatures is to be from mankind. Wild animals, they have a line; flying animals another line; wild animals are another kind, line. And you can't find anyone from any kind of creature able to think except mankind.

Is it true or not? Mankind can think because they have intellect, but a donkey has no intellect, a dog has no intellect. Intellect is for mankind, a heavenly *'ata*, heavenly grant. And we have been granted

---

[102] Mawlana is saying that there are unlimited varieties of thinking.

that intellect from our Creator because we are creatures and there must be a Creator for us.

You can't say, "I am *creating* my child in my womb," or you can't say, "My wife is *creating* my child in her womb." That is foolishness! You can't say this; no intellect accepts this! If you say this, I may say, "What about a cat? A cat gives birth to three babies, four babies, two babies or five babies. What do you think—does that cat *create* those babies in its womb?"

How the mentalities of people living under the 2008 calendar have changed! They are reverting to be like animals, that have no intellect! No animal claims that I am creating my babies in my womb, I am giving their designs in my womb. I am that one who is designing and creating my babies as male or female." Or no one can say that a cat makes its babies' colors, to be a black one or white one or grey one or mixed-up. Who can say so? What has happened to mankind to say, "No Creator"? How can they say this?

What intellect can say that a mouse arranges its mouse babies in its womb? What is this foolishness for the twenty-first century's people? But they are drunk! And I hope that now some holy people, some special people, some authorized people among mankind are going to destroy all *batil*, wrong and falsehood. I am asking from my Lord, Jalla Jalaluhu, through His most glorified servant and creature, Sayyidina Muhammad ﷺ, and through my Grandshaykh, to be able to destroy all *batil*, falsehood. I am nothing, but sometimes my mentality, that belongs to heavenly Power Stations, should fire up the falsehood of shaytanic teachings!

May Allah forgive me, and may holy people's support be with me to destroy every wrong idea, every falsehood on earth. May Allah forgive me! For the honour of the most honoured servant in His Divine Presence, Sayyidina Muhammad. If anyone can bring any *i'tirad,* objection, to this, I am saying, *"Hatu burhanakum*[103]—bring your proofs that what I am saying is wrong!"

I am the weakest servant, but sometimes I am the strongest one to destroy shaytanic ideas and teachings and practices. And I hope that, even if I am the weakest one, I am going to destroy all false ideas that are shaytanic teachings under the cover of technology. I am that one who is going to destroy their technology, *insha'Allah!* For the honour of the most honoured one in Divine Presence.

Why am I saying I am that one? Because I am the weakest one. No need for strong ones! Strong ones can take away the whole universe! This is nothing. Therefore I am saying I can do this. *As-salamu 'alaikum! Fateha!*

---

[103] *"Bring your proof."* (2:111; 21:24, 27:64; 28:75)

9

REGARDING THE LIMIT OF OUR UNDERSTANDING OF THE CREATOR

As-salamu 'alaikum. Madad, ya Sultanu-l-Awliya. We are asking heavenly support from heavenly people, whom now they are calling "holy people." *A'udhu bil-Lahi min ash-Shaytani-r-rajim. Bismillahi-r-Rahmani-r-Rahim.* By the name of Allah Almighty, All Merciful, Most Beneficent and Most Munificent. May He forgive us! We are really in need of His forgiveness.

Whether it is a short or long *sohbet*, I don't know. My heart is just in contact with one of the heavenly centers, with what They are sending to me, making me speak or making what I am saying to be clear for you. "You," that means from East to West, from North to South, mankind. Even if only thirty people or forty people are sitting here, I am addressing my speech to all mankind, and I have been permitted and supported by holy people to speak and to address all mankind. Therefore, it is not important that there are only thirty, forty people here, but I hope this speech from holy people may reach everyone.

First, I am asking forgiveness from our Lord, from our Creator, the Lord of Heavens, Allah. You must try to learn to say His Holy Name, "Allah". Say:

Allah Allah, Allah Allah, Allah Allah, 'Aziz Allah;

Allah Allah, Allah Allah, Allah Allah, Karim Allah;

Allah Allah, Allah Allah, Allah Allah, Subhan Allah;

Allah Allah, Allah Allah, Allah Allah, Sultan Allah.[104]

He is Allah, the Creator! O mankind, you must try to learn who created you. That is the most important learning for all mankind. If I ask you who created you, you can't say, "My parents created me," because if your parents were able to give you life, why have they not kept that secret of the power of life that you are saying came from your parents to you? Why did they lose that secret power, why passing away? Where are your ancestors? Just under the earth, under ground. Now they are dust. How?

Therefore, Islam first teaches people to be realists. They must ask to learn what is Reality, or otherwise they are going to be under the level of animals. A pity for mankind to fall from their honoured level to below the levell of dishonoured creatures!

Who created you? Don't run after imagination! Don't run after such a person, that no-mind person, Darwin! He was someone who never used his mind and he was imagining. Even though he was [studying to be] a priest, Shaytan made him leave his position and carried him to another level at which he found in himself courage, or Shaytan gave that Darwin a kind of courage, to come and say that we come from one-celled creatures and that we have jumped from one step to another step to be a man. And just before being men, men were apes!

---

[104]Allah, the Arabic name for God.

Here, the Shaykh adds parenthetically: "There are some words that we are using from their origins, and their origins have reached mankind through the Arabic language. It is [often] difficult to translate one word, to give a real translation of what you are saying," meaning that Arabic terms often have several meanings or subtle shades of meaning.

That is a big *ayib*, a big shame, for that person, and more than that one, that all nations have accepted what Darwin was saying. That is Reality? No! They are not saying that this was his imagination; they are putting their stamp on it that Darwin was speaking the truth. Never! What is his proof, saying "evolution"?

Imagine coming from one–celled creatures that are amoebas! Firstly, according to that one's imagining, amoebas were the first creatures that appeared in existence. I am asking how those one-celled creatures that are amoebas started to be in existence. How could it be? By themselves? They weren't in existence. That would mean that amoebas gave life to themselves *by themselves*. Amoebas are the most primitive creatures, one-celled. If that one cell has the power to appear in existence by itself, what about you, who are now the highest level of creation?

And Darwin was such a drunk person that he never said when it is going to end, that evolution. Must go on! Why was he saying that man is the last point of evolution? After that, why did he make it stop? The power that in amoebas brought fishes and other creatures, step by step reaching to mankind, why did it stop with mankind?

The twenty-first century's professors or scientists, why do they not make it more clear to people? How are they understanding? What is their foolishness? Why are they not saying that we are looking for another creature that is going to be more evolved by nature?

Ah! There is another point, "Nature." What is "Nature," O Darwin? Say! Explain to people what Nature is. Was Nature the mother of creation? Where did amoebas appear, in Nature or out of Nature? Tell me, O scientists, now the twenty-first century's scientists, were amoebas in Nature or out of Nature, and what is Nature's effect on amoebas? What was the secret power in Nature that made an amoeba, because amoebas came from Nature?

No answer! They are making people not to believe in truth but to believe in falsehood. No answer! I am asking, "What is Nature? Where it is? Where is its beginning and where is its end? Where does Nature stay? How does it command, how does it bring or create so many things? How, where it is? It is only in imagination!

The only, main, purpose of those scientists is that all of them are atheists. They follow what Shaytan, Diablo, teaching them. They do not believe in God, Allah Almighty, and they think that their beliefs give them honour. No, taking honour from them and making them to be on the lowest level of creatures through that way!

Therefore, the most important thing that you must learn, it is that, if I ask you, "Who created you?" you should say, "There is a false theory that we are speaking about now, but the reality and truth is that we have been created, we are creatures. But our Creator, no one knows about our Creator except through His Holy Names." Because, as an example, we may say that if an amoeba were to ask, "Who created me?" if we were to say, "Man created you," do you think that that amoeba could understand about you?"

Possible? *Impossible!* Therefore, we, also, if we were asking who created us, I would say, "Allah." Then we would ask, "Who is Allah? How is He, where is He?" This means that, as an amoeba would ask if we said that its creator is a man, it would be impossible for an amoeba to understand about you. No; impossible, because it has only one cell, while you have countless cells, and countless *different* cells. And it is such a foolish question for a person to ask, "Who is Allah?"

If we said, "You were created by Allah Almighty," that person might ask, "Show me!" Similarly, if an amoeba were asking, "Show me my creator," we might say, "Your creator is a man." If the ameoba, one-celled, were asking, "Where is he? How is he? Who is he?" it would be impossible, it would be impossible! Therefore, we may say, as they are saying, "We have been created by Nature," as an amoeba might say, "My creator is Nature." And so many atheists, they are saying they are coming from Nature.

Please explain to me who that "Nature" is, what that "Nature" is, and where it is and how it is. Is it possible? Do you think that it is possible? But so many professors, scientists, they are on the wrong way and making people not to say, "Our Creator, the Lord of Heavens." Therefore, every kind of curse is falling on them now

May Allah forgive us! Now, today, I think it is enough. We may continue. I hope, although I am the weakest one on that way, to take away those no-mind, atheist people because their minds, brains, are slowly, slowly drying, drying, drying; no life for their heads. A holy one, his brain and body are always fresh, always in life; one hundred per cent life power is with them. But those people who are refusing to say, "Our Lord, our Creator," their brains are becoming slowly, slowly, slowly, slowly dry, dry, dry, and finishing.

May Allah forgive us! I think that now a new entrance to understanding has just opened to destroy those unbelievers and atheists. I am the weakest one, but I hope to take down their falsehoods, to be taken away.

May Allah forgive me—forgive me and forgive you, for the honour of the most honoured one, Sayyidina Muhammad, peace be upon him and upon all the prophets who were honoured by the Lord of Heavens. May Allah forgive us! For the honour of the most honoured one in His Divine Presence, Sayyidina Muhammad ﷺ— *Fateha!*

10

The Immeasurable Honour of Being Allah's Servant

As-salamu 'alaikum! Selamet olsun![105] To be in safety *insha'Allah* here and Hereafter, as much as possible, use, say, *"As-salamu 'alaikum."* And *malaika*, angels, are also saying to you, *"Salam*, safety, here and Hereafter!"*

Destur, ya Sayyidi, ya Sultanu-l-Awliya. Meded, ya Rijal-Allah! A'udhu bil-Lahi min ash Shaytani-r-rajim. Bismillahi-r-Rahmani-r-Rahim.

That is the sign of a Muslim, to run away from Shaytan, because Shaytan is running after mankind, Shaytan is running after the children of Adam. Therefore, you must call to Allah Almighty and ask protection, or you may fall into Shaytan's trap. And Shaytan is using hundreds of tricks to make you to fall into his trap.

Don't sleep! Wake up, O mankind! Don't say, "I am powerful." No! You are weak, a weak one! You must ask for your Lord's protection. Don't forget to say *"A'udhu bil-Lahi min ash-Shaytani-r-rajim! A'udhu bil-Lahi min ash-Shaytani-r-rajim!* O our Lord, I am running to You from Shaytan's tricks!"

---

[105]Peace be upon you! May you be safe!

What is his main goal, Shaytan? His main goal is to make all mankind to be caught in his trap. Whoever falls into Shaytan's trap must go with him to Hells. Shaytan is never happy that the children of Adam should be happy here or Hereafter, no. He is so angry, saying, "Because of you, I fell, I was thrown out of the Divine Presence. Therefore, I am going to use my whole ability, capability, energy, everything. My goal is to make you fall into the same Hells, not to be happy during your life on earth or after this life in the eternal life. I am never happy that mankind should be happy eternally, no." And he is giving his oath that "I shall give as much *juhdi,* effort, as possible to make the children of Adam be in troubles with me here and in Hells there."

Therefore, beware of Shaytan! People they are writing, "Beware of the dog." On every door there is a sign, "Beware of the dog!" A dog! A dog is not such a terrible one as Shaytan. A dog may bite you and you may do *tedavi,* cure, but if Shaytan bites you, that is difficult, very difficult; no cure. Therefore, the sign of a Muslim is to say *"A'udhu bil-Lahi min ash-Shaytani-r-rajim.* O our Lord, please protect me."

Allah, He is the Protector of countless universes. People are thinking that Allah Almighty Himself comes and protects you, you, you, you. No! But our *adab,* good manners, is to call Him, and then Allah Almighty sends protectors to you. When you really ask, you can find a protector for yourself from among mankind, also, from spiritual people, holy people, but *adab,* good manners, is to say, "O my Lord, please protect me from Shaytan's running after me, and perhaps I may fall into his trap." Therefore, it is a sign of a Muslim to say, *"A'udhu bil-Lahi min ash-Shaytani-r-rajim,"* and then you are protected, you are protected.

Then, you must know that you are weak servants. And the Lord of Heavens is giving you such an honour and saying, "O My servants!" To be servants of the Lord is so high an honour, you can't find a limit for that honour—that Allah Almighty is saying, "*Fa'buduni.*[106] O My servant, pray to Me and worship Me, O My servant! *Fa'buduni*; worship Me and try to be My servant. And My servanthood is such a big honour that you can't imagine!"

Eh! If a king was asking to you to come to be his guard or servant, and was dressing you in royal clothes that belong to the guard and servants of the king or queen, you would be so proud. Do you not see the Buckingham Palace guards, how they are, looking like this, never moving their eyes? They are so proud, with those big hats and uniforms that belong to His Majesty the King or Her Majesty the Queen. What do you think if Allah Almighty is calling you, "O My servants, O My creatures, come! Come! I am distinguishing you with an honour that I never granted even to angels."

Can you understand, can you think about it? You must think about it! A million times better than to have worldly titles and honours. [Parodies:] "I graduated, I graduated from Oxford University," dressing like this and putting a cap on his head, a heedless person, wearing something on his head and saying, "I am that one!"

"Who are you?"

"I am. . . ," not saying his first name, Thomas or William or George, but he is saying, "I am a Ph.D., Dr. William!" putting first his title and his name at the end, so proud.

What is this? They are thinking that it is their high honour. Some of them are using many alphabetical letters, saying, "O Shaykh, I have so many titles that twenty-nine or thirty letters of the alphabet are not enough to show my titles," putting on eye glasses (if putting eye glasses, that means a V.I.P. person).

---

[106] *"Therefore, worship/serve Me."* (21:25, 92)

That is not an honour, but people like it. And your Lord is giving you an honour that even angels were not granted and you are not appreciating that honour! That is the limit of foolishness, the limit of ignorance! How are we running away from our Lord's magnificent honour, granted to us without anything? *Wahban*;[107] it is a gift from Allah! People are running here, running there; no one now is appreciating the honour of servanthood to the Lord of Heavens. What is going to be for them here and Hereafter? For which thing are they looking, those people? To where are they reaching? Reaching—*tauba, astaghfirullah!*—reaching sewers!

People are running to sewers, not asking to get out, to be clean, to be honoured. Instead, they are running to sewers. I am saying, "They may spend their life in sewers."

"Which one is good? New York's W.C. sewers? Is Washington better or Moscow or Ankara or Peking better?

"O my friend, from where did you reach this position, from where did you graduate?"

"O my brother, I graduated from the sewers of London."

"I graduated from the Sorbonne's sewers," or, "I graduated from the Moscow sewers."

"Do you think that there are other sewer above our sewer?"

"Yes, maybe. Maybe in Pakistan, maybe in Pakistan. Yes, if you go to Pakistan and graduate, you are going to be fighters."

"What about Turkey?"

---

[107]Free, without asking for any return.

"Turkey is also very good, their level, for fighting and killing and destroying and putting each other down. That is their honour, also."

"What about Germans?"

"Germans, mm-m-m, they are so . . . Sometimes they are using their minds and running to Berlin; sometimes not using, going to Bonn. Sometimes they are saying Rome's sewers are better."

"You tried it, O my brother?"

"I will try, but no time now. I am getting older. If I can come to this life another time, as *gurus* say we are coming so many times, next time I will come as a donkey, to run, or as a rat, and try to find out which sewer is best."

"You are right. You think there is such a thing as a person coming another time?"

"Yes, sir! It is our honour, also, that one time we are going to be dogs, one time going to be donkeys, once going to be cats, once going to be camels, once going to be jackals, sometimes going to be . . ."

"Never going to be mankind?"

"No, no, finished! We are going to run to another channel, to reach another level of life."

"Who said this?"

"*Kuru kafah*, dry head."[108]

---

[108]Here, the Shaykh adds parenthetically, *"Kuru"* in Turkish means "dry". *"Kuru"* means ones whose minds are dry.

"Yes. I hope that when I finish this time and change to the next time, I may be a guru, whose face you can't look at, so ugly, so dark."

Yes, sir! That is our situation about which they are saying, "We have reached the peak of civilization in the twenty-first century."

I am saying, "Congratulations that you are returning to the animal world! You are not going to be honoured. You are rejecting the honour of being from mankind and you want to go back to the animal world! And congratulations for your understanding and your new level that I think is lower than the animal level, even!" May Allah forgive us!

O people, all the world's people, beware of Shaytan! What we are saying, all of it, is that the aim of Shaytan is to take you away from heavenly servanthood and its honour, and to make you like the animal world and even below its level.

No one can object to what I am saying. If anyone says something, come here! I may teach him, I may show the right way. I am an authorized one to make people find their way and keep their honour, whoever has lost his real goal and the meaning of his creation, and what real honour is. I am the lowest one who may teach all mankind their honour and their situation now.

May Allah forgive us! For the honour of most honoured one in His Divine Presence, Sayyidina Muhammad ﷺ—*Fateha!*

11

For What Are You Living

As-salamu 'alaikum! It is an order from Rasul-Allah ﷺ to say more *"As-salamu 'alaikum"* among ourselves because with *salam* more blessings come. *Salam* brings blessings. Otherwise, if standing up to leave without giving *salam*, blessings do not come, as some clouds come and go but do not give rain, while some others approach and give rain.

Therefore, whoever wants heavenly rain with the blessings of Allah Almighty, say more *"As-salamu 'alaikum."* It is so important that Allah Almighty orders, *"Idha dakhaltum buyut, fa sallimu 'ala anfusikum"*[109]—when you enter a place, a home or house, say '*As-salamu 'alaikum.*'" Therefore, earlier, it was our good manners that, if someone came and knocked at the door, from inside someone would ask, "Who is there?"

"As-salamu 'alaikum," that coming person would say. It is so important to say *salam,* even when you go into a place, into a home and no one is there: *"Fa sallimu 'ala anfusikum."* If no one is there, even, you must say, *"As-salamu 'alaikum wa 'ala 'ibadi-Lahi-s-salihin."*[110]

---

[109]24:61.

[110]"Peace be upon you and upon Allah's righteous servants." This sentence, with "Peace be upon us" in place of "...upon you," is said in every prescribed prayer (*salat* or *namaz*).

It is so important, and it is *bi-sha'ir-Allah,* among the signs or symbols of Islam, to say *"As-salamu 'alaikum."* If someone does not say it, you may understand that he is not Muslim.

Therefore, we are saying, "O our attenders, may Allah bless you from His endless Blessing Oceans." As much as possible, try to get more blessings from Allah Almighty. But people, they are running to reach something from the material world, not thinking of saving more blessings. Such greedy people now! Even the Muslim world's people, they are too greedy for worldly things to ask for more blessings.

For what are you living—for Allah or for your ego? *For what are you living?* You are trying to make your ego happy or to enjoy itself. People are asking enjoyment for themselves, not asking to make their Lord happy with them. No matter how much you may do for yourself, it is going to disappear, finishing, finishing, but what you do for Allah Almighty will remain. *"Amalu salih yabqa";* good deeds remain, but bad deeds do not remain, going away.

I am sorry to say that the whole Muslim world's people, they are going in a wrong direction. Their idea, their goal, is not to ask for blessings from Heavens, but they are asking for their selves, to make their egos enjoy more and to become happy. But it is big falsehood. Wrong way, wrong way!

I was looking at a new instrument, teaching little ones letters, and words, also. I only remember from that small instrument that sometimes you press a button and a voice comes, saying, "Wrong! Wrong way! Wrong!" That is in my memory; yes.

How many times are angels addressing your souls, "Wrong! Wrong step! Wrong action"? How many times are they saying it? When that instrument was saying "Wrong," that boy was correcting, quickly correcting. But millions of people, a heavenly warning, *ikh-tar*,[111] comes to their souls, but they never correct themselves.

So many! For everything, wrong or right, Heavens does not leave anyone on earth alone. Always that warning comes from Heavens to our consciences, saying, "Wrong!" But people are saying, "I don't care! I don't care!" like Pharaoh. No matter how many times Moses said, "Come to your Lord and surrender," Pharaoh said, "I don't care!" So many times Abraham was calling Nimrod, "Come and surrender to your Creator, the Lord of Heavens," and he was saying, "I don't care! I don't care! I don't care!" And therefore the Prophet was saying, peace be upon him, "O people, if Allah Almighty left everyone with his ego and gave them a chance to be Pharaoh or Nimrod, I don't think that anyone would be Muslim." Everyone would say, "I am the Lord of Heavens," *astaghfirullah*, or say, "I am the owner of all continents. All the countries that I am in belong to me!"

Everyone would claim that he is the owner of the Heavens and earth. But Allah Almighty does not give them a full opportunity, *shurut*.[112] If giving it, everyone would claim, "I am Lord! I am your Lord!"—not an ordinary Lord but saying, "*Ana Rabbukumu-l-'ala*,"[113] not accepting to be an ordinary idol for people but saying, "I am most important! I am on top! Even if you are serving, worshipping, so many *alihat*, gods, I am the greatest one." That is Pharaoh. Therefore, *everyone* would say this.

Now, that is its *'unwan*, heading. At this time, they are saying, "We are the most civilized people, the most perfect people among

---

[111]Notice, notification, warning.

[112]Conditions, pre-conditions.

[113]Referring to Pharaoh's declaration to his people, *"I am your most exalted Lord."* (79:24)

those who passed away before our time." You can find even little ones saying, "I am this one." Everyone is just making a condition for being like a Pharaoh, a Nimrod. Everyone is saying, "What I want must be! What I want you must give to me!" fighting with their parents, fighting with their teachers, fighting with the government, fighting with everything, saying, "What I am saying, what I want, you must give to me!"

The title and most famous *tabi'at*[114] of Pharaoh or Nimrod is that they were on that way. No difference between the Nimrod who passed away and those who are now living on earth. Therefore, Allah Almighty is making among them *nufur*, hatred, everyone hating others: children hating their parents, men and women hating each other, children hating among themselves, neighbors hating among themselves, nations hating other nations. *Subhanallah!* That is hatred, just planted in people's hearts. And who is the planter, *zari'*, who is the farmer that is cultivating that hatred among people?

Now, the love that Allah Almighty granted to nations, to people, has been taken up—not taken up, but people are kicking it out and they are running after hatred. Therefore, they are saying, "The most civilized people, now!"

They are cursed people who are saying such things! How you are killing, destroying, burning? How you are saying, "We are the most civilized people"? What is this foolishness? You are killing innocent people and you do not believe that on the Day of Resurrection you should be questioned, when Allah Almighty will ask, *'Bi ayi thanbin qutilat?'*[115] O murderer! Why did you kill that little one—*why?* What was its *thanb*, sin, that you killed her, killed him, a little one?" Allah is going to ask.

---

[114]Nature, natural disposition, character.

[115]*"[And when the girl buried alive is asked] for what sin she was killed."* (81:8-9)

How are they saying, "We are the most civilized people"? They are liars, more than Shaytan! Even Shaytan, has more honour than so many people living now, the twenty-first century's people, the worst people! Shaytan should be on the first *tabaqa* of the Fire, but those people should be on the seventh, the lowest level of Jahannam, Hells!

This is a matter that I was not thinking of speaking to you about, but when my heart is in connection with heavenly powers, They are making me say it. It is the real truth, what we are saying. We do not accept those people! Killers should be punished in the lowest level of the Fire, and it is so appropriate for them.

O people, beware of Shaytan! Beware of following your egos! Allah created you and, in your creation, He put from His heavenly love. You are not using that love, kicking it out and taking from Shaytan hatred and enmity, and killing people, innocent people, burning them, shooting them. What is this?

I am calling to all nations. We are only a handful of people here. Doesn't matter! Allah Almighty is doing something to reach to East and West. I am nothing, I am nothing, but They are making my language to speak the truth. No one can say, "You are wrong."

May Allah forgive us! O people, beware of your ego! Beware of Shaytan because he is carrying you to the Fire, the fire of *dunya* and the fire of the eternal life. Try to reach eternity with your Lord's pleasure. Beware of being in the worst conditions, in misery, in the Fire!

May Allah forgive us! It is enough. We did not arrive at saying, *"A'udhu bil-Lahi min ash-Shaytani-r-rajim, bismillahi-r-Rahmani-r-Rahim,"* but such powerful Oceans' warnings are coming to all mankind.

They must come to what your Lord is sending and they must try to keep all creatures' rights!

[Parodies:] "Animal rights! Yah, animal rights!"

"What do you do?"

"I keep dogs. We like dogs so much. Therefore, we are defenders of the rights of animals."

"*Astaghfirullah!* You do not think about the rights of mankind but you are eager to keep dogs' rights?"

"Şeyh Efendi!"[116]

"What is it?"

"There are barber shops."

"Eh? For what, barbers? Yes, to shave my head."

"No, because now we are such improved people that we are trying to keep the rights of animals."

"Eh? For what?"

"We are keeping some dogs. I mean to say, Şeyh Efendi, we are very, very, very up-to-date people. You must not be now in our day because you don't know about the rights of animals. How old are you?"

"In my place there are forty cats."

"Eh, do you take your cats to the barber shop? They do like this, like this, like that, making the cats so nice."

---

[116]Turkish term for addressing a shaykh.

"No need."

"We keep our dogs and bring them to barber shops, and we are come, also. Someone must be there when bringing that dog. We have seven staff members.."

"For what?"

"To hold the dog, our dog, because we bring him to the barber shop to give him a good look. But sometimes he snaps. Therefore, two persons must hold his head, some of them must hold him by his tail, and two people for the neck and paws because sometimes he barks, also. Sometimes one of them puts a bone for him to be occupied with when they do the shaving. We are keeping the rights of animals!"

"What about mankind?"

"I don't care! I don't care! My dogs are more important to me and my cats are more important to me. Others don't matter. We would like our names to be written as a first class animal rights keeper, and we hope that maybe the Government will give us a medal. And when we pass away, they may put on our gravestone that this person was such an animal rights keeper.'"

"What about mankind?"

"Eh, what is this 'mankind'? Each one of mankind must have even a cat, to give them their rights."

Now, the meaning of the highest civilization level for them is just to be on the level of animals. And the worst thing is that some *belediyes*, municipalities, are ordering, "Whoever brings their dog must also carry a bag and a shovel. If it does anything on the way, that person must take and carry it away."

What is this? This is the honour of mankind? They are proud of such a way? *Asif!* I am sorry, so sorry, about whoever is making mankind fall down to the lowest level of creation.

May Allah forgive us! For the honour of the most honoured one in His Divine Presence, Sayyidina Muhammad ﷺ—*Fateha!*.

12

"YOU CAN'T TAKE IT WITH YOU"

As-salamu 'alaikum! Welcome to you! May all blessings and mercy be for His sincere servants. Try to be sincere servants of our Lord and our Creator, Allah Jalla Jalalahu.

Destur, ya Sayydi, ya Sultanu-l-Awliya! Meded, ya Rijal-Allah! Ashadu an la ilaha illa-Lah wa ashadu anna Sayyidina Muhammad 'abduhu wa habibuhu wa rasuluhu,[117] peace be upon him. May Allah grant us that *Kalimatu-sh-Shahadah* that is the sign of our Islam, to be with it always, here and at the time that we are passing from this life to the eternal life.

Meded, ya Sultanu-l-Awliya! We are wasting our lives for nothing. Really, everyone, particularly believers, they must try to keep the units of their lives, to give and take the most precious jewels. But we are wasting our lives. For what? For nothing!

The Prophet, the honour of all the worlds, the honour of the Heavens, the honour of all creation, what did he say? *"Lau kanata-d-dunya tazinu inda-Lahi janaha ba'uda, ma kan yati shurubatan mai bi-*

---

[117]"I bear witness that there is no deity except Allah and I bear witness that Sayyidina Muhammad is His slave and beloved and messenger, may Allah's blessings and peace be upon him," the *Kalimatu-sh-Shahadah* or Islamic Declaration of Faith.

kafir.[118] If the value of this earth was only as much as the value of one single wing of a mosquito , Allah Almighty would never give unbelievers even this small amount water to drink because they are denying the existence of the Creator."

If all this *dunya,* this our Earth, this planet with everything on it, were to be a *kurah,* ball, made not of earth but if the whole of it were to be gold or a diamond, oh-h-h, how happy people would be! So happy! But in front of Allah Almighty, even if this world were created as a diamond although its value is not as much as a wing of a mosquito, it would be so negligible that it would be impossible for us to state a value for it.

How could this earth be by itself, if you are saying that it came into existence by itself? What is this foolishness? But on behalf of science, scientists are saying, "This world, it is just in existence by itself."

How could it be? They are not saying *how,* only "by itself". "Who said that to you?" I am asking. "That knowledge, from where have you taken it—from Heavens or from the earth or from under the earth?"

I may say to them, "You are taking such knowledge because you are rats! You are taking such knowledge from sewers; *your knowledge you are taking from sewers!* That is knowledge? What is that? How could it be by itself?

O scientists, ask rats what they are saying—"We are in existence through ourselves"? Even rats are denying this and swearing at such

---

[118]"If in front of Allah the world had the value of a mosquito's wing, He would not have given an unbeliever [as much as] a drink of water from it." *(Mishkat)*

scientists. "How are you saying that this huge *kurah,* ball, came into existence by itself? That knowledge, from where is it coming? How could it be by itself?"

And you may ask, "This big ball of earth, or of gold or diamond, do you think that it has a will? Its being and its moving and the conditions on it, do you think there is a will for this ball? You can't say 'No.' There must be a will for this golden ball to turn around itself and to turn around the sun. Ask Venus, 'O Venus, who put you into that orbit? Who put you, and you are a small one? You must be far away because you are so *hafif,* light, while Jupiter is a very heavy one.'"

Scientists, they are saying that the solar system is pieces thrown out of the sun. And I am asking, "If you are saying this, that they are pieces of the sun and the sun threw them out, do you think that the sun used a base on which to put a catapult and then shot them up? There is a base, putting it on it, and then—*wooo!*—sending.

"The sun, how was its balance? If you used that base to send away some pieces, ordinarily those big and heavy ones must fall closer to the sun and small ones must be thrown far away."

And one of them is saying to me, "O Shaykh, you are . . . I understand that you are a little bit—hm-m-m. How old are you?"

"Don't ask how old I am!"

"Because you must know that small children, they are always near their mother. And therefore the sun keeps its small pieces as a hen keeps her small chicks under her wings."

"You are so, *efendim,* so wonderful a scientist!" I am saying this, so many things.

They are saying, "Everything came into being by itself." What is this foolishness? They are ashamed to say, "There is a Creator," because they are engaging their minds to Shaytan. Therefore, their heads are empty like football players'—twenty-two people who, all of them, inside, their heads are only like a football, nothing in it, empty. "Oh-ho-ho, shoot! Oh-ho-ho, shoot!"—that is it! People, either they are renting their minds or selling them. So many people they are writing, "I have a mind for sale"—for sale!

Now people who claim that they are living at a time when science has reached its limit, they are so proud, but their theories or their knowledge are going to be at the point of zero. They are ashamed to say that there is a Creator, creating and giving His rules.

Everything is within rules. Without rules you can't find anything. From the biggest galaxies to the smallest particle representing whole worlds, the atom, they are within rules. They know it, but yet they are insisting on saying, "No God!"

Hasha![19] Insisting on denying the existence of the Creator, what is that? They[120] are saying now, to prepare your understanding, that if the whole world were a piece of diamond or of gold or silver, not earth, the Creator would not give such people, who are scientists, atheists, unbelievers and secular systems' people, even one sip of water to drink.

We are making a base for our Association in order to have understood perfectly what we want to say. People are running after something that has no value. If everyone had such a world of treasures, gold, jewels, it would be of no value for that person because, when he passes away, when he dies, he is not going to take anything from that or use it, leaving and going. The angels, in whom they do

---

[119]Never! God forbid!
[120]Spiritual Headquarters.

not believe, must be ready for their last moment, coming to take that precious and honoured being among mankind. And if that person asks, "Oh, where is my world, where are my treasures, where is my kingdom, where is my sultanate, where is my presidency or prime ministership or commander-in-chiefhood," or, in such a way, "Where is what I collected? Where it is? I must take it!" the angels will say, "No. Forbidden!"

There is a big customs official, saying, "No, leave everything. Come inside!"

"Even our clothes?"

"Yes, even your clothes. Leave them there and put a white cloth on yourself and come with that. You can't bring anything from your *dunya*. Only that white suit that you are in, you may come with that because that is finally going to be dust. It is *mamnu'*, forbidden, for anyone to take anything from this life, from his treasures, to take it with him and pass away."

O people, we are wasting! Big wasters, the biggest wasters, mankind! Animals, they do not put away anything, but men want to collect and to take it with them, like pharaohs.

How many pharaohs? Hundreds of pharaohs, hundreds of Nimrods, hundreds of Neros, hundreds of Shaytan's agents, kings, emperors! And they saved countless jewels, gold, but they went with nothing in their hands. Even a ring would be taken. Anything on their ears, taken; on their necks, taken; on their hands, taken away. But people, they are like drunk ones! Drunk ones are wasting their lives for material things and they can't carry those material things with them. They are not taking care of their spirituality. And those who are not taking care of their spirituality, they are doing their worst for themselves!

And now *dunya,* all of *dunya,* is preparing itself for Armageddon, the biggest war, and the greatest mass of mankind is going to die and they will not take anything with themselves. That is the reason.

May Allah forgive us and grant us to think about such things and to give even at least a short time for our future here and Hereafter, to prepare something for the eternal life, for eternity.

O people, run to eternity! Don't run after such ways that are only making those people dust. Nothing can be carried with them. Try to save something from this life for your eternal life. You should be happy here and Hereafter, because people of *dunya,* daily they are getting more hopeless, more sorrowful, more displeased. Each day, they are looking and seeing that their life's days are getting less, less, less; not going to be one, two, three, four, five and more, but ten, nine, eight, seven, six, five, four, three, two, one. Ha-a-a-a! Zero, finished! Checkbook!

Wa min Allaha-t-taufiq![121] Allah makes us be awake! Wake up, O mankind, wake up, *wake up!* See realities and prepare yourself for eternity, for the eternal life! May Allah forgive us and bless us! For the honour of the most honoured one in His Divine Presence, Sayyidina Muhammad ﷺ—*Fateha!*

---

[121] And success is from Allah.

13

NO SENSE OF RESPONSIBILITY FOR MANKIND WITHOUT BELIEFS

A'udhu bil-Lahi min as-Shaytani-r-rajim. Bismillahi-r-Rahmani-r-Rahim. La haula wa la quwwata illa bil-Lahi-l-'Aliyi-l-'Adhim.

Welcome to you! How did you happen to come here? You haven't any mental house[122] in your country? I am preparing a balance for balancing your minds.

Ashadu an la ilaha illa-Lah wa ashadu anna Sayyidina Muhammadan 'abduhu wa habibihu wa rasuluhu. O our Lord, fix our feet on Your right path, not to fall, not to follow Shaytan. Whoever is following Shaytan must fall, must fall!

We are saying that praying is *salat.* But there is another meaning of praying: to ask from Allah Almighty, *du'a,* supplication. And Allah Almighty wants *du'a* from His servants.

If a bone has nothing inside it, a person cannot live. And the Prophet, peace be upon him, was giving an example that, as in bones there is that liquid through which power comes to our physical being, so that praying, supplication, does the same thing for our spiritu-

---

[122]Mental hospital.

78

al being. Therefore, you must pray; you must pray! And so, we are humbly saying, "O our Lord, fix our feet on *Haqq*, on Truth." If not, if He does not fix them, you may fall down, here and Hereafter.

On the Day of Resurrection, people will pass over the *Sirat*. *"Sirat"* means "bridge." It will be fire. Everyone will be asked to pass over that bridge to enter Paradise. If everything can be completed before that bridge,[123] when it finishes, you may take your way to the bridge, and whoever can pass over it will end in Paradise. But so many people who aren't able to pass will fall down into Hells; underneath it, the Fire will take them. There are some hooks that, when people are passing, will take them like this, to fall down. And you will be asked first, to your face, "Are you among believers or not?"

Therefore, first of all, mankind has been asked to believe. You must believe! It is not possible for anyone's mind to deny the Creator. Only maybe a drunk person, a no-mind person, may deny, but normal ones *must* say there is a Creator.

Earlier today, I was going around on the mountains and I was looking. I was asking those mountains, full of trees, "Do you think that men planted these wild trees here?" And you, also, in your countries, you are seeing jungles, forests, full of trees, and you can see that there is, for example, a pine tree. Next to it there is an oak tree or another kind of tree. Who brought and planted those oak trees there?[124]

---

[123]That is, the process of cleaning from sins and the dirt of this life by enduring suffering, illness, bereavement, etc., before reaching that stage of the journey.

[124]Meaning, how did all the varied kinds of trees arrive at the places where they took root--by themselves, by their own will, power and locomotion?

But people are not using their minds. They like to be no-mind ones. Even animals, they understand. The most perfect creature on earth, that is man. Human beings, they are perfect ones.

Countless kinds of creatures you are able to see, while countless kinds of very small creatures it is difficult to see. Sometimes I am seeing a very small ant, very small, coming into my books, and I am opening them, looking, seeing—so small, but so quickly running, coming like this, coming like that. If I blow on it, it quickly runs, and you can't see its feet, what is their mechanism. Who makes this? But those foolish people are saying, "Nature."

What is Nature? Is Nature a living one or a dead one, a seeing one or not, a hearing one or not, an understanding one or not? Who designed it? But those foolish *kafir* scientists, atheists, cursed people, they are still saying, "Nature."

What is Nature? Why are you not saying, "Allah, the Creator"? What is the reason that prevents you from saying "Allah"? Who made it? Say about yourself, one drop from a man, one drop from a woman—in the womb of women, who designs a person and it comes out as a man? What are you thinking? What is this foolish-ness for the twenty-first century's people? Most of them are following Shaytan! How are they denying?

Everyone will first be asked, "Are you among believers or not?" He will be asked, "Who created you?" Say, at that time, "I did not believe that anyone created me." Say, say! "Who brought you here?" Say, "I did not believe that anyone brought me here." Say!

Therefore, every religion is based on a belief, and the most im-portant pillar of belief is that you must believe that you are created. If you are created, who created you? You are saying, "I am a crea-ture." If I am a creature, there must be a Creator.

Say! This car, was it in existence by itself, no one making it? Taking you to the mental house, bringing to me! Bring here; I shall look. "What are you saying?"

"I am saying nothing, just that this car was found in my street. I am so happy to have it! I do not believe that anyone made this car and I am shouting, 'O people—a car, just found in front of my house, and I am so happy. And I believe that no one made such a thing. It just appeared by itself!"

"Where?"

"At Lefke International Mental House."

"Bring him here! Then, what you are saying?"

"I am saying that this car was found in front of my house by itself, and I am a person not believing that anyone made it."

"Come, Abu Bakr, 'Umar! Come and tie his feet and put him down! Hajji ____, bring a stick, a new one from our trees, so that when you hit him he will understand."

Not yet! "*Vur*, hit him!"

"O Director of the Mental House, I think that someone brought this car."

"Leave him! But it is too difficult, a long conversation. We have a mind. That mind is like our *dümen*,[125] leading."

Our minds are like that. Without this, you are nothing. If not for that very precious thing that is granted to you by your Creator, you are nothing, you are nothing! That has been granted to all mankind. But so many people now, they are atheists.

---

[125]Rudder, helm.

Why, atheists? Why are you saying, "No God, no Creator," while you are a creature? If you created yourself, keep your self in yourself! Why are you going to pass away? Who is making you grow older?

Day by day, day by day, day by day you are getting older. Stop it, because the period of youth is so, so beautiful! Why are you not keeping yourself to be always young? Who is forcing you to grow older? Think about it!

Why does your height reach one-and-half to two meters or so? Why are you not like giants, three meters, five meters, ten meters? Who is keeping you from it? But not thinking. They are all drunk people; they should be taken away! Therefore, the first question will be, "Do you believe in your Creator, the Lord of Heavens?" If saying, "No!" let him go down, to learn belief there!

Nothing can save people now in the worst situation; mankind has just reached the worst situation. After one foot, they are going to fall down and no one will be able to reach them to take them out, only faith. Only faith! You must understand and you must believe, or you will go away, finishing. Not millions but *billions* of people, they are ready to be taken away because they are still drunk and they are insisting on denying the existence of the Creator. No chance for them to live longer on earth!

Two times, big wars, world wars, people passing away, dying. They were, in the first war, maybe twenty million; in the second war, maybe a hundred and a few more million. But this third is coming, holy books saying "Armaggedon." We are saying "Malhamatu-l-Kubra,"[126] the biggest war, billions, billions, going, passing away and

---

[126]The Greatest Batttle/Massacre/Slaughter.

never going to be again. If there are six billion people, five will go, one billion remaining.

O people, this is a humble Association. We are not trying to show you that we know something, no. We are only warning people, warning you, as all prophets came to warn their nations. Finally, the Seal of Prophets ﷺ, peace be upon him, came, and he was for all nations and he is the last one. And then the Day of Resurrection will come and finish. For everything, Allah Almighty is making a limit. The limit of mankind here, now, according to the Prophet's tidings, is 7,000 years.

One week ago, I was looking at some fossil photographs. Scientists are saying that they are sixty-two million years old. What is this? Was that person drunk or not knowing calculation, or was he present at that time, or at the beginning of this computer?

"O Shaykh, do you not believe in our computer"?

"No, I never touch a computer. I have a small mind. If I touch it, it will make me a no-mind person. Therefore, I never ask how it works. I am saying, 'How can it be?' It *can* be because Shaytan is sitting in it, and for every computer there is one jinn. Jinn are making mankind to be much more crazy, much more idiotic. Who said this 'sixty-two million years ago'?"

Once I was in Chicago. There is a natural history museum with mammoths. They said to me, "When those two mamoths heard this [sixty-two million year theory], they began to move around. They wanted to get out because it is written on them that they are only 8,000 years old."

Where is 8,000 years old and where is sixty-two million years— such a different number of years! And then the mammoths were very angry because, as that shaytan, Darwin, was saying, step by step animals came, and then apes, and from apes people like Darwin came (he looks like an ape). And the mammoths were so angry, saying, "How are crocodiles our ancestors? What is the relationship between crocodiles and ourselves? How did our ancestors come from crocodiles? We will never accept that! Open the doors! We are coming out!"

And the doorkeeper was saying, "Be calm, because we are sending you to that ape's grandson, Darwin, to find a solution for your case. He may understand. We do not understand such a thing. Maybe crocodiles came from mammoths, and they must change that sign.

"Be calm! Now we are changing that sign, to be written on it that these mammoths are sixty-two million years old and that crocodile is from their son."

And the mammoths were saying, "It is okay. Doesn't matter now." Changed, and they are happy. "Those scientists are putting it on TV in East and West to say that these crocodiles are sixty-two million years old."

What is this foolishness? They are shaytans and Shaytan's representatives! To make people's beliefs finish, they are trying to destroy their beliefs. And we are saying, "Beware of Allah Almighty's divine anger! He may send on them a punishment from Heavens!" And still, in all nations, the Minister of Education everywhere is Darwin, everywhere Darwin. I am calling them through this magic machine in front of me, "You must correct your beliefs. It is impossible!" And people have just reached the point at which they haven't any belief; no belief for them. Those shaytans' educational system is destroying all beliefs. And people are killing, burning, destroying because they are saying, "No Day of Resurrection, no Judgment Day."

If they are saying "Judgment Day," they must think about responsibility. But they never like to be responsible for anything they are doing. That is the biggest curse on makind, that they are not accepting that they have responsibility. We understand that animals have no responsiblity, but are you on the same level as animals? *They* have no responsibility, but you have been granted a mind that makes you responsible for everything that you are doing.

May Allah forgive us! O people, try to make your beliefs strong. And those people who are trying to destroy our beliefs, may Allah take them away, and make us under holy flag of the Seal of the Prophets, the most honoured, most glorified, most beloved servant of the Lord of Heavens.

Sultan sensin, ya Rabbi.[127] Forgive us and grant Your blessings to us. We are believers, O our Lord. And keep our feet fixed on Your right path and not following shaytans or shaytanic groups from mankind. *Fateha!*

---

[127]You are the Sultan, O Lord.

14

ASKING FOR ETERNITY, NOT FOR *DUNYA*

Allahumma, salli ʿala Muhammadin wa ʿala ali Muhammadin wa sallim taslīman kathīran.[128] *Hu-u! Meded, ya Sultanu-l-Awliya! Meded, ya Rijal-Allah.*

The Prophet ﷺ was saying, *"Ad-dinu nasiha."*[129] *"Nasiha"* means "advice". The Prophet's *hadith*—that knowledge that was granted by Allah *Subhanahu wa Taʿala*[130] to His most beloved and glorified servant, Sayyidina Muhammad—that knowledge belongs to Heavens, belongs above Heavens, also. Therefore, you can't bring a limit for its meaning. No, no limit. It is like an ocean and you can't reach its beach and you can't reach its bottom.

Now we are repeating this holy *hadith*, as my Grandshaykh always did for addressing people when everyone was sitting: *"Ad-dinu nasiha."* And from that Ocean, Shah Naqshiband, may Allah bless him, was saying *"Tariqatuna as-sohbet."*[131]

---

[128]Our Lord, bless Muhammad and the people of Muhammad, and greet him with abundant greetings.

[129]"The religion [Islam] is sound advice."

[130]Allah, Glorified and Exalted.

[131]Shah Naqshband: a great eighth century C.E. grandshaykh and founder of the Naqshbandi *Tariqah*. *"Tariqatuna as-sohbet"* means, "Our *tariqah* consists of Association" of the shaykh with his *murids* (followers).

O people, we have been ordered to bring the names of holy people and to speak about them because *"Inda dhikri-s-salihin tanzilu-r-rahmah"*,[132] when you speak about a saint, blessings and mercy, mercy and blessings are coming. Therefore, each time when we are speaking, and when we were listening to our grandshaykhs, mostly they were speaking about *awliya* to make blessings come closer, closer—blessings, endless Mercy Oceans, giving us strength for our organs and power coming to our hearts, more urging power, as when spring comes, the weather brings new life to trees. Therefore, when blessings come to the hearts of people, giving, bringing, also, that secret power to make them wake up. *Subhanallah!*

Now, They are making me to speak as They like. They are my leading power; They are carrying me like this, like that, like this, like that. Now it is a proper meaning. Perhaps we said it before or it is coming in a new way:

When you ask that question, you are asking, "O Shaykh, knowledge is not something that we can touch with our materiality. Blessings are something else. And advice—for what, advice?"

We are saying, "For what, prophets? Why did Allah Almighty send us prophets? You must know it."

Allah Almighty makes it clear for some servants, when they have been granted heavenly powers to understand and to speak about it, and to make people's real being to be *taujih*, guided. Why did Allah Almighty send His prophets? This is an important question. Then we can understand the meaning of advice, the meaning of religion.

Everyone knows but not everyone believes. Some people know and believe. Some others, they are learning, knowing but not believ-

---

[132]When pure/righteous ones are mentioned, mercy descends.

ing. Some others, they only believe. Some specialized people, they know and believe. To know and to believe is excellent, the highest level.

Yes, prophets, for what did they come? What were their missions or what was the mission of prophethood?

As we learned and we believe—and what we learned, we believe in it, also—the first man, Adam ﷺ, was created and put in Paradise. Then there happened what happened, and he was landed on the earth.

The first descendants of Sayyidina Adam ﷺ, they believed that their father had been sent from Paradise to be on earth for a while. And they knew that their father or grandfather had done something wrong; then he had been sent down to a place where there was no relationship between that place and Paradise. And they knew that their grandfather Adam, peace be upon him and upon every prophet, particularly the Seal of Prophets—they knew that he wanted to get back to that level, heavenly level, to be there; they were aware of that.

Adam, he was always crying and asking to be returned to Paradise, to that Paradise for which you can't make any *ta'rif*, description, of the difference between being on earth and being at that level. He knew, but his sons and grandsons, descendants, they did not know what he knew, and Adam, peace be upon him, he was crying and asking forgiveness from Allah Almighty.

And forgiveness was granted to him,[133] and he was saying, "O my Lord, I would like to be on the first level at which I was granted by You to be. I am looking at this *dunya* as a jail, a prison. Therefore, O my Lord, make me reach my first *vatan*, homeland. *Subhanallah*, my heart is always just drawn to being in my first home, my home that You granted to me. I would like to be there, O my Lord!"

But his sons, they did not originate in Paradise; their origin was on earth. Therefore they did not understand that their grandfather was longing, longing, longing to be in Paradise. Out of Paradise, it is like Hells, or at least out of Paradise it is like a prison. Even if the prison is good, yet there are some people on earth—they are in hospitals or in mental houses or in prisons—who are longing to come out. And Adam was longing to come back to his first homeland, and he was crying.

Then Allah Almighty accepted his *tauba*, repentance, and He said, "O Adam, I will take you back to your homeland." He did not say "homeland," but, "I am calling you again to your Paradise, where you will be up to eternity." Eternity, no limit for that time. You understand this, *insha'Allah*.

And He Almighty was saying, because Adam ﷺ was also asking that his descendants should be in Paradise, "O Adam, as I accept your *tauba*, repentance, I will make you come back to Paradise. I am granting My divine blessings to you and opening Paradise for you. I am sending to your descendants, up to the Day of Resurrection, some chosen servants of Mine to call them to the way of Paradise.

---

[133]This is clear from the fact that Adam and Eve repented of their disobedience as soon as they had eaten from the Tree, saying, *"'Our Lord, we have wronged ourselves. And if You do not forgive us and have mercy upon us, we will surely be among the lost'"* (7:23), and the words, *"Then Adam learned from his Lord words [of repentance], and He accepted his repentance. Indeed, He is the Acceptor of Repentance, the Merciful"* (2:37).

"Come and go through this way. You should find yourself finally in Paradise because your grandfather is there waiting for you." Yes. That was what Allah Almighty was promising Sayyidina Adam. "I shall send some special, chosen servants, who are My messengers, with My heavenly Messages, to call your descendants to come to Paradise."

Therefore, Allah Almighty sent His chosen servants, who are prophets, to call people, "O people, come, come, come after me! I will lead you to Paradise, that no one's eyes have seen, no one's ears have heard and learned about. It is a grant from Allah to you to believe in those beliefs, taking you back to Paradise." Therefore, O our listeners, *subhanallah*, Allah is calling everyone to come and enter Paradise. But most of Adam's sons refused, saying, "We are not in need, we do not believe in an eternal life. No!"

Therefore, *"Ad-dinu nasihah."* What is the meaning of *"nasihah"*? *Nisahah*, They are making me give a wider explanation of it. It is not something to say, "I am Muslim" or "I am Protestant" or "I am the Pope" or "I am Christian, Jewish, Muslim." Important is to ask the way back to Paradise. Therefore, prophets were coming and giving that advice:

"O people, prepare yourselves to come back to Paradise, to be with your grandfather, grandmother, and for thousands of prophets to be with their followers, *mu'mins*, and their messages to be sent to millions of people to take care and come to Paradise."

Now we are living in a time when people are just cut off, cut off. They are not asking anything about Paradise. And our scholars, I am sorry to say, their new title is to be "Doctor."

"Doctor Hussain, Ph.D. What Ph.D.?"

"You do not understand such a thing."

"I must also understand."

"If you are asking to understand something about Ph.D., you must go and spend at least twenty years to be a doctor. Your head is a little bit hard. You need to spend twenty-five years to be—not a Ph.D; a Ph.D. is hgher—an assistant. Doesn't matter, because after a while you quickly forget half of it. Therefore, eh—thirty years; doesn't matter! Work on it. We shall give you an assistantship; half assistant, doesn't matter!" Like Pakistani people—three-quarters of them are doctors, yes? Our Turks—eh, one-fourth of them; doesn't matter! Arabs, they are saying, "We are not in need to be Ph.D.s We have a Ph.D. when we are born from our mothers." If you are asking Egyptian people, they are saying, "What about Lebanese people, half-Christian, half-Muslim?"

"What is your knowledge?"

"We have knowledge."

People they are trying to learn but not to believe. They are giving their whole ability, capacity, only to be a Ph.D., not to be a believer. They have that title, "Ph.D., Professor," but if you ask, "Do you believe?" they are saying, "No, I only know. I do not believe."

And prophets were asking to make people believe. Scientists and scholars are saying, "We only want to know [empirically], not to believe and not to practice. We like being doctors." And *nasihat*, that advice from prophets, makes people believe and use their capacity to come back to the line of eternity, to have *shauq*, longing, desiring so much, and *'ishq*,[134].

Some of them, they are only interested in learning, not interested in practicing and reaching the line of eternity. *Eternity!* So

---

[134]*Shauq:* longing, yearning, desire; *'ishq:* passsionate love.

sweet a word in Western people's languages. I like that word more than anything. [Slowly drawing out the words:] Eternity, eternity, *abadi, sarmadi;.abadi, sarmadi,* eternity, eternity. Such refreshment and power is coming to me! But people are dead; they are not asking. If you bring a Beirut sweet, *shini,* to a table and put it there, and put straw here in front of a donkey, it will run to the straw, leaving the famous sweet of Lebanon.

When people eat that sweet, baklava, the *sherbet,* syrup, remains. I am mixing straw with that and making people eat. Happy, very happy! If you give curry to an ox, it will never look at it, but if mixing what remains with straw and giving it to the ox, he never knows it and eats. For the sake of the straw, donkeys and cows and oxen, they are eating. And that is the way for some people, but if you give only curry, they will never eat. Does your donkey eat? Never eats, never eating *biriyani,* saying, "We don't like it, we aren't interested in it." But mankind is interested in *biriyani, chapatti, tandoori* and curry, salad and *turşu,* pickles, chutney.

"Other things?"

"Eh, we don't like them!"

Therefore, people are in seventy and more branches, according to their *işta,* desire, appetite. And prophets brought, for every kind of people, what they might be interested in. That eternity, eternity, is the highest level for which real people, when they have been glorified by their Lord, are asking.

"Eternity, eternity," so fresh a word, making my heart open! Eternal life, eternity; *ebedi, sarmadi, abadi, sarmadi*—eternity! *Ya Rabbi,* grant us it! Don't let us be like animals. They want only materials things, plants and something growing on the earth. We know that You did not create us for eating grass or meat or so many things that You are granting us on earth, and we are asking only for eternity, eternal life, to be in Your Divine Presence.

O our Lord, let us be believers! For the honour of the most honoured servant and glorified one in Your Divine Presence, Sayyidina Muhammad—*Fateha!*

This is something that is not written in the books of *'ulema*, scholars, but it is suitable for people living now in our days. And every curse is coming on people now because they have stopped asking for an eternal life beyond this life. That is the reason. They believe only in this material life on earth, nothing else beyond this, and Allah Almighty wants you to ask from Him eternity, eternity, eternal life. *Fateha!*

We are not fanatical, *muta'assib*,[135] people; I am not a fanatical person. Fanatical Muslims you can find, fanatical Christians you can find, fanatical Jews you can find, fanatical Maronites you can find, fanatical Protestants you can find, fanatical Hindus or Buddhists you can find. I am not a fanatic. I am a realist and I am speaking to each one of mankind because I am a member of the big family of mankind and I have been granted something that is different from the mentalities of all religious people. The wrong ideas of such fanatical religious people are under my feet. *Allahu Akbar!*

---

[135]Fanatic, zealot.

15

FOLLOWING THE ONLY SAFE WAY

As-salamu 'alaikum! Astaghfirullah, astaghfirullah, astaghfirullah min kulli dhanbin wa ma'siya, min kulli ma yukhalifu dina-l-Islam.[136] We are asking forgiveness from Allah Almighty!

A'udhu bil-Lahi min as-Shaytani-r-rajim. Bismillahi-r-Rahmani-r-Rahim. La haula wa la quwwata illa bil-Lahi-l-'Aliyi-l-'Adhim.

We are claiming to follow the Seal of Prophets, Sayyidina Muhammad ﷺ. That is what we are claiming, but, *shattana ma baynahuma*,[137] we are so far from keeping the advices of the Seal of Prophets, Sayyidina Muhammad ﷺ. As he was saying, *"Ad-dinu nasihah"*—the main aim of Islam, the meaning of Islam, it is to advise people. For what? To find a safe way to Heavens.

I was in London, and once I saw a big market, supermarket, and there was written on it "Safeway". You know Safeway? I was thinking that there are people advising there, showing the Safe Way.

I went there and asked, "Where is the Safe Way?"

---

[136]I seek refuge in Allah (three times) from every sin and disobedience and from whatever is contrary to the faith of Islam.

[137]What a difference there is between the two of them [i.e., speech and action].

They were saying, "Safeway is inside. Go in!"

I went, going around. *"Yahu,* is this a market or a Safe Way? For what is this?"

"How old are you?"

I said, "Over *tis'un,* ninety."[138]

"Go around and look. You can find a safe way to get out!" [Laughter.]

And prophets, peace be upon them, they are asking for the Safe Way from the Seal of Prophets. Each prophet was asking for the Safe Way, to learn it from the Seal of Prophets, because Sayyidina Muhammad, peace be upon him, is the only one who knows the Safe Way. Allah Almighty never kept a student, to teach him directly, except Sayyidina Muhammad ﷺ. No other prophet learned directly from Allah Almighty.

"Ar-Rahman, 'allama-l-Qur'an."[139] Allah Almighty, He is that One who taught that one person to whom the Holy Qur'an came, only Sayyidina Muhammad ﷺ. Other prophets, for example, Sayyidina Musa was *Kalim-Allah.*[140] *Kalim-Allah* heard Allah Almighty's divine Voice that belongs to our Heavens, hearing, learning something, but he [Moses] was not able to enter into those Oceans. Therefore, so many times Moses went to Tur Sina, Mount Sinai, and Allah Almighty spoke to him. And he was such a one, always asking questions, always asking questions.

Rasul-Allah, the Seal of the Prophets, Sayyidina Muhammad ﷺ, he was once invited [to Allah's Divine Presence], on Lailatu-l-Me'raj.

---

[138]Reckoned according to the Islamic *(Hijri)* calendar.
[139] *"The Most Merciful taught the Qur'an."* (55:1-2)
[140]Allah's word.

On the holy night that he was invited to be in the Divine Presence, the Seal of the Prophets never once asked any question to Allah— fiinished! Therefore, all the prophets, they are asking for the Safe Way from Rasul-Allah 🌸. He was teaching all the prophets and his nation, also, teaching everything that any one of the prophets, of mankind, might be in need of. He was able to answer, to show them what is the Safe Way to reach the pleasure of Allah.

Why are we asking the Safe Way? The Safe Way is that one that leads people to Allah Almighty's pleasure. That is the Safe Way. If you are going, going, going and not finding that Allah Almighty is happy with you and not pleased with you, that means you are on the wrong way, a dangerous way.

Safe Way and Unsafe Way—whoever is asking for safety here and Hereafter may ask that Safe Way from the Seal of the Prophets, the most honoured or most honourable one in the Divine Presence, and the most glorified and most praised one in the Divine Presence.

Who is that one? That one is Sayyidina Muhammad 🌸. Mankind must know that. If they are asking for a Safe Way, that is the Safe Way. Otherwise, they are on dangerous ways. They should disappear and finish, vanishing, never again coming into existence, finishing.

Therefore, the prophets' inheritors [awliya], they are followers of the footsteps of the Seal of the Prophets. All prophets must walk in his footsteps; all awliya, saints, holy ones, must walk in his footsteps. No one can be holy without walking in his footsteps and the footsteps of earlier prophets. Can't be! Whoever says so, they are liars, they are agents of Shaytan. Whoever does not walk in the footsteps of prophets, they are all Shaytan's students, Shaytan's followers, Shaytan's representatives. They should beware of Allah's anger coming on them!

We are living in the twenty-first century, and mankind has entered into a tunnel. No lights, no guides; they are going, going. Shaytan is in front of them, saying, "Follow me! Follow me! Follow me!"

I was seeing, in airports, some cars, written on them, "FOLLOW ME!"

"'Follow me!' Who, how are we following? Will we get down and follow that car?"

"No, that sign is not for you. That is for these big planes coming and they do not know about the situation at the airport. There is written on that small one, 'Follow me, follow me, follow me!' and those gigantic planes are coming and following."

"If not following, what happens?"

"Going off the runway—*uh-h-h-h*, finished!"

Yes. "FOLLOW ME!" The captain of that gigantic plane can't say, "For what should I follow this one? I have come here from a distance of fourteen hours and more, and I should follow that small car, written on it, 'FOLLOW ME'? I am not like a camel caravan driver!"

Always in front of camels there is a donkey; you know? The owner of the camels rides on a donkey in front of them and all the camels follow. And the camels are very angry, very angry. "What is this? We are like gigantic creatures! Why is our owner is riding on a donkey in front of us and we are following a donkey?" But what shall we do? This is the twenty-first century. You must follow donkeys. You can't follow big ones.

The twenty-first century's people, they threw out their *sultans*[141] and brought some ones who are like the legs or feet. Do you think that your feet can take you to the Safe Way? But people living in the twenty-first century, they are saying, "We must follow our feet's steps. We don't have our heads, so we must follow our feet."

Where did they reach with you? Your steps, your feet, to where have they brought you? Look now at East and West, carrying you to a fire-land, a burning world, no peace, and the whole world now, it is on fire everywhere because people are following the feet and leaving the heads.

Heads, they were *sultans*.[142] They threw out *sultans*, who were like the heads, and brought the feet, saying, "Eh, today there is election in Turkey, election in Arabia, election in Russia; election in Pakistan, also," whose people are saying, "We are Number One Muslims." From where have they taken that 'election'? Does the Holy Qur'an say there is election, there is democracy? *Pocracy!*

Alhamdulillah, U.K. is okay; no fighting there. Even though they are making a *tamthili* election,[143] *alhamdulillah*, there is still honour in U.K. with Her Majesty the Queen or His Majesty the King, because that title brings blessings on that country. Therefore, I am not happy anywhere in U.K. except in London. I am happy because they have a *sultan,* they have a monarch, and for the sake of monarchs those blessings are coming on them. I don't like Germany, Italy, Spain, Turkey, Russia, Egypt, Libya, Pakistan.

Pakistani people are saying [parodies:] "*Ya Shaykh,* this is an Islamic republic." In which book do you find that "Islamic republic"?

---

[141]Monarchs, kings.

[142]That is, monarchs.

[143]Following the model of an election.

Iranian people, they are saying "Irani Republic". "Islamic republic," *masha'Allah!* Where is your *imam*? Allah is saying, "There is one *imam.*"[144] He must be for the whole Islamic world, whose population now reaches billions.

Why are people afraid of China, the Chinese people? Because its population is over one billion or more, or two billion. The whole world is watching them. Where are the Muslims? Muslims, how many republics? Where is your *imam*, O Pakistani people? [Parodies:] "Eh, Bhutto, Batu, Bata[145] (they make shoes) is coming." Understand my English, sir? Not understanding? I may speak in Arabic *hatta bi-subh.*[146]

The Prophet was saying, peace be upon him, Sayyidina Rasul-Allah ﷺ, "When the Last Days approach, it is from the signs of *Qiyamah*[147] for the 'heads' to be 'feet,' the 'feet' to be 'heads.' *Za'imuhum laki'a ibnu laki'a.*"[148]

May Allah forgive us! No way for mankind to be saved except if they ask for the Safe Way, the footsteps of the Seal of the Prophets. May Allah forgive us. *As-salamu 'alaikum!*

---

[144]The *imam* is the caliph of Prophet Muhammad, the accepted spiritual authority of Muslims worldwide, whose function was to guide the Muslim nation and ensuring that its actions and the laws of the state were in keeping with Islamic principles and laws. The Islamic caliphate was abolished in 1924 during the secular dictatorship of Ataturk.

[145]The name of a well-known Pakistani shoe manufacturer.

[146]Until morning.

[147]Judgment Day.

[148]Referring to a *hadith* stating, "The Hour will not be established until the leader is the depraved son of a depraved father." (*Musnad* Ahmad, Bayhaqi and others)

Once, there was a fire on a mountain, and a lot of trees and land were burning. Then the police was investigating to find that one who had made the fire.

They found an old woman and brought her to court. The *hakim*[149] was calling, *"Çavuş!"*[150]

The *çavuş*, guard, stood up, saying, "O Your Honor, we are bringing that woman because she is the main cause of that fire."

The judge looked. "How old are you?"

The *çavuş*, guard, said, "How old are you, O my grandma?"

"I am from the time that the British government landed in Larnaca. I don't know which year it was."

"It was over one hundred years ago."

The *hakim* said, "*Çavuş*, guard, you are a no-mind person, bringing that woman whose age is over a hundred years and occupying our Court with such nonsense! Take her to her home, quickly! I was sitting here thinking that someone could carry responsibility. This is my grandmother's grandmother you are bringing, to make a case on her? Take her home!"

"I can't walk. O my son, I can't walk! Let two men hold me up and take me by car to my home."

Now I am swearing at all of them because my age, also, is ninety.[151] I am only spending, spending my mind and nothing is in it

---

[149]Judge.

[150]Guard, sergeant.

[151]Measured in *Hijri* years.

now. And your heads are also from footballs, empty. Therefore, doesn't matter! Who is going to put an *'ayb,*[152] on me? No one can blame me. I can swear! But what I am saying, it is true. It is true!

May Allah forgive me, forgive you, and send us someone whom He is dressing in the greatness of Heavens to carry people away from Shaytan and bring them to the line of prophets. *Amin!*[153] *Fateha!*

---

[152]Blame, reproach, shame, disgrace.
[153]Amen.

16

CONCERNING USEFUL AND USELESS KNOWLEDGE

As-salamu alaikum! A'udhu bil-Lahi min-ash Shaytani-r-rajim. Bis-millahi-r-rahmani-r-Rahim.

Allah Allah, Allah Allah, Allah Allah, 'Aziz Allah.

Allah Allah, Allah Allah, Allah Allah, Karim Allah.

Allah Allah, Allah Allah, Allah Allah, Subhan Allah.

Allah Allah, Allah Allah, Allah Allah, Sultan Allah!

Masha'Allah! You must know that He is *Sultan! Astaghfirullah! Meded, ya Sultanu-l-Awliya! Meded, ya Rijal-Allah!*

The Holy Prophet was saying, *"Talabu-l-'ilmi faridatun 'ala kulli Muslimin wa Muslimat."*[154] *Sahih,* right?

The Seal of Prophets, Sayyidina Muhammad ﷺ, *mu'allimu nassa-l-khair.*[155] He was sent from Heavens to teach people what is necessary for them to learn and to know and to act on. That was his real mission, to teach people. And he was saying that you must learn

---

[154]"Seeking knowledge is obligatory on every Muslim male and Muslim female." *(Hadith)*

[155]Taught people what is good.

about man's position and who created you or who created *dunya wa ma fiha*.[156] That is real knowledge. It is not real knowledge to ask to know what is not necessary to know, what is not obligatory.

Now people are occupying themselves with some meaningless efforts. Yesterday I was looking at that Shaytan box, TV. I saw that there were many scorpions; perhaps there might have been twenty scorpions, more or less, in a box. One person, whose age was maybe like ____'s and he had many assistants, he was holding a microscope, and he was taking an instrument and catching hold of the tail of a scorpion and taking out its poison.

I am saying, "For what is this? What are they learning? They are looking only at how that creature carries that poison and what is the power of that poison. And how? They they were not saying how, but we must say it."

He was occupying himself with such a thing, and I was saying, "This person must have lost his mind because his effort is only to know what is the power, what is the effect of that poison in that creature, never occurring to that person to ask, 'Who created that creature?' And that creature is on the same level, on the earth, as so many other creatures, but he never asks, 'That creature, how does it have such a terrible poison? It eats some things on the earth, and spiders and other kinds of insects also eat that. Countless creatures in the same area, they eat the same things, and it is for some a poison and for others it is a *dawa*, medicine."

We have a saying: "The rain of April falls, and every creature wants to reach even one small drop of that April rain."

"Why?" I was asking Grandshaykh.

---

[156] The world and whatever is in it.

And Grandshaykh said to me, "Because the rains coming in April bring something from Paradise."

It is a secret happening and secret event, and you can't think or you can't learn anything about the secret of those rains. The same rain is raining, and some poisonous creatures—snakes, scorpions, spiders and such poisonous creatures—they want something from those drops to reach them. And in the mouth of a snake or some other creatures, those drops are changed into a terrible poison.

And also in the oceans, creatures are coming up, up to the surface of oceans and opening their mouths to reach one drop of those holy rains coming from Heavens, and they are changing into pearls. That is a knowledge that has reached mankind from Heavens through prophets. But now so many foolish scholars, as I said to you, are catching hold of the tail of a scorpion and taking some drops from its poisoned tail to look at what it is.

Why do you not listen? It is not something that you have been ordered to learn, no. You must try to take your wisdoms from holy books. Holy books are full of wisdoms, but *their* knowledge, it is like something to be thrown into the rubbish, dustbin.

'Knowledge,' it is not real knowledge. It is a shaytanic way to divert mankind from true Reality and make them lose their minds, their capacities, their mentalities on something that is rubbish—rubbish, because they are not saying, "This is from the Creator."

And now people are occupied, all of them. "We are learning. Our children just finished O level, E level, T level, K level, X level." Then, "My son is going to university to be a doctor or to be a Ph.D."

Understand what I am saying? You must try to learn from prophets' knowledge that has reached us from Heavens, not to occupy yourself with what an ant eats, how it carries it. [Parodies:] "If an ant carries a wheat seed and it is too big, heavier than its own body, how does that happen?"—*such* knowledge.

A person was saying, "I know everything. You can ask me!"

Then another person was saying, "O my master, for so many years I have been thinking about something. It is so important to me."

"What is that?"

"I want to learn. If you know everything, I am asking: People they are wondering how an ant carries a heavy piece of wheat so easily. They may ask. But I am asking you something else. It is a much more unusual question, and I would like to know. But no one is giving a real answer."

"What is that?"

"You know that an ant has two parts, the head side and the lower side. I was always looking and wondering—its intestines, are they in the head side or the lower side."

"I have never heard such a question or given such an answer, never! Making me change all my knowledge now! O person, from where you are coming?"

"I am coming from the *badu*.[157] Always I am with ants. I am looking at this side and that side, and the joining place is at zero point. How does it carry that, not leaving it, as a train leaves some cars and takes others?"

"What . . . ?"

---

[157]Bedouins.

That person wants to learn what is the power of a scorpion's bite, making a person, if he does not die, at least scream, cry for twenty-four hours from that one little spot from a scorpion. That is much more important than ants.

People are working on something that is, we are saying, *ma la y'ani*, useless. The Prophet, peace be upon him, ﷺ, he was saying, *"Min husni Islami-l-mari' tarkuhu ma la y'anihi."*[158]

Now all nations are doing research and spending millions of dollars, wasting their energy, their time and their riches for useless matters. What is this? If you do not believe in that scorpion, take one and put it on your hand. Try it; it is better! Why are you doing like that? That person also had a white beard. That means no mind.

You have come to learn who created you. Where were you one hundred years ago? Was anyone here in existence? No! After a hundred years, where are you going to be? You are between two areas of non-existence. This area is non-existent, and that, afterwards, is going to be non-existent. How have you appeared between two areas of non-existence? Ask this, learn this, and bow to Him who has done that, who has created you in such a way. Use your minds for that! That is real knowledge that makes you reach the Creator of Heavens and Hells, the Creator of Heavens and Paradises and universes and endless galaxies.

But for people, it is easy to take a scorpion. What is this with which you are wasting your time? *"Talabu-l-'ilmi faridatun 'ala kulli Muslimin wa Muslimat."* *Asif annu;*[159] I am sorry to say that now Muslim territories are also in same way, wasting their time, running and

---

[158]It is from the excellence of a person's Islam that he leaves alone what is useless/futile for him. *(Muwatta, 47.1.3)*

[159]I am sorry.

following no-mind Western people's minds, leaving the real sources of knowledge and wisdoms that have come from Heavens. And Allah Almighty is saying, "I am giving you, O My *habib*,[160] the Holy Qur'an and wisdoms."[161] Therefore, they are falling into such a terrible, terrible situation. They can never know how to get out because they have fallen into a bottomless well, *kuyu*. They can't find anything to take them out, no, and they do not know what they are going to do.

I am the weakest servant, but I may say, I may give a real answer for them. And such a thing is a real knowledge, heavenly knowledge, that no one may be able to object to.

O people, you have come to learn. Therefore, when you pass away and you are buried in your grave, angels will come, asking from you, "What did you learn?"

The first question, "What did you learn? *Man Rabbuka*"[162] "Who created you?" the first question. Then, "Who led you to the Lord of Creation? Who was that one? What did you learn that he was granted?"

Don't say that his knowledge, knowledge known since fifteen centuries, is unacceptable knowledge. No, you are wrong! They brought gold from the time of the pharaohs but they did not say, "This is old gold. We must throw it away." What prophets brought,

---

[160]Beloved—that is, Muhammad ﷺ.

[161]2:231, 4:113.

[162]"Who is your Lord?" As mentioned in a number of *ahadith*, this is the first question every newly-deceased person is asked during his or her questioning in the grave by angels (Bukhari, 2:422, 2:450; Abu Dawud, 4735; *Mishkat al-Masabih*, 0130).

that is a real pearl of knowledges. You must come and hear and listen and obey to be a perfect one in creation.

May Allah forgive us! For the honour of the most honoured one, Sayyidina Rasul-Allah ﷺ—*Fateha!*

17

THE IMPORTANCE OF CLEANLINESS

As-salamu 'alaikum! Ashadu an la ilaha illa-Llah, wa ashadu anna Muhammadun 'abduhu wa habibuhu wa rasuluhu ﷺ. *A'udhu bil-Lahi min ash-Shaytani-r-rajim. Bismillahi-r-Rahmani-r-Rahim.*

Meded, ya Sultan-l-Awliya! Meded, ya Rijal-Allah! Whoever does not believe in [Islamic] saints who are holy ones, their faith is very weak, never growing.

Allah Almighty, why does He put saints among people? They are really heavenly springs on earth. Those who want to drink or to clean themselves physically, they run to taps, running to find spring water for drinking and cleaning. Just like that, those who want to reach their heavenly stations or who want a cleaning must find a way to clean themselves because servanthood, first it needs a cleaning. Therefore, Islam came to clean people, their physical being and inner personality, also. *"An-nadhafatu nisfu-l iman,*[163] cleanlinesss," the Prophet ﷺ was saying, "is half of our belief," so that everything is just built on cleanliness.

You can't do anything without *wudu*.[164] If you want to pray to Allah, you must clean yourself. *Abdest,* ablution, that is first. If anyone comes and says, "*Ashadu an la ilaha illa-Lah wa ashadu anna Say-*

---

[163]"Cleanliness is half of faith." *(Hadith)*
[164]Ablution (Arabic, *wudu;* Turkish, *abdest*) for prayers.

yidina Muhammadan 'abduhu wa rasuluhu," that makes a person to be clean inwardly. So many orders are coming from Heavens, but first a person must say, *"La ilaha illa-Lah, Muhammadan Rasul-Allah* ﷺ.[165] We accept, *ya Rabb!* You are our Creator and You are the only One. And also we believe in what You sent us. Sayyidina Muhammad ﷺ is Your representative and You sent him to us to prepare us for eternal life in Your eternal kingdom. That is his mission." And then we say, "We are Muslims."

Then, we have been given some orders. And first of all, after saying *Shahadah*, the heavenly order says, "Go and wash yourself. Take a shower, *ghusl*"—the first order, because you can't pray without washing yourself. Therefore, the Prophet is saying, *"An nadhafatu mina-l-iman,* cleanliness is from our faith." You must do this.

For what conditions you use a shower or ablution, they are well-known. You can learn them. Washing takes away from you the darkness that surrounds you, because every unbeliever is surrounded—like a silk worm, just covered. Without washing yourself that will never go from you.

Washing is so important in Islam, cleanliness! Islam came to make people clean in their souls, clean in their spiritual beings; Islam came to make you pure in your actions and it makes you clean during this short life, with so many heavy burdens on you. That *ghusl,* major ablution, takes away every heavy burden from a person, and he or she is going to be a strong one, ready to be a servant to Allah Almighty.

This is a humble meeting. It is a free place, because all prophets proclaimed their prophethood and never asked anything from peo-

---

[165]"There is no deity except Allah, Muhammad is the Messenger of Allah."

ple. But some people, they said that prophets had come to collect the benefits of this world and they accused them.

Prophets were pure ones, coming to people, to the base of people, the lowest level on which most people are walking, and prophets did not come to be up but to be down. Even though their real beings were from Heavens, they were coming, coming, coming to the lowest level of people and sitting. Each prophet was sitting with common people. Anywhere—in the streets, in gardens, in fields, in homes, anywhere—they came down to reach people's lowest level, to catch them, for hunting or for saving mankind from Shaytan and his tricks. They were asking to clean people, and cleanliness is not only the cleanliness of what you are wearing.

Yes, you must wear clean clothes, but Islam came to clean you from the satanic virus. Shaytan is running and putting his virus for mankind, coming to all your organs, and that virus is making man dirty, dirty. Even if they take a bath seven times daily, they are not going to be clean till they follow the main orders of Heavens against that virus. If you do not save yourself from that virus, one day that virus may kill you!

And heavenly people, who are holy ones, they belong through their hearts to Heavens and through their physical being among common people. Therefore, don't say for the Prophet, as Wahhabis are saying, "The Prophet was an ordinary person."

Astaghfirullah! No, no! But Wahhabi people, they are not thinking about it. They are saying, "He was like ourselves." No; he was pure from that virus, but you are full of the virus!

Shaytan, at every second, throws at you some new, unknown virus. Why? Not to become a clean one! And those who have the virus, they are not clean ones. Can't be, can't be! By washing, that virus will never go. But the virus may leave a person when he says, *"La ilaha illa-Llah, Muhammadu Rasul-Allah* ﷺ.*"*

And Sayyidina Muhammad 🌸, he was not an ordinary person. If you are saying, "He was like ourselves," what does it mean to be a holy one? What would his relationship to Heavens be? Do you think that you have a relationship to Heavens? No. Then why are you saying, "He was like me"?

Therefore, they are always objecting. The people of Ignorance Period,[166] they were saying, "Why does that Book come only to Sayyidina Muhammad 🌸? Why does the Lord of Heavens not send a Book to each of us?" They were such dirty ones, their minds full of the shaytanic virus! And Islam came to make you a pure one. *"Allah yada'u ila Dari-s-Salam."*[167] Allah Almighty is inviting you to His Divine Presence in the eternal life. Dirty people can't enter!

This is a humble meeting. And we are trying to say something through our Masters,[168] Masters who were following heavenly, holy people, prophets, step by step. And heavenly beings are coming to make people walk in their footsteps because walking in their footsteps takes you to Paradise. But shaytanic footsteps take you to Hells, to the Fire. We must understand this point. And They are saying, "We are not coming to you to ask for anything of this material life—gold or jewels, or to be kings or *sultans* over you. No, we are, like you, from mankind, only we have been dressed in a heavenly dress."

Sayyidina Muhammad 🌸, he was from mankind, but he was dressed in honour and glory from Heavens. Therefore, if he looked

---

[166]The Period of Ignorance of the divine guidance prior to Muhammad's prophethood.

[167] *"Allah calls to the Abode of Peace."* (10:25)

[168]The chain of Naqshbandi *awliya* (grandshaykhs) reaching back to Abu Bakr as-Siddiq 🌸 and, through him, to the Prophet 🌸.

at someone, that one might fall down from *nadharu-l-haybat*.[169] If he had looked at a person with his *mandhar,* true appearance, no one would have been able to look at him, no one. It would have been impossible.

But the Prophet came down, down, down to the level of common people. Yes, there is a helicopter. A helicopter comes, comes, comes in front of you, also, but don't say, "This helicopter is like me. A helicopter is like us because it is on earth like ourselves." No; after a while it may begin to leave your level and go up. And prophets commonly were with common people, but don't think that they were like you. If they were like any one of ourselves, what would have been the benefit of being dressed in the honour or title of being prophets? Prophethood is something else. That prophethood makes a person be in connection with heavenly beings.

A helicopter may leave people, going up to 5,000 feet or more, but it isn't able to go up higher. But prophets, they may be with you at your level. Then, in *tarfatu 'ain,* a blink of our eyes, they may be up, finished! And the big mistake of people now is that they think that prophethood is nothing, or that prophets were people like ourselves and they were speaking on some subjects, nothing else, and their speeches are written in books. "When we read them, we are going to be like them."

How can you say we are like prophets because you are learning their statements, their messages, in books,? But they are now such proud people!

"Who is that one?

"A Doctor of *Shari'ah.*"

---

[169] An awe-inspiring glance.

"A Doctor of *Shari'ah*? Eh! Then, anything else? We are not in need to follow anyone. We are only hearing those prophets, and prophethood has ended. We are now their *khulafa*.[170] What they brought, they brought. Now we are also looking in those books so that there is no difference between ourselves and prophets. *La fadl*,[171] no higher rank for them! What they said, they said, and what they said, we are reading now in those books. Then we are going to be like them."

The biggest mistake, biggest mistake! And now that biggest mistake, Shaytan is using it to make people not believe in any holy sources, holy books and holy ones. People now are just finished! They are not asking for holy ones, and holy ones are escaping from them, hiding themselves, because they are saying, "You and I are all the same. Why am I going to respect you or for what shall I ask to learn something from you? *I* can learn and *I* must be a respected one!"

Therefore, Wahhabis never accept *awliya*. They have lost the most beautiful and most powerful relationship between Heavens and man, *awliya*. And for hundreds of years the Muslim nation, *ummah* was respecting them, making *maqams*[172] for them, and saying, "Those people were closer to our Lord. They were pure people, and now they are in the Divine Presence. We may visit them and ask for heavenly support through them."

Now Muslims are following the Wahhabi way and destroying old *kubbes*, domes, and *tekiyahs* and *dergahs*,[173] saying, "No need! We are not in need!" Therefore mankind is becoming closer to the ani-

---

[170]Successors, deputies.

[171]No superiority.

[172]*Maqam*, a saint's gravesite highlighted to reverence his status.

[173]*Tekiye* or *dergah*. A place of learning and retreat for followers of a Sufi shaykh.

mal level instead of becoming closer to heavenly beings. Animals' most distinguishing sign is to be wild; the animal world, all animals, they have more or less wildness. Therefore, those people who are denying holy people who are closer to their Lord, they are coming closer to the animal world, and animals are wild creatures.

And now, look at all mankind, how they are! Are there more calm people or more wild people? Day by day, you are hearing from East, West, North, South, among Arabs, Turks, Europeans, Western countries, Eastern countries, that there is fire, killing, killing, killing.

Allah never ordered to kill! Rather, Allah Almighty is ordering, "Make people live, make people happy, make people be in satisfaction and peace in their lives." But now people, they are growing in wildness, wild people, even though they are describing and saying about themselves, "We are the most civilized people."

That is their civilization—to kill everything, every living creature, and killing human beings, killing innocent people, killing little ones, old ones, and *'ajiz*, helpless, weak people! That is their civilization? *That is Shaytan's civilization!* But Allah Almighty promised to the Seal of Prophets, "O Muhammad ﷺ, I will send someone to clean earth from those wild animals, beasts!" Beasts—more than wild; they are becoming beasts! Allah should kill them, should take them away!

O people, come, come, and keep the rights of Allah Almighty's people, Allah Almighty's servants! Help them! Help them! Whoever hurts Allah Almighty's creatures, they are not Muslims, they are not *mu'mins*, they are not believers! They are Shaytan's people!

May Allah forgive us! For the honour of the most honoured one in His Divine Presence, Sayyidina Muhammad ﷺ—*Fateha!*

18

"O MY SERVANTS, GIVE TIME FOR THINKING"

As-salamu 'alaikum. Happy? Thankful to Allah? Really? No one is making any objection to Allah Almighty's orders? Understand? No one is objecting to what is happening? All of you are pleased with Allah, heh? No one is complaining?

Aferin![174] All of you are Paradise people! *Masha'Allah!* Here, you are saying nothing, but when I go back to that room, one thousand complaints!

As-salamu 'alaikum! Welcome to you, *ayyuha-l-ghafilun,* welcome, heedless people! You are unhappy because you are not millionaires of euros. Eh! You are unhappy, saying, "I have not changed my old car for a new one."

"Yes, sir! Everyone changes to a new car each year."

"For what? I can't do that!"

Ask him! Ask him, if you can ask, "Why you are not saying, '*Alhamdulillah,* thanks to Allah that He did not create us as donkeys.'" Donkey are complaining? _____, each day that person makes one

---

[174]Bravo, well-done!

116

hundred complaints! Happy? Here happy; outside, no. That is *nifaq*. What is *'nifaq'*? Hypocrisy!

Allah Almighty is saying, "I will not leave My servant untried, and I am going to try everyone." Even prophets; the most difficult trials were for them, although they had miraculous powers. But the Lord of Heavens did not give them permission to use them except only when He said, "Use it!"

Everyone must be tried. Why? Tried, like an examination from the first class, if you want to be in the second class. And people, from the first floor up to the second floor, must be tried, and Allah Almighty may send every kind of trial. He tries you and then gives to you. This life is a very short life, but you will graduate for eternity.

Here you are going to be tried. Then you will taste of dying. If you pass, in front of you is unlimited life, eternal life. But people, ninety-nine per cent and more, they are really unbelievers. They do not believe in eternity, while in every heavenly religion that has come, prophets brought news about eternity from Allah Almighty.

Suddenly you are opening your eyes. You are finding yourself on this earth, on *Dunya*. You are *hayran*, confused, not knowing where you are, where you are going. "How did it happen? I am in existence, and I see that yesterday I was a little one. Then today growing, then growing more, and then . . . ."

It is not limitless growing. After a point that is the top point of our lives, we begin to come back down, down, down, and then we disappear. "I see that people are appearing, then disappearing. What is this?" wanting to bring a solution or an understanding or to know something, but seeing that he is surrounded and can't understand how he appeared here.

A hundred years ago, none of us was in existence; no appearance. Now we see that we are in existence; we appeared: How did we appear from a dark, very narrow place in our mothers' wombs? How did we appear, and after a time that is just appointed for everyone, when that time finishes, we are going to appear in another place.

The first place is the wombs of our mothers, and we appear there, from beginning to end, for nine months more or less, and then we appear in another place. We come out of our mothers' wombs, and that is our second appearance. We find ourselves in another world, and we do not know anything. And then, day by day, our understanding power gets to be more complete.

Then we come into another appearance. The age of majority, that is another appearance. "What has happened to me? My senses have changed. Who changed them? How were they changed?" And as he grows up, his appearance get more and more and more developed.

Oh-h-h! Reaching a level at which he feels that his appearance is becoming weaker, weaker, weaker; coming down, coming down, coming down. And one day, he looks and sees that his appearance in this life is going to finish because he looks around himself, first asking, "Where is my mum, where is my dad?" No answer! Their appearance has finished. "What happened? Where am I going? Who made me? Who brought me from invisible worlds? Who brought me into this world with a new appearance?"

People are not thinking about it. Change, change comes in each second. You are not the same when you breathe in and breathe out; the one before and the one after, two breaths are not same. One brings something to you, the second takes something from you.

People are not thinking. They are runing after this temporary life, and one day they are falling down. Their appearing here has just finished, and no one knows, when they give their last breath, what has happened. But another appearance is just beginning.

You can't bring a solution to those points. Only that One who makes you as a man or woman, who asks you to appear, who gives you an appearance, He knows. And He has sent some ones, saying, "O My prophets, you are on behalf of Me. Speak to mankind because they can't bring an answer or solution about themselves, about their appearing and then disappearing."

But people now, they are drunk, drunk. They never think about such important points. They only think about the appearances of this *muwaqqat*, temporary life; only this temporary life is important for them. They never ask about the permanent life.

Therefore, Allah Almighty is sending some ones who are able to get in touch with your understanding level and who want to make you understand something about your future after disappearing from this life. What is going to happen, you can't think about it and find an answer.

Therefore, we are here now. Particularly among the twenty-first century's people, their concern or their mission is only to look around themselves but never to think how everything around ourselves that we are in happened. How it happened, no one is asking. People are like drunk ones, really drunk, not using their minds. And the Creator who created you and every living creature, who created the earth and skies and Heavens, up and down, He is asking, "O My servants, give time for thinking!"

Even for one minute, think about it! To think, what is its value? The Prophet was saying, "For a person to sit down and think for one hour is more powerful and lovely to Allah Almighty than a person's praying to Allah for seventy years."[175] That is more powerful for people because the key to unknown appearances, the key to unknown worlds, comes through our thinking power.

You can think. Men can think, but animals, they do not think. No need for them to think, no. They are occupied with their needs, running like this, like that. But men, they have been granted a will to think and to do, to think and to make, to think and to ask for a way up to where their thoughts bring them.

You must try to do it. You must not stay at the same stage or on the same level. The Lord of Heavens, He does not want you to be on the same level. You must try to improve, improve in your spirituality, for approaching His Divine Presence.

Therefore, He ordered His prophets to call people to be servants of the Lord of Heavens who created them, and gave good tidings to His prophets that the servanthood that we have been granted, that is an honourable dress for you among other creatures. And prophets are calling you, "O people, come and dress in that heavenly, glorious dress of being servants of the Lord of creation!"

---

[175]The saying "An hour's reflection (*fikratu sa'at*) is better than worshiping for sixty years" is narrated as a saying of:

    1. Abu al-Darda' by Ibn Sa'd in his *Tabaqat* (7:392), Ibn al-Mubarak in *al-Zuhd* (p. 332), Hannad in *al-Zuhd* (2:468), Ahmad in *al-Zuhd* (p. 139), Ibn Abi 'Asim in a*l-Sunna* (p. 129), Abu Nu'aym in the *Hilya* (1:209), and al-Bayhaqi in the *Shu'ab* (1:135-136);

    2. Ibn 'Abbas by Abu al-Shaykh in *al-'Azama* (1:298);

    3. al-Hasan al-Basri by Ahmad in *al-Zuhd* (p. 272), Ibn Abi Shayba in his *Musannaf* (7:190), and Abu Nu'aym (6:271).

But people have lost their way. The whole world now, including the Muslim world, has lost its way. All of them are occupying their hearts with something that is not going to be for anyone. You may try, you may work, you may reach so many treasures, but they are not for you. When you pass away, that is just cut off. You will leave your treasures and go.

O people, run to Allah! Follow His prophets to be in peace here and Hereafter. If not, you are going to suffer. People are suffering; now the whole world's people are suffering. Powerful people are suffering; weak people are suffering; rich people are suffering; poor people are suffering; learned people are suffering; unlearned people are suffering; workers are suffering; chiefs of big manufactories, they are suffering; beautiful ones are suffering; weak ones are suffering; powerful ones are suffering; women are suffering; men are suffering; little ones are suffering; big ones are suffering. Look! Everywhere now, everyone is suffering.

But there is one group of people whom suffering never touches. Those who are running to their Lord's Divine Presence, they are not suffering. Others, all of them, are suffering. But they are drunk; they are not yet understanding that they are suffering. That is another big suffering, not to know that they are suffering.

May Allah forgive us, and may He send us now someone from among heavenly people to direct our ways. Instead of people going to the sun-rising direction, they are running to the sun-setting direction. Why do you not run to sun-rising direction, always running to the West, West, West? And, *subhanallah*, Allah Almighty is putting something in the hearts of Western people, that they are always thinking or dreaming of reaching the East, the sun-rising direction. But *bil-'aks*, on the contrary, our people are running to Western countries, while Western countries' people, their souls are just taken to Eastern countries. Yes, *subhanAllah!*

Therefore, Western people, they are fortunate, because I don't think that you can find anyone who does not dream of reaching Eastern countries and being there and living there. But I am sorry to say that now every Muslim country's people, including Arabs, Turks, Pakistani people, they want to be like Western countries, so that Western people, they are fortunate. Those who dream of being in Western countries, they are unfortunate people.

Understand? Look, _____ is an Arab but he never wants to be like an Eastern person. Look! No moustache, no beard, and the latest, new-fashion clothes, open here, and shaved. He is so happy! Eh! Turkish people, also. "We must be like Western people. We will never accept to be like Ottomans! They are very old-fashioned people. We must be new-fashioned!" Europeans, good fortune for them that their hearts are running to Eastern countries, from where the Star of Prophets and Sun of Prophets and Moon of Prophets came.

May Allah forgive us! *Subhanallah! Ya Rabbi,* forgive us and send us someone to correct our ways, our minds, our direction, to You. For the honour of the most honoured one in His Divine Presence, Sayyidina Muhammad 鸞—*Fateha!*

19

GUARDING AGAINST SATANIC DELUSIONS

As-salamu 'alaikum! O our Lord, forgive us and grant Your blessings to Your weak servants.

A'udhu bil-Lahi min ash-Shaytani-r-rajim. O our Lord, keep Your weak servants from Shaytan and his traps, not to fall into them. Whoever falls into Shaytan's traps, it is so difficult to get out—so difficult! Therefore, you must be careful not to fall, not to be caught, by a trap of Shaytan. Guard yourself, because Shaytan has hundreds and hundreds of traps, put everywhere.

"Bismillahi-r-Rahmani-r-Rahim," that is our sword. Always carry that sword, because if a person goes to a battlefield without a sword, he may be killed. If he carries a sword, people will take him into consideration. Therefore, we must be careful and awake, not sleepers. Otherwise, you may be quickly taken as a prisoner or injured or killled. Therefore, we are saying, *"A'udhu bil-Lahi min ash-Shaytani-r-rajim. Bismillahi-r-Rahmani-r-Rahim."* May Allah protect us!

Follow His holy orders; you will be in safety here and Hereafter. Don't say, "I know, I know, I know." You don't know; you know nothing! You may be *ghalat,* mistaken. Therefore, we are saying, *"A'udhu bil-Lahi min ash-Shaytani-r-rajim. Bismillahi-r-Rahmani-r-Rahim,"* and we are coming into a protected area.

If you go into an unprotected area, something must touch you that you are not going to be happy with. The Prophet, peace be upon him, the most praised servant and most glorified one in the Divine Presence, Sayyidina Muhammad, he was saying, *"Ittaqu mawadi'a-l-tuham,*[176] you must keep yourself from falling into a trap."

There may be so many advertisements, or not so many. Perhaps all advertisements are calling people to be caught in one trap. Advertising, that is its meaning. They are advertising every kind of thing, everything; they are even advertising cat food. A cat needs advertising? Without that advertising, it jumps on the table, eating as it likes. It needs advertising? But such clever ones, men, they are doing advertising for everything, and in every advertisment there is one or more traps. When you enter that field, you must be caught by any one of hundreds of traps.

The first to fall into Shaytan's trap, who was he? Adam, the first. What about for ourselves? Every time, daily, daily, a hundred times we are falling! If Adam ﷺ fell into a trap, what about you? And he was saying,

"O my sons and grandsons and my descendants up to the Last Day, I am warning you and saying, 'Beware of Shaytan!'"

Eh! We are writing, "Beware of the dog"—yes? "Beware of the dog," they are writing and people are looking at that. If they come nearby, quickly they will go far away. Perhaps that dog may bite them; they are taking care. Which of us is careful of Shaytan, and each day hundreds of traps are catching our legs, hands, heads, beginning from the first ones?

Shaytan, don't think that he is an idiot. Ooh-h-h! You are an idiot but Shaytan is not an idiot! Therefore, he is always looking,

---

[176]"Guard yourself against the places of blame."

looking—not looking at the flock, no. Shaytan is saying, "I have nothing to do with sheep, with the flock. Where is the shepherd?"

"I am here."

"What are you doing?"

"Sleeping."

"Yes, you must sleep more because it is a safe valley. You take your rest!" This is his *nasihah*, advice, to shepherds. And he is coming with the same thing to the shepherds of nations. He is saying, "Do this! Don't do that!"

"What am I doing?"

"You are doing the best!"

"For me or for my nation?"

"No, no, sir! Nation, they are the flock. You must always consider your ego, your self! Make them sleep and you do as you like."

Ha-a-a, Shaytan—Shaytan does not go to the 'feet'! No need; coming to the top ones, saying, "Do this, do that, to be camouflaged, because something may be against you"; coming to the top ones, coming to kings or *sultans* or emperors or presidents or prime ministers or their ministers.

Satan is very clever; he has satanic cleverness. From the beginning up to today, he has camouflaged himself, and no one asks, "Who is that one?" camouflaging, so that people think, "That is our best friend and best advisor. We must ask our advisor what we can do."

Sayyidina Adam was just cheated by Shaytan. Up to today, hundreds of kings, *sultans*, thousands of powerful ones, Shaytan is making them fall into a valley that they aren't able to get out of.

Now every country is in flames, Muslim territories more than Western countries. Look! Everywhere that there are Muslims, there is a fire, Shaytan making Muslims kill each other. For what, for what? *For Allah?*

Allah Almighty may ask Kenyan Muslims, may ask Afghan people, may ask Iranis, may ask Turkish ones, may ask Iraqi ones, "Why were you carrying those weapons? What was your aim? Why were you killing? Why were you making trouble? Why were you running in the streets?" Is it not blameworthy for you to run in the streets, O Muslims, and shout for democracy, not saying, 'Oh, we are asking for *Shari'at-Allah*,[177] the holy commands of Allah'"?

Why are you not going in the streets [to call for *Shari'ah*]. You are calling shaytanic words! Why are Muslims not going to mosques? Do they not know that Allah Almighty is looking at those people who are in mosques? And *"sharru biqa'ul-ard al-aswaq."*[178] Arabs, say to your people not to look in mosques but to look outside; otherwise, my stick is ready! After the stick, my sword; we have a sword, also! Don't look at mosques, look at what is happening in *aswaq*, streets, marketplaces: what they are thinking, why they are shouting, to whom they are shouting—shouting to Allah or shouting to Shaytan?

Did you see or did you never see those people who are making a demonstration, carrying the Holy Qur'an in their hands and saying, "We are asking for heavenly rules"? Did you hear or see that anywhere? How are they Muslims, how would Allah Almighty support them? They should be taken away! It is not the surface of world

---

[177]The Islamic *Shari'ah* or sacred Law of Islam, derived from the Holy Qur'an and the Prophet's practices and injunctions.

[178]"The most evil place on earth is the marketplace." (*Tabarani*)

that is changing but people who are in *hukm*, in power. Allah should change them. The time is over!

The first, first *kırbaç*, whip, is coming on Muslims and their heads! Keep *amanat-Allah*,[179] His oath that He sent us, the heavenly oath from Heavens.[180] Keep it! The Prophet was saying, "If there are 12,000 believers who are supported by their Lord, no power on earth can take them away or defeat them. Finished!" But we are not finding even *ithna 'ashar*, twelve, people. What is this?

The time is over and heavenly punishment is approaching, approaching, approaching, as heavenly punishment approached that nation that Allah Almighty punished through that day, *yaumu-l-dhulla*.[181] Overhead is open, open! Unbelievers want protection so that if someone sends something, it will not fall on them, but they are not asking for divine protection. If Allah sends a punishment, no one can prevent anything.

O people, come and join that group that is supported by heavenly powers. Don't trust in *kufr*, don't trust in unbelievers! Trust those who believe. They are, all of them, supported. Now no one among Eastern or Western countries can be the victor if Allah Almighty protects and gives His heavenly support. No one can be victorious or win! This must be well-known.

Subhanallah, Allah Almighty is letting people make such instruments that, although we are sitting in an unknown place on earth,

---

[179]Allah's sacred trust.

[180]Allah's promise to support the believers; see, for example, 8:66, 3:13, 123-125, 150, 173-174 and numerous others.

[181]*"The overcast day"* (26:189), on which divine punishment came to the rebellious people of the Arabian prophet Shu 'aib, whose story is told in 26:176-190.

our declaration is reaching throughout East and West, so that no one will say, "Never did any warning, heavenly warning, reach us, O our Lord!"

This is reaching, *subhanallah!* They are proud of such instruments, yes, and they are saying, "We are much more powerful than Muslims because Muslims, some of their people, are *mutaakhkhir.*"[182] All unbelievers, they are saying, "We are so strong, powerful, with such instruments, but Muslims, they can't do it!" Yes, Muslims, they are not in need of such a thing to make their sound reach everywhere!

Sayyidina 'Umar, on the *minbar*,[183] was saying, *"Ya Sariyat, al-jabal, al-jabal!"*[184] Was he using *this* instrument? But no more faith among Muslims. They are official Muslims,[185] not real Muslims; they are by-name Muslims, not real Muslims! They are saying, "Europeans are making such a. . ." while Sayyidina 'Umar, on the *minbar* for *Juma'* prayer, was calling aloud to the head of the Muslim armies, saying, *"Ya Sariyat, al-jabal, al-jabal!"* And between Madinatu-l-Munawwarah[186] and that mountain is three months' walk!

Do we have power? We have power that we are not using yet! Leave them to be proud of such instruments of theirs. Real power,

---

[182]Behind, backward, undeveloped.

[183]Pulpit.

[184]"O Sariyah, the mountain! The mountain!" This relates to the following incident: During 'Umar's caliphate, while he was giving a *khutbah* [sermon] in Medina, he suddenly called out, "O Sariyah, the mountain! The mountain." Sariyah, who was the commander of the Muslim army in Syria, heard this command in the midst of a battle and retreated toward the mountain, thereby saving his troops from being massacred.

[185]Salaried government employees.

[186]Medina.

Allah 'Azza wa Jall ata lil-Muslimin, ata lil-Islam; [187] Allah granted unexpected powers to Muslims! At that time, it was enough. Now we have power. We can stop all weapons factories or flying towers of *pulat, çelik,* steel. We have power!

We do not fear them, and we are such smooth and very soft ones now. [188] But when Allah is saying, *"Ash-shida'u 'ala-l-kufaru,"* [189] *ash-shida'u* means that *mumins* are like lions; when they are ordered, they are like lions! Lions can carry a whole deer and zebra and ox or so many, so many animals; lions can carry them in front of themselves and escape. Muslims, we are Muslims! If looking at Muslims, armies going to fall down!

They are thinking that Islam is something easy, an easy thing, and they can do to Muslims as they like, and *ghafil,* heedless Muslims, they are fearing the weapons that Europeans and the non-Muslim world are inventing and making. No! Your heart must be with your Lord! Allah Almighty is saying, "I am sending the Holy Qur'an and I am that One who is taking it on His responsibility to protect it." [190] Who can take away Holy Qur'an? No one, no one, no one!

O people, O all the world's people, beware of Shaytan, not to be cheated by Shaytan. Shaytan is asking people to fall into fire here and Hereafter, and we are asking forgiveness from Allah Almighty, for protection here and Hereafter. For the honour of the most honoured one in His Divine Presence, Sayyidina Muhammad, *sallallahu 'alaihi wa salam*—*Fateha!*

---

[187] Real power, Allah Mighty and Glorious gave to the Muslims, gave to Islam.

[188] Conciliatory rather than standing up for principles.

[189] *"Vigourous against the unbelievers."* (48:29)

[190] Referring to the verse, *"Indeed, We sent down the Reminder [Qur'an] assuredly We shall guard it"* (15:9).

20

LOVING THE HOLY ONES WHOM ALLAH LOVES

A'udhu bil-Lahi min as-Shaytani-r-rajim. Bismillahi-r-Rahmani-r-Rahim. La haula wa la quwwata illa bil-Lahi-l-'Aliyi-l-'Adhim. Meded, ya Rijal-Allah!

Here is our brother, Shaykh Gibril Fuad Haddad, a famous author and authority in Holy *Hadith* and what is related to the knowledge of *Hadith ash-Sharif*,[191] and we have been honoured by him for three days, four days. And he is asking to understand something about secret knowledge in Islam.

And we are saying, "By the Name of Allah Almighty, Most Merciful, Most Magnificent and Most Beneficent." May Allah make us say something that will be like a guidance for all mankind. Allah Almighty can make an ant talk, and He, Almighty Allah, if He wants, He can make, in an ant's language, an address to all mankind, as is mentioned in Holy Qur'an.[192]

And we are saying, "*A'udhu bil-Lahi min as-Shaytani-r-rajim. Bismillahi-r-Rahmani-r-Rahim.* O our Lord, forgive us! Forgive Your

---

[191]Noble *ahadith*.

[192]Referring to 27:18-19, reporting the conversation between the prophet Solomon and an ant.

weak servant; forgive Your most beloved servant's *ummah*, nation. We are in need of Your blessings, and we are asking also for support from the beloved ones who are *awliya*—for support from Them so that we may be able to address all people.

Islam came with a message, from the earliest time of the prophethood of the Seal of Prophets up to its end. Therefore, each address that came through the most beloved and glorified servant of Allah, Sayyidina Muhammad, it is for all the nations of mankind.

And it is from his holy teachings to nations that Allah Almighty likes His servants to be in love with His *awliya,* with His holy ones. That is a very important pillar in Islam, that Muslims must look for holy ones in the nation of Muhammad, peace be upon him, and be in love with them, give their love to them, and high respects, also.

That is one of the most important pillars that Islam is teaching mankind. O mankind, you must look for holy ones. Who are holy ones?

Once I was passing through Switzerland on my way to Germany, and in that country there is a famous monastery on the way, and the name [of the holy one there] is Nikolaus von der Flühe. Always, when I was passing by, his spiritual being was asking me to come down and visit him, a holy one. He was feeling refreshment every time that I was passing through there and going down and visiting him.

Once I was passing and coming, and on the stairs after visiting I saw a person who looked like he must be a priest. I greeted him. He also greeted me, and I said, "Your Holiness is looking after this holy place?"

And he answered, "I am sorry, O Shaykh, I am not a holy one."

"Why?"

"You know why," he said.

And I asked, "What about the Pope?"

And he said to me—I am not lying, *insha'Allah;* I am speaking the truth—because I was asking what about the Pope, His Holiness: "Never! Never! Because," he was saying, "the holy one is inside, in whose service I am here." And he was indicating to me who is holy or not. I was ashamed to ask, "What about me?" fearing that he would say, "You are also like the Pope."

"O Shaykh, you know something. I know why you are coming here. I have never seen a Muslim authority or *'alim,* scholar, or *imam* coming and visiting here. Therefore I understand that you are not an ordinary one of those people."

I said, "Allah knows. Why are they not holy ones?"

"O Shaykh, for people who are official, officiality sends away sincerity, and sincerity, when it leaves a person, he can't be a holy one. One of the most important conditions, *shart,* to be a holy one is to be sincere. Those people, they are all official people, and among official people you can't find a holy one." He said this. And I left him and went on.

Now we are coming to our speech that is from powerful heavenly ones, from holy ones, holy ones. They are saying that the first condition for believers is that they must look and must try to find a holy one because Allah Almighty, He loves His servants to love what He loves. And those are *awliya.*

Second, there is another condition for believers. The first condition is to love those whom Allah loves. And the second condition that They are saying is important for improvement in spirituality, in heavenly *maratib*, levels, is to hate those people whom Allah hates. Two legs, *Muhabbatu-l-awliya, bughdun 'ala a'dai-Lah*.[193]

I am sorry to say that, as we are saying from *turath Muhammadi*, the heritage of the Prophet that we are on, a hundred per cent of people, even in the Islamic world, they have left *awliya-Allah*, holy ones, and they are fighting holy ones and saying bad things about them. And secondly, all people are running after *mabghud*,[194] hated ones. They are embracing them, and *awliya*, kicking them out.

This first happened in the holy land, Hijaz.[195] They destroyed even the graves of *Sahabah*, with whom Allah Almighty is happy here and Hereafter, and to whom He granted His divine pleasure, saying, "I am pleased with you."[196]

We have an *adab* in Islam: That person who is an honored one and also a holy one, in our real *adab*, we are not permitted even to touch their cats. Even cats, no; they belong to *them*. Sometime cats come and sit on their *jild*,[197] *sajadah*, prayer carpet. You can't do like this [gestures] because it is sitting near that holy one. That makes that holy one unhappy. Then how about their followers, or how about Prophet's beloved *Sahabah*, Companions?

And they are destroying their graves! Allah should take down their kingdoms! And everywhere that people are not asking for *awliya-Allah*, holy ones, those people should disappear, be taken away, be carried away!

---

[193]Love of *awliya*, hatred of enemies of Allah.

[194]Detested, hateful, odious.

[195]The Saudi province in which Mecca and Medina are situated.

[196]As stated in 48:18, 9:100, 58:22.

[197]Sheepskin.

I was looking today at that TV, and there was a program showing that American or Western technology is making some planes
without a pilots, flying by themselves. They can never be caught,
and their forms are so *'ajaib*, so wondrous, how they are flying,
bombing. And they are saying, "Laser bombing." You know that,
the latest technology, a red ray coming on anything—oh-h-h! I was
looking, I was trembling. Then Grandshaykh was saying to me, "O
Nazim Efendi, why are you trembling?"

"*Ya sayyidi*, these are huge ones! We have nothing."

"We have nothing? We have *something!* They have nothing, *we*
have something! What we know, they do not know. *'Y'alamuna dha-
hiran mina-l-hayati-d-dunya,'*[198] right? They know something that belongs to this world, but we have something beyond this level of
technology. We have something else.

"Do you remember that at the end of the Second World War,
French armies were bombarding Shamu-sh-Sharif?[199] [Grandshaykh
continued]. And I showed you from Mezze that the French army
was bombarding Damascus with the biggest ones. One reached the
tomb of Sayyidina Yahya,[200] just coming on it, and a hand appeared,
and it took that bomb and threw it away. I showed you this. Why
are you afraid? What is their technology?

"By that power, Allah Almighty *sakhkhara lahum,*[201] gives them
permission to do this, to do that, but they will never reach above

---

[198] *"They know [only] what is apparent of the life of the world."* (30:7)

[199] Damascus, Syria.

[200] Sayyidina Yahya is John the Baptist, a prophet of Islam, the relative and precursor
of Jesus Christ, the last prophet descended from Abraham through the lineage of
Jacob. The burial place of Sayyidina Yahya's severed head is in the Umayyad
Mosque in Damascus.

[201] "Subjected to them," a paraphrase of 45:13.

Heavens. They are always below Heavens. Those who have heavenly powers, they are up; those who are not granted it, always they are down. Don't worry!"

These words made a settling, pleasure, peace in my heart. Then I was okay, I was not afraid of what they were doing. "You, if I order you, 'Put your finger like this,' all of them may fall down."

But people, they are not understanding Islam, not understanding the power of a *wali*. They never understand the holy power that is in *awliya*, holy ones. And the Christian world says, "The Romans caught Jesus Christ and put him on the cross." What about *awliya*, at every time? And Jesus was prepared.[202]

This is some secret knowledge that we are speaking about. You can't find this in their books or other books. We will not making it more clear [than this], but Jesus Christ, when he was invited to rise up to Heavens, he was prepared. Not even from one kilometer's distance could anyone have been able to put a foot toward him to catch him.[203]

What are they thinking about Jesus Christ? What is that, no-mind people! If Jesus had used that power, opening it, he could have burned East and West when he was ready with Archangel Gabriel to take him up! They are understanding nothing!

---

[202]The meaning here is that because the rank of a prophet is higher than that of a *wali* (although *awliya* possess heavenly powers), Jesus' power was greater than that of any *wali*. And Jesus, peace be on him, had "been prepared" by heavenly training for his role and the proper exercise of his powers.

[203]According to Islamic belief, Jesus, peace be on him, was not crucified. *"They did not kill him nor crucify him, but it was made to seem so to them. . . .Of a certainty, they did not kill him. Rather, Allah raised him to Himself, and Allah is Almighty and Wise"* (4:157-158; see also 3:54-55).

And I am saying also for Sayyidina Hussain[204] ⬥, about whom they are saying that they cut off his head: Do you think that he was alone there in Karbala? Seventy kings of jinn with their countless armies just surrounded that place! And the soldiers of Yazid caught someone else but they did not know. *"Wa lakin shubbiha lahum."*[205] He was not Sayyidina Hussain.

Christians are saying, "Jesus Christ is the *kuzu,* Lamb [of God]." Lamb, what lamb? How was he a lamb? Sayyidina 'Isa was a lamb? Sayyidina Hussain was not a rooster, to have his head cut off!

This is a secret. The time is over now; people should understand! In East and West, permission is not given to anyone to speak about this except Grandhaykh. Therefore, *". . . Anna-l-quwwata lil-Lahi jami'an," sadaqa-Lahu-l-'Adhim.*[206] True or not? Allah Almighty can do anything!

When Nimrod threw Sayyidina Ibrahim, peace be upon him, into the fire,[207] an ant was running. A person saw that it was so quickly running. "O small creature, where you are running?"

Not answering. Then, after a while, he saw that ant coming back. It said, "O my Lord's servant, I couldn't answer you the first time because I was carrying in my mouth water to extinguish the fire of Nimrod."

---

[204]The son of 'Ali and grandson of the Prophet, who was martyred at Karbala in Iraq.

[205]*"But it was made to appear so to them."* (4:157). Another possible reading is, *"But he [another person] was made to resemble him to them."*

[206]*". . .That all power belongs to Allah. . . "* (2:165), Allah spoke the truth.

[207]21:68-69.

Sadaq, he spoke the truth! That ant's answer, it was one hundred per cent right. It was enough to take away, to extinguish, the fire of Nimrod, what that ant was carrying in its mouth. People never understand the working of Allah's Will. *Subhanallahu-l-'Aliyu-l-'Adhim, wa anna-l-quwwata lil-Lahi jami'an!*[208]

What happened in Hiroshima, where Americans threw that first atomic bomb? Some months ago, they held the sixty-third year's anniversary at that place. What happened there? An atomic bomb, dropped by an airplane, made Hiroshima down—up, up and down.

They are saying, "Yes, okay," to that. But if I say that Allah Almighty extinguished the fire of Nimrod by an ant's mouthful, *dharraH,* atom, of water, they are saying, "Oh! It can't be!" That can be, this *can't* be? What is this?[209]

The first *munkarat,* the first deniers of Islam,[210] have come into Islam at the end of the world now, and they should be punished. Therefore, they are killing each other.

May Allah forgive us! I think that it is enough. *Fateha, Allah yahfadhna!*[211]

---

[208]Glory be to Allah, the Most High, the All-Mighty, and all power belongs to Allah.

[209]That is, modern man sees no problem in rejecting and deriding the extinguishing of Nimrod's huge fire by a tiny droplet of water carried in the mouth of an ant. At the same time, the fact of the complete destruction of a large city by a nuclear reaction of the tiny particles we call atoms is accepted unquestioningly.

[210]Denied, disacknowledged, deemed strange, disapproved.

[211]May Allah protect us!

21

ASKING THE RIGHT QUESTIONS

Welcome to you! *Shukru lil-Lah*, we are thanking Allah, and we are saying, *"Ashadu an la ilaha illa-Lah wa ashadu anna Sayyidina Muhammadun 'abduhu wa habibuhu wa rasuluhu."* Then we are Muslims.[212]

Now we are living at a time when ignorance has reached everyone, and so many people are not using their minds and they are objecting to some aspects of Islam. We are asking from Allah Almighty not to be among those no-mind people, and we are saying, *"A'udhu bil-Lahi min ash-Shaytani-r-rajim. Bismillahi-r-Rahmani-r-Rahim."* That is the sign of being Muslim.

We have been ordered to run away from the most dangerous and difficult enemy of mankind, Shaytan. We must ask protection from Allah Almighty. If you are trying to fight or to defend yourself *by yourself*, it is impossible. Instead, we must ask protection, and we are asking for Allah Almighty's shelter to be in safety.

You must not forget that you are servants of Allah Almighty. Who created you? Ask who designed you, O man! You must ask this and you must try to teach yourself as well as your children. But Shaytan is doing his worst for all mankind, using hundreds and thou-

---

[212]Meaning that when one makes the preceding *Shahadah* or profession of faith, he/she has accepted the basic premise of Islam of belief in the Creator and in His Last Messenger ahd Message, and accordingly is a Muslim.

sands of tricks, and putting countless traps for mankind to make them forget who they are, how they are in existence. Shaytan is trying to make people not to remember, making them to forget.

People are not asking. They are asking so many useless, tasteless questions, but the main question that man must ask is, "Who am I, how am I in existence, from where have I come?" No one is asking, and universities, educational systems, they do not care about holy books, heavenly books. They are not using them or asking.

How are people going to learn? They are teaching so many nonsensical subjects in hundreds of books, and [in actuality] they are teaching students only to deny and teaching them not to ask, "Who am I?"

So many branches of their knowledge, they are not knowledge because all *real* knowledge, if you use it, must take you to the Divine Presence of Allah Almighty. That is knowledge. There are so many branches, but if you accept *that,* you are going to find the roots of knowledges.

But now people, they are only using and looking at the outside appearance of trees. They are not interested in how that apple came into existence, how that tree that we thought was a dry tree in winter time, thinking, "This is finished. No more leaves or fruits or flowers on it. We are seeing that that has just dried," could be alive. And when springtime comes, they are surprised, saying, "Oh! Yesterday we were thinking that that little tree was just dry. How is it now beginning to bring out blooms and leaves, and giving such a beautiful view, beautiful show? How did it happen?"

There is dry earth and rains are coming on it, and that dry earth begins to bring out so many plants, so many kinds of flowers and plants and trees. What happens? It is only earth, and rains are coming on it from above. How can it be?

They are not asking. They are just saying, "Eh, that is an apple tree," or, "That is another kind. So many fruits, just awakening. We thought that it was a dried one, but now we see that it is growing new leaves, new flowers, and after flowers there will come so many kinds of fruits." They are not thinking about it.

Mankind now, they are drunk ones, and drunkenness is coming from their heedlessness, coming from their ignorance, coming from those people's not using their minds. If they used their minds, they would find so many things. But they are not using them. They are only looking at the outward aspects of everything.

Then, we come to mankind. Mankind, how do they come? What happens? Mum and dad sleep together, and then after nine months and some days there comes a child. They do not think about it, "Who is able to do this?" not asking. That is their only knowledge; they never, never think or ask to learn anything. They are saying, "Nature, Nature." You are also 'Nature'! Their ways will lead to Hells with their 'Nature'!

Perhaps most of you were not born when I went to Madinatu-l-Munawwarah, the Prophet's holy city, with my Grandshaykh, maybe now more than fifty years ago. I went with my Grandshaykh for seclusion in that holy land to whose earth Allah Almighty gives holiness.

We went from Damascus, taking our cars to reach the Prophet's holy city, and we passed through deserts full of *raml*, sand, nothing on it, and came. Then, we made, as we were ordered, seclusion. Seclusion takes people from outside to themselves. Now, most people's eyes are outside, around themselves. They are forgetting themselves and their interest is in what is around them.

No! Begin first from yourself. Look at yourself; *then* look at what is around you. Seclusion takes man from outside to his real being, inside. Therefore, no one can be without a *dalil*, guide. If no guide, no one knows anything.

You must find a guide for guidance because you can't find the way to yourself without a guide. Therefore, seclusion, it is the most important thing that makes us reach ourselves. If you live seventy years, eighty years, ninety years or more or less, but you not find a guide and you go, knowing nothing about yourself . . . Therefore, Allah Almighty sent His prophets to make you know who you are, taking you from outside to inside, taking you to yourself. Otherwise, you are ignorant, like so many kinds of animals.

Now people, they are thinking, "Oh, Doctor ____," "Doctor ____," "Doctor ____," "Doctor ____!" So many doctors, and they know nothing. Therefore, Allah Almighty sent the first prophet, Sayyidina Adam, as the first guide for his children, and after him there came more prophets from his grandsons, grandsons, grandsons, reaching up to the Seal of Prophets, Sayyidina Muhammad ﷺ. Finally, he came to take people to themselves, to make them know who they are.

The last and greatest guide for mankind, he was Sayyidina Muhammad, peace be upon him. If life on earth were to go on up to eternity, he is enough, he is enough to be a guide for the billions, trillions of people who may come. His guidance was just granted to him in the Holy Qur'an, and the Holy Qur'an is enough for every nation throughout the centuries up to eternity. No need for a new guide to come with a new holy book; no. The Holy Qur'an is enough to take you to yourself. That is important!

Yes, we were going [to Medina] for that purpose, to make a way. My Grandshaykh wanted to make a way from me to myself. I was in seclusion for three months, and I went back to Damascus when I finished. Grandshaykh was there; by his orders I came. And I saw that on those sandy plains, sandy lands, there were countless colored flowers.

How did it happen? Because once, while we were in seclusion, there came a rain. That rain gave life, by the holy command of Heavens, and they were like such beautiful, beautiful lands, with every kind of flower. *Subhanallah,* the sun was giving different colors. In Europe you can find lands with flowers, but they are not so many different kinds—maybe five kinds, maybe ten kinds. But in those countries, the sun, by the holy command of Allah, gives so many countless colors, so many plants. I was thinking that it was like an embroidered carpet, so beautiful!

Therefore, I am saying, "Why are they not asking, 'How did that happen? What is the secret power?'"

They are saying, 'Nature.'. That is 'Nature'? Nature is under the control of an angel. I am ashamed to say that if Allah Almighty looked only once at the earth, this earth would be Paradise.[213] And His territories, divine territories, are countless!

O people, come and learn, before the Angel of Death comes to you to take you from this life to the graveyard. Try to learn something! But people, they are only learning how they can reach material aspects during this life and their only goal is how they can give their physical being pleasure. Getting more money—for what? To give their physical being more pleasure! And it goes against them. If a person does not take so much care of his physical being, he may live,

---

[213]That is, Allah does not look at this insignificant world but assigns it to intermediaries to manage and care for.

after seventy, up to eighty, ninety, hundred. But those who want to give more pleasure to their physical being, you go and look in the cemetery on the day of their death. They do not reach more than fifty or sixty years. O people, think about it!

May Allah forgive us! It is enough for anyone who can think about it. If not using his mind, he is like an animal. Animals they do not think. The main *farq*, difference, between man and animals is that man thinks, animals do not think. And those who do not think about such subjects, their level is the level of non-thinking creatures, animals.

May Allah forgive us and grant us from His endless blessings to follow prophets and their inheritors. For the honour of the most honoured one, Sayyidina Muhammad, peace be upon him ﷺ— *Fateha!*

22

You Must be Patient or You Must be Thankful

As-salamu 'alaikum! Ahlan wa sahlan, welcome to you! We are all His servants. As the sign of servanthood, we are saying, *"A'udhu bil-Lahi min ash-Shaytani-r-rajim. Bismillahi-r-Rahmani-r-Rahim."*

Don't trust in yourself, no! You may trust in Allah. But it is difficult for you to reach trust in Allah Almighty. You may trust the most beloved and most respected and most glorified servant of Allah Almighty, who represents Allah Almighty.

Must be a representative! If no representative, how would we reach Allah Almighty? Therefore, He put and made Sayyidina Muhammad ﷺ as His representative. He is Allah Almighty's representative.

If you do not know His representative, how are you going to know Allah? It is impossible, impossible! Therefore, secondly, we must give our utmost respect to Allah Almighty's representative and His deputy, who is named in *"La ilaha illa-Llah, Muhammadur Rasul-Allah"* ﷺ.

You can't find anyone else's name in front of which is written His Holy Name, *"La ilaha illa-Llah,"* but there is written on the Divine Throne, *"La ilaha illa-Llah, Muhammadur Rasul-Allah."* Therefore, you must try to reach His representative, the most beloved and most glorified one whose name is Muhammad, peace be upon him, whom Allah Almighty respects.

What about you? Why are you not giving your real respect to that one who is respected by his Lord, the Lord of the Holy Throne, the Lord of Heavens and all creation? What is the reason? What is the reason that you are not giving your most high respect to the most glorified servant of Allah Almighty? He never said that I am your Lord. Sayyidina Muhammad, he never claimed that I am your Lord, only saying, "I am His servant and I am under His command. What He, Allah Jalla Jalaluhu, says, I am trying to fulfill."

You must try, O people living on earth and eating from every kind of pleasure, Allah Almighty's favors, endless favors to you! Why are you are not giving that respect to that one who is respected from pre-eternity up to eternity, Sayyidina Muhammad 靆?

Now people are forgetting spirituality, they are not interested in their spirituality. All men, their interest is just for their physical being, nothing more after that; finished! They are saying, "When our physical being disappears, we will disappear. Nothing more."

That is a shaytanic teaching for men. And creation is going on, *istimrar*, continuously, never stopping, from pre-eternity up to eternity. You must be happy and you must be most interested in yourself, how you are in existence, how mankind found themselves on earth. Their existence is from outside or from this earth? What do you think?

You do not think; people do not want to think. Therefore, they are drinking, drinking, drinking till they are drunk. When they are drunk, drunk ones never know their right hand from their left hand. Perhaps people are carrying that drunk person to his home, and he may say [parodies:] "To where am I coming? This is my home? No!

I was in Buckingham Palace. Where are you bringing me?" Dreaming, dreaming; when drinking, dreaming. "I am in Buckingham Palace. Bring me to my palace!" No mind, finished!

And people now, they never ask from where they are coming. If you ask, he will say, "I am coming from Buckingham Palace, and my grandfather was King George the Fifth and my grandmother was . . . To where are you bringing me?"

"This is your palace."

"Where is it? Written on it, 'W.C.' Uff! Bringing me to the W.C.!"

"This is your palace. When you come in the morning, you may find your palace." *Tauba astaghfirullahu-l-'Adhim wa atubu ilayh!*[214]

People are drunk, drunk! Shaytan is making them not accept anything except physical pleasures for their physical bodies. Beyond that, they are not accepting anything because they are fully drunk, fully drunk! People they are good ones if they are not drunk. When they get drunk, they are no longer good ones—finished, because drinking makes their minds stop, and they run to drink in pubs.

For what? To forget the heavy burden of their material being. That makes them drink so that they may forget. But when they come to themselves, they are saying, "Oh! Why I am here? Why I am here? I am that one who last night was in Buckingham Palace, and tonight you are bringing me to the W.C. center!"

"Yes, come! We are going to write on you, 'W. C. Center of Victoria Park in London.' You may sit on a chair and you may collect from people. When they come, *wsh-h!* Take one pound from big ones. You should be up tonight as you like. Tonight you may go to

---

[214] I seek forgiveness of the Almighty and I repent to Him.

your 'Buckingham Palace.' Now work here! At nighttime we will take you there."

That is most men's goal, to be in palaces and to fulfill their physical enjoyment, nothing else. What is this? Animals, they are much more honourable than mankind now, who are living in sewers, rats that are living in sewers, yes! But they are not saying, "This is a sewer and it is a dirty place." No, they are saying, "Oh, so good!" and fighting each other like rats in sewers, dirty channels. They are very happy and fighting. One rat is very angry with the other rat. "Why are you coming here? This is my territory! If not going back, I will bite you till you die!"

People, they are mostly now—you may say *all* mankind—fighting for sewers, the dirt channels of this life, no more. And the Lord of Heavens is saying, "O mankind, I have not created you to be and to live in sewers, dirt channels. I created you to be in honourable places—to be there, to be always honoured. And yet you are running away to the sewage of dirt channels?"

We must try to understand something, or people should go and find their graves so dirty-smelling, such dirty places, that if a live one were put in it for one minute, he might die. But it should be his up to the Last Day!

O people, you have not been created for *dunya*, for the sewage of dirt channels, no! You have been honoured by your creation, that your Lord created you and honoured you to be the most honoured creature on earth, in Heavens. Try to reach that level! Try to reach, or you should find your grave in such a dirty channel that for even one second, no one may be able to live in it.

You are welcome! You are servants of my Lord, coming here, and I am welcoming you because I have been ordered to welcome His servants. I am trying, but mostly it is difficult to meet everyone and to speak to them separately, and it is so difficult to fulfill their wishes.

Yes, I am trying to meet one after another of my guests. But when I am calling, "Come!" they are saying, "O Shaykh, we are leaving today. Yes, we would like to meet you!" Yes; coming and sitting, and some of them saying to me, "O Shaykh, give me an advice."

"*Yahu!* How many days were you here? Not any advice all that time, but now you are asking advice from me? Were you sleeping when I was with people, trying to say something?"

"Doesn't matter, *ya Shaykh!* We are Pakistani people, we are democratic people. Therefore, we are trying to bring democracy to your 'mental house.'"

"*Yahu*, rhe 'mental house' never acceps democracy. _____, can there be democracy in our place? In the mental house you saw, is there democracy?"

And coming—others are coming, particularly ladies, sitting, and they are speaking the most after certain nations that also have a medal for speaking. If they begin, from morning up to evening, from evening up to morning, Pakistani people are never ending, and saying this and that, this and that. "My family, my daughter, my son, my husband has left, making me . . ."

And I am saying, "Quickly finish this and go! I am fed-up from this! You are also bringing all the dustbin, all garbage, bringing here! I can't sleep at nighttime because you are saying so many things and injuring my heart, and I can't sleep." In such a way! They are thinking that only *they* must speak. It can't be!

When we are saying something here, you must keep it! It is enough for all nations! Don't come and say to me this or that about *dunya*. No, it is no good. Therefore, twenty-four hours are not enough for me to answer people. Sometimes I am swearing, I am getting angry. When I am getting angry, they are very happy [laughter], making Shaykh to be angry.

O people, speak and give a short report about what you are in need of. If you do not find it through our meetings, then you may ask. But our meeting, it is enough; no need to ask. They [Spiritual Headquarters] are saying, "You must be patient or you must be thankful."

For everyone living on earth, some of them must be thankful, some of them must be patient; no middle course. If anything is disturbing you, try to be patient till Allah Almighty changes it. And ask the reason, and the reason is what we are speaking about now. Keep it! They [Spiritual Headquarters] are saying, "O people, try to be with Allah. You should be happy! Don't be with Shaytan or with *dunya*. You should be sad always!"

That is the summary. But people are asking this, asking that. I am saying, "Be with Allah!"

"How can I be?"

"Find those servants who are always with their Lord's Divine Presence. Look at them and take what you are in need of. Then you may be with Allah. Don't make a long conversation, no. *You must be thankful or you must be patient.*"

May Allah forgive us! We are trying to teach or to train ourselves how we may be able to save ourselves from the hands of Shaytan and his deputy, our ego. Try and ask for support from Allah

Almighty in front of Shaytan and your ego. You should be happy here and Hereafter.

O Allah, forgive us! And you must think that you are in need of forgiveness at every moment. O our Lord, forgive us and grant us from endless blessings, to make You, O our Lord, pleased with us.

Try to make your Lord pleased with you. That is most important. All the prophets were calling people on that point. "O people, come and try to make your Lord pleased with you, nothing else." If your Lord is not pleased with you, what is the benefit of having all the treasures of this world? Nothing!

May Allah forgive us and bless you! For the honour of the most honoured servant, glorified servant, of Allah Almighty, Sayyidina Muhammad ﷺ—*Fateha!*

23

KEEPING OUR OATH TO ALLAH

As-salamu 'alaikum! As-salam Allahi 'alaikum wa rahmatahu wa rid-wanuhu![215] *Meded, ya Sultanu-l-Awliya! Meded, ya Rijal-Allah!*

A'udhu bil-Lahi min ash Shaytani-r-rajim. Bismillahi-r-Rahmani-r-Rahim. Destur, ya Sayyidi, ya Sultanu-l-Awliya. Meded!

Rasul-Allah, peace be upon him, he was saying, *"Ad-dinu na-sihah."* Therefore, it is the most important pillar for Islam to stand on. If that pillar is broken down, no more Islam. Therefore, now, no more Islam because that pillar has just broken down.

Allah Almighty sent Islam, and it is His biggest grant to His servants, *din-Ullah*, the religion of Allah. For what did *din*, for what did Islam, come?

Islam came to teach people that they are servants and they must keep the heavenly orders of Allah Almighty. When they do not take care to keep heavenly rules, they are going down, down, until reaching the deepest and most terrible place in the Fire.

Now people, they have left *din-Ullah*, the heavenly faith to which all of us gave our oath on the Day of Promises.[216] Before

---

[215]Allah's peace be on you, and His mercy and His pleasure.

coming to this life and being dressed in these clay bodies, our souls were free throughout the endless territories of Allah Almighty. And He said to souls, "*Alastu bi-Rabbikum?* O My servants, I created you. Do you accept that I am your Lord, the Creator?"

All of them said, "*Bala,* yes, O our Lord! You are our Creator."

And then, "Do you give your promise that you will be My servants?"

All souls, they said, "*Bala,* yes, our Lord! O our Creator, You are our Lord and we are Your servants, not anyone else's. We are *Your* servants. That is our oath. We are Your servants."

Right or wrong, what we are saying? This is a declaration for all nations now. From here, I am asking. I am zero, before one [01], but when They put one in front of me [10], I am going to have full power. Now I am one, after zero. If putting one in front of me, I may take this world from its orbit, throwing it away! We will have power when I am going to be one in front of zero. Now I am one behind zero, zero.[217]

I am sorry to say that all nations are running after nationalism, running after some foolish ideas that they have taken from Shaytan, Sadanas. They are making Sadanas as their Lord. They are never listening to any other one, only saying, "Sadanas is our everything!" And people now, they are in endless troubles, endless problems, endless

---

[216] *"And [mention, O Muhammad,] when your Lord took from the children of Adam, from their loins, their descendants and made them testify concerning themselves, [saying to them,] 'Am I not your Lord?' [Alastu bi-Rabbikum]?' They said, 'Yes! [Bala!] We have testified [to that]* (7:172). This 'event' in the spiritual world is known as the Day of Promises.

[217] The Shaykh's meaning is that he is normally .....0000001, endlessly nothing, but if Allah, the One, is in front, then he is 1000000.....

miseries. They are in the worst position since the beginning of this life on earth up to this day—the worst position. Can't be worse than this!

All prophets, including the Seal of the Prophets, peace be upon him and upon other prophets, said about the Antichrist, "The Antichrist is that one who is fully the representative of Shaytan." And Shaytan's goal is to take everyone from their Lord and bring them to the Dajjal, to the Antichrist. Shaytan is trying to do that.

Finally, when people are hopeless, they look and run to find someone to save themselves, and they are now in such a position. All nations, all governments, all states are hopeless. They can't find any way to save themselves or their people. Look, each day! And Shaytan is saying, "Now is the best time to involve myself among the children of Adam as a savior—to show myself as their savior now, and then I will carry them to Hells here and Hereafter." And all nations, all people, are denying the existence of their Lord, their Creator!

I was surprised recently. You can see Buddhist people, those people who are such silent ones. Buddhist people, they may be seen as such humble people, showing themselves as the best people, showing themselves that they are only for their Lord, showing themselves that they are only servants of their Lord. And they are claiming that Buddha is their Lord, *astaghfirullah,* and they are claiming that they are followers of Buddha.

I must swear at them. "You are going to be *wahshi*,[218] worse than wild animals!" Buddhist people, they thought that they were such peaceful ones, putting such a thing here and here [over the

---

[218]Wild, untamed.

shoulder]. And now I am seeing on that Shaytan's wizard box, TV, they are in the streets; hundreds and thousands of Buddhist people, running like beasts.

How can it be? To where are they calling people—to run to the streets? What do they want? Do you think that they are not happy with their ways? Looks like this, unhappy. They are unhappy. Therefore they are running.

For what? What do they want? Buddha was always sitting like this, thinking, sometimes sleeping, sometimes sitting there, sometimes standing up. Do they see that Buddha was running in the streets and calling people, "Come with me to reach the Himalayan Mountains or Nepal" Why running in the streets?"

Try to be a servant only of your Creator. You are claiming that you are calling people to Buddha. For what? Is Buddha going to give you Tibet or China or Bukhara or Kashmir? No. How are they claiming they are Buddhist people? They are running in the streets like llamas!

It is not right! What was your oath to your Lord—to be servants to Him or servants to countries? All are on the wrong way; they have lost their ways! I am talking about Buddhist people, I am blaming them because they are saying, "We do not eat meat because meat makes people be like beasts. We are eating only a little bit of vegetables." What about what you are doing? You are eating vegetables and you are also going to be like beasts!

There is their chief, Dalai Lama. What is his name? He is ordering them to run in the streets? If he is ordering, he is wrong, also. Once, he sent to me in London a person to have an interview with me. I was looking; he was putting this equipment, everything. "I am coming on behalf of the Dalai Lama to speak to you."

I was saying, "You are not on my level to speak to you. Say to your teacher that he may come to me. I may give lessons not to one Dalai Lama; to seventy Dalai Lamas I may give their lessons. Don't speak to me! He may come and .anyone who is asking may come!" I am zero, before one, but when They put me after one, I may swallow the whole world and everyone in it. It is not difficult for us.

Their chief is ordering to them to run in the streets? What do they want? They claiming, "We are only for our Lord." If you are only for your Lord, why are you running in the streets? For what are you asking? Ask from your Lord! Don't ask from governments! Governments—eh, every kind of shaytan is going to be in government.

O people, wake up! Before a heavenly punishment comes on you; wake up! Keep your position! Otherwise, no shelter except the Lord's shelter. Nothing can shelter you but only your Lord's shelter!

That person in Iraq who was saying to people, "I am your Lord," he made like big cities underground to shelter himself and his treasures. What happened, what happened? O people, wake up! If Allah Almighty's vengance comes, no shelter for you! Try to be Allah Almighty's servants, as we gave our oath to Him, "You are our Creator and we are Your servants."[219]

I heard that his Holiness the Pope went to Australia. I am asking, "For what did he go?" People were saying, "He went to bring peace to people." Capital for His Holiness! What did he do? Why did he go to Australia? From his throne he can call people. He must say what I am saying now; he can't say anything else. He must say, "O people, remember your oath that you gave to your Creator. You

---

[219]97:172.

are His servants, so *be* servants!" Did he say such a thing? No. He may come to Cyprus—may come, yes!

O people, I am sorry. I am only shouting at my bad ego, and I am putting my ego in front of me and I am swearing at it. You are free to keep what we are saying to you or not. You are free.

There was a holy person at the time of Harun ar-Rashid, perhaps one thousand years ago or more. People never saw that one smiling or laughing. But one day a person came and said to the caliph, "We just met Bahlul Dana. He was laughing!"

"Quickly bring him to me!" the caliph said.

They brought him and the caliph said, "O my brother! Never have you been seen smiling or laughing. What happened to that?"

"O our *sultan,* today I was in the slaughtering place, and I saw so many sheep or goats hanging by themselves. And then I was happy and I laughed because I had been thinking that I was going to be responsible for others. I was so sad, but now I see that each one is just hung with its legs up. Therefore, what people are doing, it is not for me [to carry], no."[220]

Therefore, you must take care of yourself. You are a servant. Try to keep your servanthood. Don't look at this, that, what they are doing; no. You must try to look and to arrange yourself to be a good servant, to keep your oath to your Lord, Almighty Allah. Then Allah is going to be happy with you. If He is happy with you, everyone is going to be happy with you, here and Hereafter!

---

[220] The meaning is that, as everyone will return to Allah singly and alone, each soul is responsible for its own actions and accountability with Him.

For the honour of the most honoured and glorified servant of the Lord, Allah Almighty, Sayyidina Muhammad ﷺ—*Fateha!*

24

THE SECOND BASE OF ISLAM: BELIEVING IN THE PROPHET

As-salamu 'alaikum! A'udhu bil-Lahi min ash Shaytani-r-rajim. Bis-millahi-r- Rahmani-r-Rahim.

The worst and most dangerous enemy of mankind, of the children of Adam, is Satan. You must teach that first to your descendants, after teaching them to say "Allah Allah Allah." That is going to be their first word, the holy Name of Allah, and we hope that, at the end of their lives, the last word coming from their lips will be "Allah Allah Allah."

We must change our ways from A to Z from Europeans. For Muslims, we must change everything, even, according to *"alif ba ta. . .."*up to *'ya.'*[221] If not changing, all people living on earth should be destroyed.

They are destroying each other. Heavenly curses are approaching. You must leave, you must leave the wrong way, you must leave *kafirlerin adetleri, kuffar's* habits. We must change everything that we are wearing, eating, doing, reading—everything!

---

[221]From the first letters of the Arabic alphabet up to the last.

All houses of Nimrods,[222] we must take them down! *Ardu-l-Lahi wasi'ah*,[223] Allah Almighty's earth is so big. Why are you building one story over another—*why, why*? Angels are calling those people and saying, "Why, O son of Adam? What is the reason that you are making your buildings higher, higher, higher? Are you going to follow the way of Nimrod, are you claiming to be a Nimrod?" He built such a huge tower, the tower of Babylon. Why? Or like Pharaoh: he was saying to his prime minister (all prime ministers, they must change their ways, also), "O Haman, build for me a huge tower! I would like to go up and see where is that Lord of Abraham."[224]

Bismillahi-r-Rahmani-r-Rahim. Bismillahi-r-Rahmani-r-Rahim. People who forget *"Bismillahi-r-Rahmani-r-Rahim"* are forgotten. Those who are forgotten, curses are coming on them from Heavens, and not curses like the curses coming on those people, Qaumi Namrud [Nimrod's people], Ashshuriyin [Assyrians], Kaldani [Chaldeans] or the famous tribes on the Dijle [Tigris].[225]

Therefore, people, and particularly the Egyptian people, when they accepted to leave *Shari'at-Allah*, taking away their *malik, sultan,* and accepting one who was a representative of Shaytan, Shaytalin[226]—and who was another one, Shaytalin,[227] before him? Lenin, Stalin, both of them, and Mao, they were representatives of Nimrod and Shaytan, coming to Egypt through that 'Abdul-Nasser, who

---

[222]Tall buildings, skyscrapers.

[223]*"Allah's earth is spacious."* (4:97)

[224]See 28:38.

[225]Here, Maulana comments parenthetically, "Dijle, [Tigris]; Furat [Euphrates]; Nil Mubarak [the Blessed Nile]. *Bir daha var, efendim, üç,* four rivers, Amu Derya. They say that those four big rivers are coming from Paradise."

[226] Wordplay on Shaytan and Stalin.

[227] Here a wordplay on Shaytan and Lenin.

brought communism there and did his worst for the Egyptian people, taking away what Allah had sent to people, bringing the pillars of the sultanate of Shaytan.

Our people, they did it. The Arabs followed them; they followed, and they, all of them, are cursed! Iranian people, also, they are under a curse, saying, "We have so much power," because there is no republic in Islam, no parliament in Islam, no government cabinet. All of them now aren't able to do anything for Allah till they come to *Shari'at-Ullah* that came from Heavens. If they do not come to *Shari'at*, curses will come. I am very fearful for this new year, *Hijri* new year.

There is the Islamic calendar. It is correct. Other calendars have no strong base; no base, no base. That is everything, as now in Christianity they are changing as Shaytan tells them, and then no value for that European calendar, no. The Islamic calendar is always on a strong base.

What is that strong base? The Seal of Prophets, who was born in unknown deserts and grew up, is the base. Europeans are no-mind people, Christians more than them! It is forbidden for non-Muslims to look at the base of Islam. Sometimes I am saying, "O people, what does your intellect say if someone says, 'On Venus, there are such high mountains and oceans, and this and that.'"

I am addressing NASA. It is not really NASA, but it is NASIYA, from *'nasiya,' 'nisyan,'* forgetting, forgot. Therefore, they are saying, "We are NASA people," forgetting everything that came from Heavens.

160

I am saying, "What is your opinion if a person says, 'There is something on Venus,' and you say, 'Yes, yes, yes!' and then I tell you about the moon, full moon, but you say, 'We do not believe'"?[228] That is their mentality. Europeans and Christians and non-Muslims' mentality is like that.

Who is the nearest prophet to our time? Sayyidina Muhammad ﷺ. You say the names of prophets who lived about four thousand years ago; you believe in them, although only their names remain in your books, and I don't think that any people are following them, no. But you look at Sayyidina Muhammad ﷺ, whose way two billion people are following, and you say, "You are not a prophet." What a mentality! I am fighting them!

Therefore, now, all nations, are responsible because they are not thinking about it. Jesus Christ, peace be upon him, was a prophet, and six hundred years after him, there came another prophet whose name is blest and about whom good tidings had been granted to nations.[229] And you are saying, "He is not a prophet"?

---

[228]The meaning here is that while people are willing to accept as facts ancient fragmentary evidence, theories or incomplete scientific findings, they consistently refuse even to consider as factual a matter pertaining to religion and spirituality that is backed by innumerable pieces of sound evidence and logic—that is, Muhammad's truthfulness and credibility.

[229]The name "Muhammad" and its derivative, "Ahmad," means "the praised one." Various Biblical prophecies are believed by Muslims to refer to Muhammad (see Deut. 18:15, 18-20; Isa. 42:1-4; John,1:19-24, 14:16, 26, 30, 15:26, 16:7-16). And a Qur'anic verse reads; *"And mention, [O Muhammad], when Jesus son of Mary said, 'O Children of Israel, indeed I am the messenger of Allah to you confirming what came before me of the Torah and bringing good tidings of a messenger to come after me, whose name is Ahmad."* (61:6)

161

Then who would be a prophet now? And where is Jesus Christ's *Evangelo* [gospel]?[230] We are not asking for the *evangelo* of Mark, of John, of Matthew, of Luke.

Once I went to the biggest book shop in London—big, all kind of books. I entered the section that is for Christian books. I said, "I am looking for an *evangelo*."

"Yes, sir!" quickly bringing four books to me.

"What is that?"

"This is the *evangelo* of Luke, this the *evangelo* of Matthew, this the *evangelo* of John, and this the *evangelo* of Mark."

"I am asking for the *Evangelo* that was sent to Jesus Christ!"

"We are sorry but these are our holy books."

Finished! I am not in need, because the *Evangelo* did not come to Luke or Matthew or John or Mark. No, the *Evangelo* came to Jesus Christ. You may say, "He is God's Son," or other things; it doesn't matter to me. But I am asking, "If Allah sent Jesus Christ to save nations, what was there with him? The holy books of Matthew, John, Luke, Mark?"

How would you ask me to be a Christian? The Lord of Heavens sent Jesus Christ and sent him the *Evangelo*. Where is that *Evangelo*? Finished! Like a spring; there is just a tap but no more water is coming. They are putting one, two, three, four pipes, but not even one of them is running, never giving satisfaction.

---

[230]The *Injil*, the Gospel revealed to Jesus ﷺ, mentioned in the following Qur'anic verses: 3:3, 3:48, 3:65; 5:46 [5:49 in Yusuf Ali's translation], 5:66 [69], 5:68 [71], 5:110 [113]; 7:157; 9:111; 48:29; 57:27.

Therefore, my addressing is to the whole world. Sometimes I am nothing, zero before one. And sometimes They are making me zero after one. I am something at that time! I am weak, with perhaps two legs on the floor of the grave, but my words, no one can reject them, no one can defend their ideas. Even though now Christians, Muslims, Jewish people have big foundations for their religions, I see that no one can give anything to our spirituality, and we are hungry and thirsty.

Dunya is nothing! If the Pope remembers what happened throughout the two thousand years of other popes, he must think about it! Now fifteen centuries of Islam have passed, but still Jewish people are not willing to say, *"Muhammadur Rasul-Allah ﷺ."* Why? Is anything wrong? Is anything wrong in the Holy Qur'an? Say! If they should claim that, then by morning they should receive a divine lesson!

Now it is a very terrible time, and heavenly powers should be used. And people will go from the earth, like the Children of Israel. When they did wrong, Allah Almighty ordererd some of them to kill the ones who did that wrong thing.[231] Now, therefore, so many of those people who are not coming to real belief, real Islam, they should be killed by each other.

May Allah forgive us! O people, come to yourselves! And our new year that we were speaking about, the new year of Islam, begins from the holy night, the fifteenth of Sha'ban al-Mu'azzam[232]—not tonight, not tomorrow night, but after tomorrow night, the night of Saturday reaching to Sunday.

---

[231] Mentioned in 2:54.

[232] The eighth month of the Islamic calendar, preceding Ramadan.

Therefore, O people, whatever is going to happen during this year up to next Laylatul-Bara'a, the holy night of Bara'at—everything that should be on earth, written by the Will of our Lord, our Creator, should appear. Guard yourself! Guard yourself!

No one can escape from heavenly vengeance. It will come and find them. May Allah forgive us! Prepare yourself for that third night, anywhere you may be and pray to Allah! If you can pray one hundred *raka'ats* that night, Allah Almighty will grant you what is best for you here and Hereafter.

Try to be servants of your Lord. That is the teaching of Islam, and I don't think that other religions are saying that what I am saying is not true. In all holy books it is written, "O people, remember that you are servants." May Allah forgive us and accept our prayers. *Fateha!*

25

TRY TO BE AMONG THE PEOPLE OF PARADISE FOR THE ETERNAL LIFE

O people, *as-salamu 'alaikum!* *A'udhu bil-Lahi min ash-Shaytani-r-rajim.* The biggest *bela*, curse, on mankind, is from Shaytan. Therefore, we have been ordered to run away from Shaytan. But people now are running to him.

Sometimes I saw in airports a small car, written on it, "FOLLOW ME!" For what was that "FOLLOW ME"? And I saw a gigantic plane coming and beginning to follow.

Now mankind is not running away from Shaytan but they are running *after* Shaytan, to follow that cursed one. If you follow a cursed one, what should there be—coming on you blessings or curses? Therefore, we must say, *"A'udhu bil-Lahi min ash-Shaytani-r-rajim. Bismillahi-r-Rahmani-r-Rahim."* This *"Bismillahi-r-Rahmani-r-Rahim"* is our sword, our sword for defending ourselves. It is so easy but it looks so difficult.

Shaytan never gets hopeless when he is running after a person. Some days, he says, "One time I may catch him. And I will catch that one drinking."

Shaytan comes to that one. "O my best friend, please taste and smoke! Very useful, because if you do not smoke, no one will say that you are a complete young one, from our time's youth. Smoke!"

"My head is turning!"

"Don't worry! Today it may turn but tomorrow it will be okay. Take!"

Shaytan is teaching people *sharr*—cursed doings, cursed by Heavens. For anything that you do against the rule of Heavens, curses are coming on you quickly, as lightning comes on you, destroying something from you.

O people, O people, welcome to you! Welcome to you! Your egos never like to come here and they get so angry, also. "Why are you taking me to that place? No one is there for dancing. Even 'No smoking' is written there and they are putting some rules. Why are you taking me to that place?"

Therefore we must say, *"A'udhu bil-Lahi min ash-Shaytani-r-rajim."* Then we must say, *"Bismillahi-r-Rahmani-r-Rahim, Bismillahi-r-Rahmani-r-Rahim, ragh-man li-Shaytan, ridan li-Rahman!*[233] *Bismillahi-r-Rahmani-r-Rahim! Bismillahi-r-Rahmani-r-Rahim!*

Why are you throwing stones in Mina [during *Hajj*]? Why? What does it mean? That Allah Almighty wants to teach us that we must always throw stones at Shaytan. When he comes and wants to take you away from the blest way, throw with *"A'udhu bil-Lahi-min ash-Shaytani-r-rajim!"* and say *"Bismillahi-r-Rahmani-r-Rahim."* That one must know that we are servants of our Lord who created us.

---

[233]In spite of Shaytan, for the pleasure of the Most Merciful.

Who can say that there is no God? So many foolish ones! I may ask, "If no God, who brought you into existence? How did you come into existence—by yourself? You were invited to come here? How are you saying, 'No God'?"

To say "No God," it is so easy, but it is so bad, the worst words that mankind can say. That makes heavenly anger fall on them, and heavenly anger, when it moves, no power—your missiles, your destroyers, your such-and-such weapons, *silahlar*, atomic weapons, and every technology that you have, it is nothing if heavenly anger moves to come on earth.

O people, we are a handful of people here, and tonight we are reaching, *insha'Allah*, one of the holiest nights, Laylat al-Bara'at,[234] about which the Prophet, peace be upon him, was saying, "After the Night of Power, no other night can be as valuable as the Night of Bara'at."

Where is the *imam*? Read *Suratu Ha Mim!*[235]

[After the recitation:] *Masha'Allah, masha'Allah!* Blessings just reached us, *al-hamdulillah!* And we are asking forgiveness and guidance from our Lord, Allah Almighty, to be sent to us throughout this year so that we may follow His most beloved and glorified, best servant throughout creation from pre-eternity up to eternity, Sayyidina Muhammad ﷺ. That is the way that mankind can save itself. If not, it should be taken away. And this night, tonight, is going to be a

---

[234]The night of the fifteenth of Sha'ban, the holy night during which the divine decrees for the coming year are apportioned.
[235]The forty-fourth *surah* of the Qur'an, *Dukhan* or *Ha Mim*.

change in what will happen during the entire year, and we hope that our names will be on the tablet of Paradise people, not on the tablet of Hells' people.

O people, *dunya* is a dark *dunya*. No one is happy now with *dunya*. Those who are giving their love for this dirty *dunya*, *dunya* is dark place, dark place, but Shaytan and our ego are urging us, "Oh-h-h, you must try to be forever in this *dunya*!"

What is the result? Melting, melting, melting! Those who are asking to be with Allah Almighty, Allah is giving them real existence—*haqqani*, forever, up to eternity, eternal life.

Eternity! Such a sweet word in Western languages I have not seen! Eternity, eternity, *ebedi, sarmadi, daimumi!* No word gives my soul such enjoyment and pleasure as that word, "eternity, eternal," gives.

Eternity—try to reach eternity! If not, you will go back to the worlds of darkness; you won't see anything. Some creatures, they are living in darkness, dark places under this earth, and it is not easy. It is such a big trouble for a person to be imprisoned in darkness. And such happiness and enjoyment for those people who want lighted worlds, invisible worlds, to reach more and more pleasure and lights. Divine lights will come on them forever, forever, forever, never-ending.

Dirty *dunya!* Dirtiness is in it, yet people are asking to reach here, there, to be this, to be that—such weak faith, such weak beliefs. It is not right! Come, little by little, to accept, and try to be in eternity for the eternal life, in the blest countless Oceans of creation. Come and ask for that! Don't be for *dunya* but try to be for the Creator of Heavens.

May Allah forgive us! *Fateha!*

26

FIGHTING YOUR EGO DURING RAMADAN

Meded, ya Sultanu-l-Awliya! Meded, ya Rijal-Allah!

Allah Almighty is saying in the Holy Qur'an for all nations, *"Wa dhakkir, fa inna dhikra tanfa'u-l-mu'minin.*[236] O My most glorified and most honoured one in My Divine Presence, you, O Muhammad, remind My servants, because reminding may give them some lights to show them their way, to know where they are going." That is a heavenly order from Allah Almighty.

And we have now reached Holy Ramadan, the fasting month, the most glorified month among the twelve months. Tonight is going to be the first night of the holiest month of the year, *shahru-r-Ramadan*, the holy month of Ramadan. Tonight, believers are going to pray *tarawih*,[237] twenty *rak'ats*, and tonight, *insha'Allah*, we are going to intend to fast tomorrow according to the holy command of Allah Almighty. That is our intention. We are asking from Allah Almighty to give us enough strength to keep the holy order to His servants to complete thirty nights' *tarawih*.

O our Lord, *qawina 'ala ta'atika, ya Rabbana, hatta yuaddi shay min jihattina an yuqaddim dharra mina ta'at li-huduraka, Rabbana. Qawina, ya*

---

[236] *"And remind [O Muhammad], for indeed the reminder benefits the believers."* (51:55)

[237] The nightly *sunnah* prayers of Ramadan which follow *'Isha*, the prescribed night prayer.

Rabbana, 'ala ta'atika. Atina maqdara[238] to be able to control our egos. The biggest curse comes on people when their egos are over them.

The biggest mistake for men is to make their egos their commander; I am not saying *'sultan'*. To be under the command of his or her ego, that is the biggest curse for a person. When you make your ego commander over yourself, you are cursed forever, never cutting off! The month of Ramadan gives a chance to people to be able to leave their egos and to fight their egos and to be able to control their egos.

Subhanallah! Subhanallah! People now are running in the streets, everywhere. In East and West, everywhere, people are running and saying, "We don't like this prime minister," "We don't like this government," "We don't like this *sultan*," "We don't like this president." No one is thinking of saying, "We don't like our egos to be in power." Everyone is so happy to serve his or her ego; no one is saying, "My ego is not good! I must fight, I must bring it down, and I must put my heavenly power with my soul, to look after myself." No one, no one! Everyone is so happy to be under the emirate, to be the obedient servant of their egos. No one is asking to fight, to take their egos down and put their spirituality in power.

Everyone is giving power to his ego! How should this mankind, the children of Adam, be happy? They are asking to burn themselves, nothing else! They are preparing that because their commander is their ego that is the representative of Shaytan, and Shaytan is ordering their egos, "You must kill, you must burn, you

---

[238]Empower us, O Our Lord, to Your obedience. Until we are able to put forward one atom's weight of obedience to Your orders. Grant us strength.

must take them away, you must be the only one on earth! Don't give any chance to anyone else!"

Therefore, curses are coming now. If people do not change their ways, curses will come to take away four out of five, one remaining. If the population on earth is five billion, four billion are going to die, one remaining.

It is a very terrible time now. Therefore, I have been ordered to remind all nations, if my words reach all nations: It is not an honour for men to kill men! It is not an honour for men to burn a man! It is not honour for men to destroy countries! They haven't any right to kill even an ant because an ant has a right to live. You can't kill it! You may say, "O my Lord's creature, leave and go." That is a heavenly order, and it will never give you any harm, no harming.

Now men are getting to be such oppressors, killing everything, wanting to kill everyone. Therefore, Allah Almighty is sending on them such creatures that they may only feel their effects, but it is impossible to see them or to do anything to them. Doctor, yes? A virus—can you see, can you touch, can they do anything against it? *'Wa khuliqa-l-insanu da'ifa.'*[239] But people are running to fire! They are hearing and listening and obeying only Satan's commands.

This Ramadan has now just arrived, and it is a last chance for humanity to put their hegemony on their egos, to take power away from their egos and to give spiritual power to their souls. If not doing this, don't cry about what is going to happen. Billions, not millions—*billions* will go! Fasting is fighting against your ego, to take power from your ego and to give it to your soul, to your spirituality. If not, you will go, also. That is what we are saying.

---

[239] *"And We created the human being weak."* (4:28)

And you are a handful of people here, also. I don't know if during Holy Ramadan there is going to be something [calamitous], but after Ramadan, I think that there should be something. For Holy Ramadan, maybe Heavens is delaying the curses and looking at Allah's servants, what they are doing, but in Shawwal[240] the holy will of Heavens may be in action. When coming into action, it is not going to stop till heavenly vengeance reaches all nations that are making their egos *sultan* and not obeying the orders of the *Sultan* of Heavens.

Therefore, whoever is asking to come here, I may say to them what the Prophet said, peace be upon him, the day of conquering Makkah-l-Mukarramah: "Whoever goes to the Holy K'abah, the K'abah is a shelter. Whoever goes to that one's house,[241] it is a shelter. And anyone going into his home and closing his door will be sheltered, also."

Therefore, I am saying now for all our visitors who have come: If you are here for three days, one week or ten days, you must prepare yourselves to reach your homes. Here, it is not a sheltered place for all nations. Therefore, we have been ordered to say to people who have their homes and their children that they must hurry during Holy Ramadan to get back to their homes and do what we said. They must close their doors, only going out for the obligatory service that they may do. Then they must be in their homes. I don't like anyone to move now from Europe, from East, from West, from America, from Australia, to come here now because Cyprus may be closed and no one can move from here. Then they should be in a worse condition, half their family here, half their family there. I have been ordered to give a warning to people.

---

[240]The month following Ramadan.

[241]The house of Abu Sufyan, the leader of the pagan Quraysh of Mecca, who had accepted Islam just prior to the opening of Mecca to Islam.

Yes. If *dunya* is as it is now, it doesn't matter, but *dunya* is not going to continue in such a way. All nations, they have lost their minds. No intelligence; they do not know what they are doing, only following shaytanic orders. Therefore, I am not responsible [for those who remain here after this]. From the beginning, I am saying, "Anyone who has finished their visit, they must hurry to go to their homes and keep themselves there, and it is going to be a shelter for so many people.

May Allah forgive us and bless you for Holy Ramadan. For the honour of the most honoured one in His Divine Presence, Sayyidina Muhammad, 鐥, may Allah forgive us. *Bi-hurmati man anzalathu ʿalayhi, Surata-l-Fateha!*[242] Those who are not fasting, who are not praying, who are not obeying, cursed arrows are coming on their heads. No one can save them!

---

[242]By the holiness of the one to whom it was sent down—*Surat al-Fateha!*

27

THE KEY TO SAFETY IN THE STORM: SEEKING SHELTER WITH ALLAH

A'udhu bil-Lahi min ash Shaytani-r-rajim. Bismillahi-r-Rahmani-r-Rahim. La haula wa la quwwata illa bil-Lahi-l-'Aliyi-l-'Adhim.

I was talking to Shaykh Adnan about *nasihat,* to call you to obey heavenly orders. Today he is moving from here. *Insha'Allah,* we hope that his *barakah* is going to be with us.

Then, there are coming to me now some inspirations for addressing people, not only for you but for all mankind. And the main purpose of *nasihat,* advice, it is to save humanity.

This is a very important point, to be well-known: to save mankind, who have been ordered to keep their honour, which is humanity. This must be well-known, but I never heard anyone say this up to today.

For what did prophets come? For what did holy books come? What is the importance of prophets, and *awliya,* also, saints? The answer is in such a short sentence: To save humanity. From whom? *"Inna-sh-Shaytana lakum 'aduwun, fattakhidhuhu 'aduwa!"*[243]

---

[243] *"Indeed, Satan is an enemy to you, so take him as an enemy."* (35:6)

Allah Almighty is saying, in His endless Greatness and endless Power, and through His endless Greatness Oceans, through His endless Wisdom Oceans, "O people, O My creatures! There is a dangerous enemy, a most terrible and dangerous enemy to you." That is Shaytan, Diabolo, also Sadanas, may Allah Almighty make that terrible enemy far from us! *"Khudhu hidhrakum*[244]—take your defense, because that terrible enemy is attacking you. You can't know from where, from which direction, he will come on you, so terrible! Therefore, keep your guard! You must keep your guard from that terrible, terrible enemy!"

And Sadanas' main target is to destroy humanity. Humanity is the highest level of creation on earth, and Sadanas wants to take humanity from its highest level to the lowest level. Humanity is swimming in heavenly lights, and Sadanas wants to make humanity extinguish their *nur*, their lights, and to bring them *tahta-th-thara*, '[245] underground, which is dark darkness, dark darkness, *a'udhu bil-Lah!*

His main goal, it is to bring humanity away from heavenly lights, *nur*, and to carry them, to take them, to put and to imprison them in that dark darkness, *a'udhu bil-Lah, Allah, ya Rabb!* And Allah Almighty sent His beloved ones, and the most beloved one, Sayyidina Muhammad ﷺ, peace be upon him, sending thousands of His blest people, heavenly people, to save humanity from the traps of Sadanas, Shaytan.

La haula wa la quwwata illa bil-Lah! Each one of the prophets came to save humanity, but Sadanas, Shaytan, is using countless tricks and putting countless traps, and calling people, "O people, follow me!" as in airports there is written on some small cars, "FOLLOW ME," and those big aircraft are following.

And Sadanas, the big Sadanas, is one, but his descendants are reproducing. It is in our traditional knowledge that has reached to me, also, that one leg of his is male, one leg is female, and it mates itself with itself and gives birth to shaytans. *Na'udhu bi-Llah! Na'udhu bil-Lah! Na'udhu bil-Lah!*[246] Therefore, that cursed one is urging men to mate with men, women with women—the dirtiest level, thrown out of humanity. He wants to carry them to that level! *La haula wa la quwwata illa bil-Lahi-l-'Aliyi-l-'Adhim!*

And now, the whole world is running after Sadanas! Its nations, governments, they are running to keep Sadanas' *ta'alim*, teachings and practices, everywhere. Everywhere now, the twenty-first century's people they are *musabaqa*, competing, with each other about which is going to be the first to follow Sadanas. *La haula wa la quwwata illa bil-Lah!* And humanity is just finished; in the twenty-first century humanity is finished, caught by Sadanas. As Pharaoh was tying slaves, the first one to the second, the second one to the third, now Sadanas is tying all nations, tying one to the next, and in his hand is a whip. *"Yallah!!!*[247] You must go this way! You must do this way, that way!" in order to destroy humanity, making mankind destroy its honour. And now, no honour for mankind on earth! No, not any honour for mankind because people have lost the level of humanity and have fallen, all of them have just fallen. *Aman, ya Rabb!*[248]

What is the *maqsad*,[249] mission, mission of all prophets? Only to save humanity, to keep the honour of humanity, nothing else. But even the Pope, *patarikas* [patriarchs], *hahams* [rabbis], Muslim *'ulema*

---

[246]We seek refuge with Allah!

[247]Come on! Get along!

[248]Safety, O Lord!

[249]Destination, intention, goal, aim, purpose.

[scholars], they are not yet understanding the main purpose, and they are fighting each other for this or that.

Look what we have lost and try to save what we have lost, to find it! Allah sent all prophets to save the honour of humanity. Why, *why*, are you fighting?

You are fighting for what? Russians, Americans, Arabs, Israelis, Iranis, Pakistanis, Indians, Chinese, Turks—for what are you fighting? For whom are you fighting? To save humanity? What is this?

"No," they are saying. "Democracy." Therefore, now, terrible days are coming. They are going to reach all people who are only slaves or labourers for Sadanas, coming now.

People are saying, "Oh-h-h! A hurricane is coming again, coming to America!" That is nothing! Look now, what is coming—a hurricane, how it is going to be! Out of five, one will remain. If all mankind now is five billion, that hurricane, that Armageddon, will come and swallow up four billion. Only those who are hearing and listening to the holy command of Allah Almighty, *"Khudhu hidhrakum!* Take your precaution! Guard yourself! Guard yourself!"* will remain.

There are some red signs, "Danger area! Don't approach! Danger! Caution, precaution." But people—*wo-o-oh!*—are running to it! Whoever runs to it will fall down! They are afraid of a hurricane but they are not taking any *tedbir*,[250] precaution, for Armageddon.

Armageddon! For a hurricane, people are trembling, but no one is thinking about that Armageddon hurricane that should take away not millions, *billions!* That is going to be! Only those who are

---

[250]Measures.

running to Allah, Allah will shelter. Whoever runs and asks for a heavenly shelter, they should be in safety. Otherwise . . .

For the nation of 'Aad, Qaumu Hud, *jabbarun 'anid,* [251] Allah Almighty ordered the Angel of Hurricanes to open a very small hole from that terrible hurricane. Then Allah Almighty ordered Sayyidina Hud to make a circle and sit there, and those who believed in him to be there. Yes, they were sitting.

Therefore, I am saying, a heavenly shelter may shelter you. 'Aad, they were tall like the Statue of Liberty, people like this, *jabbar.* They were saying, "We are not afraid of anyone!" The hurricane took them up and threw them down; finishing. Only the ones who were sitting with Sayyidina Hud, they came out of that terrible hurricane like from Paradise!

Now, O people, no one can save themselves by any means. The only shelter is for whomever runs to Allah. Therefore, it is a declaration for all nations from here, from a humble place. All prophets, they were sitting in small places and speaking to some slaves, some weak people, but their declaration just reached through East and West.

Here is a humble place. It is not that I am thinking, but my *ya-qin,* certainty, is for this declaration to reach everywhere, everyone. If not, they are going to be taken away. Laylati-l-Bara'a has put on the seal; finished!

---

[251] *"Willful tyrants"* (11:59). See Qur'an, 7:65-72, 9:70, 11:50-60, 26:123-139, 29:38, 38:12-14, 41:13-16, 18, 46:21-26, 50:12-14, 51:41-42, 53:50, 54:18-21, 69:4-8, 89:6-14, for the story of the pre-Abrahamic tribe of 'Aad and the divine punishment that overtook them for their disobedience to Allah's commands.

May Allah forgive us! This is the holy month, Ramadan. I don't think that during this holy month there is going to be something, for the honour of the Seal of Prophets and for his nation, but after Ramadan, I can't be able to give any guarantee to anyone. Whoever is against Sadanas should be sheltered. Those people who are running after those satanic ones, they should be under heavenly vengeance, going to be taken away. May Allah forgive us!

Just now, it is coming from our Masters, grand masters, to address you in the presence of a big saint, Shaykh Adnan Efendi Hazretleri, so that he should be a witness for what we are saying here. Allah is *Ahkamu-l-Hakimin*.[252] Those who are running away will never come back. Those who are keeping their positions, their servanthood, who are trying to keep the level of servanthood, should be saved and sheltered. May Allah forgive me, forgive you!

O people, write on big signs, "O people, save humanity!" O mankind, O mankind, try with your whole ability to save humanity! Whoever is running to save humanity, they should be under heavenly shelter. Others should be taken away; finished! *Fateha!*

Write in Arabic, in Turkish, in English, saying, "O people, save humanity! Don't follow Sadanas!" Write and put everywhere! People, they are running through the streets, saying, "We don't like war!" No, it is not enough! If you don't like war, you must say, "We are trying to save humanity from Sadanas and his followers." *Fateha!*

---

[252] *"The Most Just of Judges."* (11:45)

28

THE EASIEST OF DIVINE PUNISHMENTS

A'udhu bil-Lahi min ash-Shaytani-r-rajim.   Bismillahi-r-Rahmani-r-Rahim.

Meded, ya Sultanu-l-Awliya! Meded, ya Rijal-Allah! Bi-barakati 'ala shahru mubarak, Ramadana-l-Mubarak, alhimna rushdana wa a'idhna min shururi anfusina, ya Rabb![253]

By the Name of Allah Almighty, All Merciful, Most Beneficent and Most Magnificent. *Meded, ya Rijal-Allah!*

Always ask for heavenly support! If no heavenly support, our world can't move. If no heavenly support, no rain. If no heavenly support, oceans are going to dry up. If no heavenly support, all countries are going to be deserts. If no heavenly support, all animals are going to die. If no heavenly support, mankind is going to finish, no life for them.

Even though we are rebellious ones, Allah Almighty is granting, granting. *Subhanallah*, glory be to Allah from pre-eternity to eternity! O people, keep your obedience to your Lord, Allah Almighty, the Lord of Heavens! Allah *Jalla Jalaluhu*, Allah Most Glorious, He is not

---

[253]By the blessing of this blessed month, blessed Ramadan, inspire us with guidance and protect us from the evil of our egos, O Lord.

like His creatures. He is the Creator; we are creatures. Try to keep high *adab* with your Lord, Allah Almighty. May Allah forgive us!

O our Lord, we are rebellious, disobedient creatures. We are leaving our Lord's commands and following the orders of Sadanas, Shaytan. How we can hope for peace on earth? It is impossible! But for the honour of His most beloved one, Allah Almighty is granting from His endless Favor Oceans, and He is looking at what His servants are doing—if they are thankful, if they are saying, "No God except You, O our Lord, the Lord of Heavens, the Lord of everything—You, Allah! We are asking forgiveness! Forgive us!"

It is the holy month, Ramadan, the fasting month. For what are we fasting? Fasting is an obedience; it is the most important obedience and worship and servanthood to Allah.

First of all, He, Almighty, is calling His servants, "O My servants, come and give servanthood. Leave everything, and hear and listen to what your Creator is saying." This sound of calling people to servanthood, it is like waves, covering everywhere, reaching everyone's ears, calling, "O My servants, come and give your obedience to Me! Come, keep My servanthood because you are servants of Mine."

This announcement never cuts off. Every moment, every second, this announcement is covering the whole world, saying, "O My deputies whom I created and I honored,, and you promised to Me that you were going to keep My servanthood—O My servants, come and give your servanthood to My Divine Presence. If you do not hear and listen, I will punish you. Before you die, before coming to Me, I am going to punish you!"

"The easiest punishment, I will punish you with the easiest punishment. If you do not listen to Me, I will punish you, and that punishment it is so easy, very simple. I will not give a big punishment to you, no. But I will punish you!"

O our Lord, You are our Lord. Your command is *the* command and Your orders must be obeyed. You have the right to punish disobedient ones.

"I am punishing you, O disobedient servants, in a very, very simple way." What is that?

If I could ask people—if I asked the Pope, if I asked the Patrik [Patriarch], the Haham Başı [Chief Rabbi], what would they say? Perhaps this my speech may reach their ears. I am saying also to the Dalai Lama. "I am asking you, also: What is that *çok hafif*, very simple punishment, most bearable punishment? No, I am not giving a big punishment, but I am giving the most bearable punishment."

[Parodies:] Tell what that is, O Pope? There is also Shaykhu-l-Azhar,[254] there is also the Mufti of Makkah-l-Mukarramah, there is the Dalai Lama, there is Haham Başı. I am asking and seeing what would be the lightest, most bearable, punishment. If looking in books, in seventy months, seventy years, they are not going to find it.

It is one word that our Grandshaykh just put in my heart, heavenly knowledge. Yes, we may tell it now because no one is able to mention a more bearable punishment for the twenty-first century's people.

"Say!"

"Yes, sir!"

"I am taking up peace from earth to Heavens. No peace for them!"

254The shaykh of Azhar University in Cairo.

True? True? True? That is the most bearable one. No peace, no peace for any country, for any nation, for any level of people. No peace for governments, no peace for nations.

Earlier, nations they were fighting their neighbours, but now they are fighting among themselves, yes. True? Eh! No peace in your cities, no peace in your homes. Which one can say that I am at peace in my home; I am in peace, living in peace with my family, with my children, with my neighbours, with my workers, with my business—who can say, "I am at peace"? Which government can say, "We are happy with our nation?" because nations are black sheep, white sheep.

Heh-heh! The black sheep are saying, "No, we must be in power because our color is better than yours!"

The white sheep are saying, "No! We are more important than you! We are white ones. We can't bear you!"

This sheep, that sheep. Heh-heh! Nations! Democracy, *pocracy!*

"Heh? What happened?"

"We are trying to take away some people. We must try to be Number One, Number One on earth!"

Americans are saying [parodies:] "You are saying that to me, while *I* am here? You are going to be Number One? What about *me?* You are forgetting my majestic power!"

Russians are saying, "No! Who are you? If I roar, you are going to die!"

Yes, sir. *Merhaban, ahlan wa sahlan, ya shahru Ramadan!*[255] No peace! Yes, coming now: no peace, even within yourself, with yourself. You are not in peace with yourself; quarrelling; two *qutub,* poles, inside ourselves: One belongs to Heavens, to the lights of Heavens; one belongs to darkness. They are quarrelling. The black one that we have within ourselves, that belongs to Shaytan, saying, "You must obey me. I don't like that you should obey anyone else, no! You must be my obedient servant! Kill and seize, burn and seize, destroy and seize what I am asking!"

No peace in yourself because you do not believe in the holy orders of Heavens. You are forgetting your Creator, and this is the most bearable, punishment with which Allah is punishing you. *"Hu-wa-l-Qadiru 'ala an yab'atha 'alaikum 'adhaban min fauqikum au min tahti arjulikum au yalbisakum shi'an wa yudhiqa b'adakum basa b'ad."*[256] Yes, *within yourself;* making you two blocs.

Now the whole world is running to be in two poles, two camps. The Prophet was saying, "People are going to be in two camps, one East, one West; one believers, one unbelievers, and they are going to punish each other." No peace, no peace! Peace has been taken up. Once, this world it was in peace because people heard and listened to heavenly orders and obeyed, and Allah Almighty granted them peace—within themselves, in their countries, in East and West.

O people, listen and obey! If not, you are going to be taken away. First, peace was just taken up from the earth. This Cyprus, the Turkish part, is fighting; a handful of people, they are nine par-

---

[255]Greetings, welcome, O month of Ramadan!

[256]*"He is the [One] Able to send upon you affliction from above you or from beneath your feet or to involve you [in] sects and make you taste the violence of one another."* (6:65)

ties, fighting each other. Women are fighting men, men fighting women, women fighting women, men fighting men; everywhere fighting, no peace! Understand my English or not? Therefore I am asking, "What is the most bearable, most simple punishment?"

When they leave off listening to heavenly commands, Allah punishes them, taking away peace. And they get to be like beasts, wanting to kill, to drink others' blood, wanting to be Number One everywhere, wanting the whole world to be under their command, and all of them are going to be chairmen of Satan. A big assembly for Shaytan, and everyone wants to be chairman there! *Insha'Allah*, I am not on a chair—no chair; no one is making me be chairman. They are saying, "Eh, dustbin! Throw him away!"

Everyone now is unhappy, no one is happy now. No one is happy! At the least, when you see people's *rahatsızlık*, people's *idhtirab*, miseries,[257] it makes you be sorry; you can't be happy. When you look at that TV, no good news; everything makes you fall in misery. Therefore, when you read newspapers, everything gives you a kind of misery, making you be in trouble—everything! You look like this, you can't be happy; you may look like that, you can't be happy. In your home, you can't be happy; in the streets, you can't be happy; in your country, not happy; in East and West, not happy. People, they are in trouble; no peace, no happiness. Happiness has just been taken up.

La ilaha illa-Llah! La ilaha illa-Llah! La ilaha illa-Lah! O our Lord, O our Lord, for the honour of this holy month, send us what You promised to Your most glorious deputy, most glorious beloved one. For his honour, You promised to send us *that* one to take away

---

[257]*Rahatsızlık:* discomfort, uneasiness/ *idtirab:* trouble, disturbance, unrest.

from the earth everything that belongs to Shaytan, Sadanas, and to bring Your holy orders, to keep to them.

O people, ask during this holy month! Therefore, there should be so many, so many events, coming that a person can't carry. Ask from Allah Almighty not to see, not to hear and not to be touched by heavenly vengeance. This perhaps may be the last chance for all nations, during this holy month, for what they are doing. Maybe crises and miseries and problems on earth are going to increase, reaching the top point and then going to explode.

May Allah forgive us! O people, run to Allah! We must run to Allah, we must try to keep the holy orders of Heavens as much as possible. Then you should be sheltered by the heavenly shelter. If not, nothing can shelter you.

May Allah forgive us! *Tauba, ya Rabbi! Tauba, ya Rabbi! Tauba, astaghfirullah!* This is the holy month that helps you and urges you and forces you to keep the holy orders of Allah Almighty. Make your will power more powerful to keep the holy orders of Heavens. If you are not fasting,[258] you are going to be destroyed like dust, no one asking.

May Allah forgive us! O our Lord, *tauba, ya Rabbi! Tauba, ya Rabbi! Tauba, astaghfirullah! Shukr, ya Rabbi! Shukr, ya Rabb! Shukr, alhamdulillah! Bi-jahi Nabiyika-l-Karim, ya Allah,* "*ub'athu lana malikan yuqatil fi sabil-Illah,*"[259] to take away satanic powers and defeat them from Your servants, and this world to be as You like, the flag of Islam, the flag of *Tauhid,*[260] the Unity of the Lord of Heavens, everywhere. *Amin! Fateha!*

---

[258] That is, without an Islamically-sanctioned reason.
[259] *"Send us a king, and we will fight in Your way."* (2:246)
[260] The Oneness of Allah.

29

WHO IS A HOLY ONE?

Ya Rabbi, ya Allah! Tauba, ya Rabbi! Tauba, ya Rabbi! Tauba, astaghfirullah. A'udhu bil-Lahi min ash Shaytani-r-rajim. Bismillahi-r-Rahmani-r-Rahim. La haula wa la quwwata illa bil-Lahi-l-'Aliyi-l-'Adhim.

As-salamu 'alaikum! I don't know whether I gave *salam* or not. Therefore, to be *mutma'inu-l-qalb*,[261] I am saying another *"As-salamu 'alaikum!"*

Now I know that I have given *salam*, we shall say, *"Alfu salat, alfu salam 'ala Rasul-Allah*.[262] *Ya Sayyidi, ya Rasul-Allah*, we are asking for your *shafa'at*, intercession." And we are saying, *"A'udhu bil-Lahi min ash Shaytani-r-rajim. Bismillahi-r-Rahmani-r-Rahim."*

We are running away from Shaytan. And where must we run? Allah *Subhanahu wa Ta'ala* is saying, *"Fa-firu ila Llah,*[263] run away from Shaytan. Run to Allah who created you and brought you into existence."

---

[261]To make the heart comfortable [that *salam* was given].

[262]A thousand prayers, a thousand *salams*, on the Messenger of Allah ﷺ. O our master, O Messenger of Allah!

[263]*"Then flee to Allah."* (51:50)

Who brought you into existence? You came by basket from Heavens to this world, like a parachute, everyone coming from above by parachute? Do you think so?

Edepsizler, alçak kâfirler![264] Not for you, this swearing—for those who are denying everything beyond their minds. Their level is under the level of donkeys and animals! Animals, they know who created them, but those creatures, dirty creatures, they do not know or they are too proud to say that the Lord of Heavens created us.

May Allah forgive us! Till they are coming humbly and saying, "O our Lord, we are Your creatures. You created us; we are Your servants. You may order and we are going to listen and obey," no way for their future, no way for their happiness, or no way, generally, for peace on earth.

Where are those proud people who think that they are something, *öğüniyor?*[265] Where are those people who claim that they are the chief of Christians, chief of Protestants, chief of Orthodox, chief of Catholics, chief of the Anglican Church, chief of Jerusalem? Haham Başı and the chief of Muslims—where are they that they are so proud? Where are you with your so-ornamented clothes, to be different, a little bit different, from other people? You are such a person, so proud!

[Parodies religious leaders:] "O people, come to peace! Don't quarrel! Be quiet! Don't run in the streets!" They are not saying this, also, but they are such proud ones, with their clothes that make people think they are something, another kind, not from common people. "We are up, up, up!" Whoever makes himself, by himself, up, high, high, higher, will come down, down, down.

---

[264] Ill-mannered, base unbelievers!
[265] *Övüniyior*, boast, brag.

_____, you also have such people [in Spain]? Big monasteries, big holy ones! No holy ones, never!

Holy one; who is a holy one? Holy one, that is the one who knows who created him and what He is asking from him or from them. Those are holy ones, not those who are making a show with their clothes and making people think about them that they are holy ones.

Our Christian brothers, they are blaming Muslims concerning Muhammad ﷺ. Say, "He is the boss of creation, the most honoured one, the most glorified one." And Muhammad, peace be upon him, is also the prophet of Allah to all nations.

We are not making a distinction, we are not saying that only Sayyidina Muhammad, peace be upon him, is our prophet, that prophethood is only for him. We are saying that we believe in all the prophets, beginning from Adam, Noah, Abraham, Moses, Jesus Christ and 124,000 prophets. We are saying "Yes!" and we are not fighting against prophets. Fighters against their prophets, they should be in Hells! [

Now they are blaming Muslims and all creation's prophet, Sayyidina Muhammad, that he used a sword to make Islam to reach East and West. What about you, O Christians? Jesus Christ, did he at any time use even a knife? Who is inventing so many dangerous nuclear weapons. Is Jesus Christ signaling to them, "O Christians, you are on the right way because you are making nuclear weapons"? Is Jesus Christ signaling, "You are okay"?

I must ask the Pope, I must ask the Patriarch, I must ask all Christian bishops: Is Jesus Christ signaling that you are on right path? Why are you blaming Sayyidina Muhammad, peace be upon him, that he used a sword? Sayyidina Muhammad, he wasn't a lamb, as you are making Jesus Christ to be. Sayyidina Muhammad, peace be upon him, he wasn't a lamb to sit down and to give his neck, "Cut my neck!"

Be truthful or you should lose! Understand? Wrong, anything wrong? Yes; Allah is the Witness, Allah is looking! I don't think that anyone throughout East and West can speak on this point except a very, very weak person. I am someone who is on the lowest level. I am the lowest level person and I am saying this. They are claiming they are at the highest level; they can say anything. Even though I am an old person, a weak person, below every level, if they are saying, "You are wrong," a lesson should reach them that it may be they won't reach till tomorrow. Allah may take them away.

This world is not empty. The One who is turning this world just prepared everything in its most perfect position. They are saying, "This—who is this shaykh?" He is the lowest person, but he may hold a secret power from Heavens. That secret power may destroy everything that they have invented and brought to take away peace from the earth. That one about whom you are saying, "This one is nothing," Allah may keep that power though that person. *Allah Allah Allah!*

O people, we are only saying something that no one may be able to object to. It is so clear, so clear! May Allah forgive me and forgive you, also.

O people, who is a believer? The one who believes in truth. Who is a Muslim? A defender of truth. Try to be defenders of truth, O people! Then Allah Almighty will help you and protect you and shelter you. If not . . . !

May Allah forgive us! My anger is only against my ego. You, you are free to be angry with your ego or not; you are free. But I am fighting with my ego and angry with my ego. May Allah help me! *Fateha!*

30

THE CONSEQUENCES OF DISOBEYING ALLAH'S ORDER

Meded, ya Rijal-Allah! O holy ones, we are asking your support! You are supporting Heavens. Without your support, Heavens will fall on people.

A'udhu bil-Lahi min ash-Shaytani-r-rajim. Our Lord, we are running to You from Shaytan and Shaytan's tricks and traps, not to fall into any trap because he is putting his traps everywhere.

Bismillahi-r-Rahmani-r-Rahim. When you say *"Bismillahi-r-Rahmani-r-Rahim,"* you are dressed in big honor, endless honor. Kings' and emperors' clothes, they are going to be like the clothes of a worker in sewers.

You have just been dressed in the dress of being His servant. When you say *"Bismillahi-r-Rahmani-r-Rahim,"* you are signaling that I am a servant of Heavens. Whoever does not say *"Bismillahi-r-Rahmani-r-Rahim,"* he is signaling about himself that I belong to sewers. I do not belong to Heavens, I belong to sewers that rats run in."

People they never see lights in those dirt channels; they never smell good things, only dirty things. Therefore, those people are going to be taken away. They can't enter the holy level of Heavens, just kicked down. Therefore, O people, say *"Bismillahi-r-Rahmani-r-Rahim."* That is the sign of being Muslim, the sign that you belong to heavenly service on earth.

May Allah forgive us! *La haula wa la quwwata illa bil-Lahi-l-'Aliyi-l-'Adhim!* O our Lord, keep our feet on Your right way! The right way leads towards Heavens, the wrong way towards Hells; right steps lead to Heavens and heavenly lighted areas, wrong steps take you to shaytanic channels. That sewage, there is every kind of dirt in it.

O people, come and listen! Come and surrender! Some people are coming and saying, "O Shaykh, we are asking to go to Heavens, but we would like to be Naqshibandi or to be on the steps of Heavens without becoming Muslim."

Who is teaching you that foolishness? Those dirty words, who is teaching you? Without Islam, how are you asking to reach Heavens? Which prophet was saying that he is not *muslim*?[266] Did any prophet say, "I am not *muslim*"? Without saying "I am *muslim*," how were they prophets, how could they be messengers of Heavens? How can they be enlightened people without being *muslims*?

What is *muslim*? They never ask what it means; they are only allergic to it. That word, "Muslim," is making an allergy for them.

Accepting Islam is the way to Heavens, or how will you be able to enter Paradise?" If you are Christian, Jesus Christ was Muslim! The Pope, is he Muslim? If not, how will he reach Jesus Christ! Haham Başı, the Chief Rabbi, if he is not Muslim, Paradise is not open! You must be Muslim! "Stop! Checkpoint!" asking for identity card. "Muslim? Pass, go!"

---

[266]Islam stresses that the one true faith since the beginning of man's life on earth has been Islam, revealed by a succession of prophets who all brought the same divinely-revealed message of Allah's existence and Lordship and man's accountability to Him, "Here, *"muslim"* with a small *"m"* is used to denote the true prophets and believers before the advent of the Prophet 鏡.

"Not Muslim? Go back!"

They never ask, "What does it mean, 'Muslim'? 'Muslim' means someone who surrenders to Heavens. *"Aslamtu,* I am just giving my own will to heavenly peoples' orders. No will for me without Their wills. I am trying to be like Them." If you are trying to be like Them, you must give up your will. You must leave your will, and you should be like them and you may pass. If not, no.

From where did democracy come to your country? You are Pakistani? Did Allah send democracy or did Allah send the Holy Qur'an, Holy *Shari'at?* Where are your *'ulema,* learned people? What is this foolishness?

Turks, as well. They are saying: "Democracy, democracy! Like cream on milk, so beautiful!" People put it on bread, spreading it, first putting butter on it, then putting honey. Now, for people, democracy is like that. Therefore, they are eating themselves.

Allah is saying, "O My beloved one! If they go against My holy orders from Heavens, I will make them be enemies to each other,[267] and they should harm each other, and even kill one another. No peace for them and no *aman.*"[268] That means it is forbidden for them to live peacefully; no peace for them. Always they may harm each other. They should say, "This is the best way!"

Congratulations, Pakistani people! Democracy for you! And Turks, congratulations! Americans, congratulations! Iraqis, congrat-

---

[267]Viewed from a global perspective, democracy is against Islam because Islam stipulates a single, central authority that governs in accordance with the rules of Allah *(Shari'ah)* rather than the rule of the majority and manipulation of power through political parties and special interest groups.

[268]Safety, security, peace, shelter, protection.

ulations! Iranis, who are claiming that they are Muslims and making democracy, congratulations that you are on the wrong way!

A group of people, they are selling democracy to nations but they are not democratic themselves. There is one nation that never says, "We are democratic," but they are saying to people, "Come and take this poisoned food. Eat! You should find so much happiness and pleasure in yourself," as Shaytan was advising Sayyidina Adam and Eve, saying, "Eat from this tree! You should be so happy! Without eating this, you can't reach the peak of your pleasure. It can't be complete, your pleasure, if you do not eat from this! Eat and it is going to be complete, your pleasure in Paradise!"

And they ate, and quickly Archangel Jibril took the crown from the head of Sayyidina Adam, and Archangel Mikail came and took this holy robe, the glorious robe—taking them, and Adam was like new-fashioned people who are trying to be naked.[269] And so the dress of honor in which Allah had dressed Adam ﷺ and his wife, it was taken away, and they were looking, looking at themselves, so ugly.

Clothes give people identity. Without clothes, how would those people be? So dirty, so ugly! What are we saying? A heavenly dress is covering you, covering your shame, but people are running after democracy, saying, "Democracy is giving us full freedom to do as we please. Therefore, we are trying to be like animals, to do everything, and we are not ashamed. We are saying that we just reached the top of civilization."

---

[269]Here the Shaykh adds parenthetically: "They so regret that they are not like animals. "For what do we dress? We must try to be like the zoo's inhabitants, who are our ancestors," a gorilla or chimpanzee or orangutan. "Why are we not like animals, naked?" They are trying to be like animals; they never like to put on any clothes."

O people, surrender to the holy commands of Allah Almighty that He granted to you, dressing you in a dress of honour and crowning you, also, with the crown of being like kings in the entire world among other creatures. But Shaytan is making people not to be ashamed and not to think and not to accept any good thing that comes from Heavens.

Everything that comes from Heavens, that is most perfect. Everything now by which people are not accepting heavenly commands, they are dressed in a dress of ugliness, a dress of shaytans. Now, therefore, I am saying that Pakistan, Turkestan, Ajemistan, Afghanistan, Hindistan, Arabistan's people, they are eating themselves. That is their civilization. Allah Almighty is giving them honour and sending them heavenly orders to continue their honour. When they leave that, they are going to be the worst creatures on earth.

May Allah forgive us! O people, come and accept Islam. That means to surrender to your Lord, Allah Almighty. "O My beloved one, most beloved one, O My most glorified, glorious servant! If they do not listen to My heavenly orders and run after their most dangerous enemy, Shaytan, Sadanas, I will make them be enemies to each other and kill each other, and no safety for their lives, no pleasure for their lives, and no peace for their lives!"

And now we are in it. We are saying, "Democracy is best," and leaving the holy *Shari'at-Ullah*, the holy commands of Heavens, and people now are killing themselves and doing every dirty thing and becoming more ugly, more dangerous ones. Who is ordering a person to put a bomb on his stomach and make it explode? Who is saying this? Which prophet said this to them? Jesus Christ said it? Sayyidina Musa, Moses, said it? Rasul-Allah ﷺ said it? Abraham said it? Noah said, "Kill yourself! Put on something, and kill yourself and others"? This is from heavenly teachings or from shaytanic teachings? Sadness and sorrow for mankind that they are on the wrong way!

Therefore, out of five people, one is going to live, four are going to die! It should be the last and most terrible war, Malhamatu-l-Kubra, which is mentioned in Islamic books, as well being mentioned in other holy books before Islam. Armageddon— Armageddon is coming and it will kill four out of every five people, one remaining.

Therefore, O people, come to Allah! Run to His prophets to take you to Allah, to your Creator! Give your Creator most high respect! As much as you can, do it! You should be in safety and under the divine shelter. If not, you know; you know what to expect.

May Allah forgive us and send us quickly a person with heavenly identity to take away people from falling into the worst position here and Hereafter. *Amin! Wa salamun 'ala-l-mursalin, khususan 'ala-s-Sayyidi-l-Mursalin, wa-l-hamdulillahi Rabbi-l-'alamin, wa-salamun 'alaikum!*[270] *Fateha!*

---

[270]Amen! And peace be upon the messengers, especially upon the Chief of the Messengers [Prophet Muhammad], and all praise is for Allah, Lord of the worlds, and peace be upon you all.

31

SOMETHING THAT RUNS FROM HEART TO HEART

Destur, ya Sayyidi, ya Sultanu-l-Awliya! Meded, ya Rijal-Allah! As-salamu 'alaikum!

Are you hungry? Fasting? *Mash'allah, mash'allah!* Eh, *Allah kabul eylesin!*[271] May Allah *Subhanahu wa Ta'ala* accept our humble servanthood. *As-salamu 'alaikum! A'udhu bil-Lahi min ash-Shaytani-r-rajim. Bismillahi-r-Rahmani-r-Rahim. La haula wa la quwwata illa bil-Lahi-l-'Aliyi-l-'Adhim.*

O people, *"Ad-dinu nasihah."* For our religion or all religions, the meaning is to give advice.

What is advice? To call people to goodness, to call people to the best life here and a blest life in Paradise, eternally. Therefore, all prophets came and advised people, calling, "O people, come! Come to me and listen to me!"

And they were special people or people not on our level. Some people belong to Heavens; their interest is in Heavens. Some others,

---

[271]After completing the prescribed Ramadan fast, it is *sunnah* to fast six additional days during the month of Shawwal. *"Allah kabul eylesin"* (Tr.) means "May Allah accept it."

their interest is in this world, in *dunya*. And Allah Almighty took an oath from all mankind. Before their creation, before they came to this life, Allah Almighty took an oath from their souls, and He said to them, "O My servants! I created you and I am your Lord. Do you accept Me who created you as your Lord?"

All of them said, "Yes, O our Lord! We accept You as our Creator and we are Your servants. Only You are Lord and we are servants to You."

"All of you are witnessing, each of you for the other? In front of My Divine Presence, all of you are going to be witnesses for each other?"

They were saying, "Yes, our Lord. You are our Creator. You are our Lord and we are Your servants."[272]

Eh! Then what happened? Then we came here. We came through the wombs of our mothers and grew up, and when we reached maturity, our egos awakened, getting up and saying, "I do not accept anything! I accept only that I am here and that my parents brought me into this life, and beyond that I do not accept anything. I do not accept unseen worlds or an unseen *varlık*, existence. I accept only what I see."

That is the beginning of being a follower of Shaytan. That is Shaytan's teaching to them: "Don't accept anything. Accept only yourself! You must live as you like, you must be free! You must not be like a servant, no. Each of you, you must be your own Lord! Your ego must be accepted, and you must accept that your Lord is your ego. Beyond that, don't accept! Unseen things, don't accept!"

---

[272]Referring to the Day of Promises, mentioned in 7:172.

Therefore, Allah Almighty, from the time of Adam, peace be upon him, began to send some special people, sending from His side messengers, messengers to make people wake up. "O people, wake up! Don't deny unseen worlds, and don't deny the Last Day and Day of Judgment, when you will be held responsible for everything you did here during this life."

But they are saying, "No! We do not understand the Last Day or Judgment Day or the Day of Resurrection. We do not accept such things. That is *asatir*,[273] fairy tales!"

Then the Seal of the Prophets came, and he said whatever is necessary for mankind because his nation, *ummah*, is the last nation, and his nation is going to reach up to the Last Day, Yaumu-l-Qiyamah. During his period it is going to happen,[274] and the whole world will reach its last day. Therefore, religion means calling people and making them remember, or at least to say, "I do not remember but I accept my commitment to Allah."

Here, there is a handful of people. You are coming from East, from West, from North, from South, for the *munasabat*, occasion, of 'Eid al–Fitr.[275] For the holy month of Ramadan you have come here, and today is the second day of 'Eid. And we are also trying to remind you, and myself also with you, that servanthood is not only for Ramadan. From the beginning up to the end of our lives, we have been offered to be servants, obedient servants, to our Creator, to our Lord, Almighty Allah.

---

[273]Legend, fable, myth, tale, fairy tale.

[274]"His period" means from the time of his proclamation of his prophethood up to the end of this world.

[275]The Festival of Fast-Breaking at the end of Ramadan, one of Islam's two major festivals.

You are coming here, and it is a good *ithbat*,[276] proof, for every-one that there is something reaching from man to man. That is a spiritual reaching, a spiritual relationship. You do not see wires reaching to your hearts, no, but something is running from heart to heart, and you are coming here for that reason. And the twenty-first century's foolish philosophers and materialists and atheist professors and scientist doctors, they are trying to deny it, but there is no proof for them. This is a clear proof that there is a connection from one person to another.

By what way? I am not calling you, "Come here, Dr. ____, Dr. ____," no, but sometimes it is like lightning. Therefore, their deny-ing is foolishness and ignorance for them. That is clear. Do you think that I sent to you an e-mail or z-mail or k-mail or v-mail or a-mail or g-mail or x-mail or y-mail, a twenty-eight, twenty-nine letter mail I sent to you? Still, you have come. This is such a clear proof, but those people, they are like Shaytan. Shaytan was looking and seeing and denying, and becoming a cursed one.

Therefore, now, all scientists and learned people who do not accept what we are saying, they are going to be blamed and and di-vine anger may fall on them. Allah Almighty saying: *"Kullu shayin 'in-dahu bi-miqdar, kullu shayin 'indahu bi-miqdar.'*[277] For everything there is a scale or measure, there is a limit. When reaching that limit, you can't go any further. It is the last, final limit for you.

Their last limit was that they were trying to do something against the order of the Creator, the Lord of Heavens. They tried; I heard recently. I have not heard before of such foolishness as those foolish scientists and doctors and learned people were trying to do,

---

[276]Proof, confirmation, evidence.

[277] *"All things with Him are according to a due measure."* (13:8)

something that is against the Lord's Will. Just one month ago I heard what they did.

For so many years they have been digging under the Alp Mountains, to do something there because they have a foolish idea or foolish theory. They are saying, "The beginning of this universe was from one atom, and that exploded and then there happened whatever happened." Yes, the Big Bang theory! You never heard about it?

That theory is *zaten*, in any case, foolishness, and then, to try something, as they are imagining, asking to do something to see what is happening. And that is *tajawuz, tajawuz al-hadd*[278]—that is, attempting to reach from servanthood to the authority of Lordship.

That is something that even Firaun, Pharaoh, was not thinking about doing. They are, each one, equal to seventy Pharaohs! Pharaoh never thought that he can do such a thing, Pharaoh never said that this world came from a Big Bang. Even Nimrod did not say, Nero did not say this! Who is saying this? Only Shaytan is saying it! And our professors now, our scientists, are saying, "Ooh-h! This imagining is very suitable. This we must say to people!"

What are they trying to do? They are trying not to say to people, "There is God," they are trying to make people say, "No God." That is their final aim, not anything else.

And now for how many years have they been digging under Switzerland a huge tunnel?[279] You never heard about it? And this

---

[278]To exceed; *tajawuza-l-hadd:* to exceed the limit.

[279]Referring to the failure of the super collider, reported in an article by United Press International on September 19, 2008. The article states, "A power failure shut down the powerful Large Hadron Collider particle accelerator earlier this week," in an "experiment that seeks to recreate conditions one-trillionth of a second after the Big Bang to help scientists understand how the universe formed. The underground machine spans the Swiss-French border." The problem occurred when a "power

Footnote continued…

was the last chance that they were given because they had reached the final point of their authority that, after this limit, belongs to the Lord of creation, the Creator. And they tried to do something as a proof, so that everyone might see or might hear, to make people say, "No God!"

Perhaps one month ago I heard that they did this. And there came to me an order to send one unseen servant. They were trying to make it on Sunday. That night there came to me an order, "Send on them a jinn to do this."

I was very angry. And they were saying, "Tomorrow we will do this, we will do that, we will do this."

Before the sun rose, that jinn reached and made a sign, like this. And when they came to do the experiment, they couldn't switch on the electricity. "What happened?" Calling each other: "Hello! See what happened! Open the power station!"

"Yes, sir, we are ready. We opened the power station, also, but no response."

"What shall we say to people after we did such big advertising for it: 'Today we are testing our Big Bang's foolish theory.' What shall we say to people?"

"I don't know."

"We are 365 people. Each day, one of us was responsible. And we must connect them."

---

interruption in the transformer affected the European Center for Particle Physics' refrigeration plant, meaning protons couldn't be beamed around the facility, Swissinfo.com reported Friday. . . .Officials at the facility said the problem has been corrected and the refrigeration chamber was being cooled. They couldn't say when the beaming would resume."

"Yes, I just reached everyone. And they are astonished, saying, 'Can't be! What is there?'"

And the last one there, he was saying, "O our brothers! I saw, when I was pressing that button, a very strange and huge creature. No one can imagine its design. And my hands began to shake like a ship on an ocean; unable to stop. And it did not happen!"

And they were saying, "What shall we say to people?"

"We can say that there was only one button. We lost it and we were looking where it fell down in that huge tunnel. When we find it . . . blah-blah-blah." [Laughter.]

That is the final point at which now there is going to be taken from them every power, every power, and soon there will come another order, that Sahibu-z-Zaman Mehdi 🕮 will call, "*Allahu akbar! Allahu akbar! Allahu akbar!*" taking away that authority. No more electricity and its power, the authority to use it taken up from people, finishing.

Now they should see, they should see! They have reached the final point. And therefore, the Lord of Heavens sent one command to that saint that the whole world is under his authority, saying, "Keep them away! Keep them away! And what We granted to them of electrical power, just take it back, and this *şalter*, switch, put it down—finished!" After a while, when Mahdi 🕮 says, "*Allahu ab-kar!*" that is going to finish.

O people, we are not created for nothing, and we are not created from nothing. The Lord of Heavens created us, and He is asking us to understand and to give our most high respect for His servanthood—to be His servants, to keep His rules as a humble servant. Yes!

And finally, we are doing *something*. And our Muslims, also, now, they are very ignorant ones. They think that when they pray twenty *raka'ats* each night and fast half-a-day or less for a month in holy Ramadan, they did something.

It is just coming to me to remind myself and you, also, that when Allah Almighty created Archangel Gabriel ﷺ, He put in front of him the mirror of divine power—a mirror; he could look in it and see himself. That mirror was not like our mirrors, no. When he looked and saw the beauty that had been granted to him by Allah Almighty (no other angel like Archangel Jibril, so beautiful), he stood up and prayed two *rak'ats*. In each *rak'at* he stood for 20,000 years. And when he gave *salam*, he was so happy that he had done something for his Lord as a thankful servant.

And there came, "O My Archangel Jibril! Not 20,000 years, but if you could do each *rak'at* for 20,000 billion years, it would be, in front of My Greatness, nothing!" And Archangel Jibril fell into *sajdah*.

And then Allah Almighty gave the good tidings of His most beloved, most honoured prophet, Sayyidina Muhammad ﷺ, saying, "O Archangel Gabriel, you did those two *rak'ats* for 40,000 years. When the Last Days approach, the last period of life on earth, I am going to send My most beloved servant's nation. They will pray two *rak'ats* so quickly, so quickly, and they will not collect their hearts to think that they are in front of their Lord, always thinking about *dunya*, also. But their two *rak'ats* are going to be more precious in My Divine Presence."

Why? What is the reason? Without Archangel Gabriel's asking, Allah Almighty said, "Because, O My servant Archangel Gabriel, you prayed of your own accord. But they will pray on account of My orders, to keep My orders." So important!

You must know, O mankind, who is ordering to you to make *sajdah* and to pray. Who is ordering you? You must know that. Allah Almighty was saying to Archangel Gabriel, "You did it on behalf of yourself because you were so happy to see your beauty and *nur,* but those people, my most beloved one's *ummah,* they will pray because I ordered them, 'Pray!'"

O people! Leave ignorance and accept Reality if you would like to be happy here and Hereafter! To reach eternity and eternal life, keep to your Lord's order. Don't say, "I am not free for praying now"—no! Leave it and pray!

"Ya ayyuha-l-ladhina amanu, idha nudiya li-s-salati min yaumi-l-Jumuati, fas'au ila dhikri-Lah.'[280] O people, when you hear that call to you to pray, *fil-hal,* immediately, leave your work and run to His service, to His servanthood. O people, if you would like to live happily here and with honour, and to be in Paradise forever in the eternal life, eternity, keep His orders. If not, you are never going to have any value. Animals' dirt has no price. Those people are going to have less value than the dirt of animals!

May Allah forgive us! *As-salamu 'alaikum! Fateha!*

'Eid mubarak![281] O our Lord, keep our feet on *Haqq.* Fix them not to fall. First, Allah Almighty's servanthood! He did not create

---

[280] *"O you who believe, when it [the adhan] is called for the [weekly congregational] prayer on Friday, then proceed to the remembrance of Allah . . . ."* (62:9)

[281] A blessed 'Eid!

you to be servants of *dunya*, He created you to be His servants. That is all.

No pope can make an objection to it, no rabbi can make any objection on that point, no head of religions can make an obection on that point. They must put their heads down. I am putting mine. Pray for me that I can do my *sajdah*, that He takes the problem from my knees, because I am not happy to sit on a chair and to pray with my head. I like to put my forehead on earth for my Lord. You ask that He takes this away. *Fateha!*

32

THE NECESSITY OF HAVING A TRAINER IN HOLINESS

As-salamu 'alaikum! As-salam qabla-l-kalam.[282] You must say, you must give *salam*. Then you may speak. Without saying *salam*, don't speak! And *salam* is the sign of Muslims. No other word can be put in its place, no.

Salam, it is a living word that came from Heavens.[283] Other greetings that people are saying, they are only like imitated words, no power in them. *Salam* is from Heavens. When you give *salam*, there comes to you power from Heavens and you feel a good feeling. When it rains on a tree, it opens. Like that, *salam* gives *mu'mins* new life. *As-salamu 'alaikum!*

A'udhu bil-Lahi min ash-Shaytani-r-rajim. Bismillahi-r-Rahmani-r-Rahim. Without a base, what you are building will fall down. The base of everything that you want to do is that you must say, *"A'udhu bil-Lahi min ash-Shaytani-r-rajim. Bismillahi-r-Rahmani-r-Rahim."*

---

[282]*Salam* before speaking.

[283]The Prophet 🕌 said that when Allah Most High had created Adam, He said to him, "'Go and greet that group of angels; then listen to that with which they will greet you, your greeting and the greeting of your descendants.' Then he [Adam] said, '*As-salamu 'alaikum*—peace be upon you all,' and they replied, '*As-salamu 'alaika* [the singular form] *wa rahmat-Allah*—peace be upon you, and God's mercy,' adding [to Adam's greeting], '*Wa rahmat-Allah.*'" (Bukhari, 4:543, 8:246)

We are living for Allah and we must do everything for Allah. The big mistake, biggest mistake, of mankind is that they are forgetting their Lord and they are trying to do something for their egos. And we are asking for holy support from Heavens, and you can't find holy support except from those people who are on the way of the Seal of Prophets, Sayyidina Muhammad ﷺ. That means you can find support from holy people. And holy people, who are they? Those who are following the holy ways of that most holy one's *Shar'iat,* heavenly rules.

To be a holy one, it is not a thing that is granted to people by people. Holiness comes from Heavens; if it comes from Heavens, you are a holy one. Don't think that if millions or billions of people say to you, "This is a holy one," you are going to be a holy one. No!

A man, a servant, must try to learn *how he can be a servant.* Yes; everyone must learn how he can be a servant. By yourself, you can't be a servant. Don't think that by reading religious books you will learn servanthood, no. Servanthood can be learned through a holy one. You must follow a holy one so that then you are going to be a holy one. Don't think that when you read the books of holy ones you are going to be a holy one, no.

You must try to learn servanthood first from the lowest level of people. What is that lowest level of people? Who are they?

Lowest level people, they are of two kinds. One of them is at the last level; that means he has put his ego under his feet. That is one kind, and the second meaning of holy ones is those who are taking holy breaths from heavenly people. You must find a person who is at the lowest level, the lowest level. You must come to him because he has put his ego under his feet, the lowest level, and become a holy one.

In other words, a holy one is someone who has put his ego under his feet and is following heavenly masters. You can learn from him how you can be a servant. Therefore, we are saying, "You may read one thousand books, but to read one thousand books does not mean that you are putting your ego under your feet—no." A student can't be a doctor by himself, by looking at books and keeping in his mind so many things. He must be under a doctor, so that that doctor can teach him. *Then* he is going to be a doctor; otherwise, no one is going to be a doctor by graduating from universities or other higher schools. No, no! And we must try to keep holy ways, to be a holy one.

We have been invited to be holy ones because Heavens never accept unholy ones, accepting only true holy ones. Therefore, every person who reaches the age of majority must try to learn how he can be a holy one. Holy ones, they are welcome in the Divine Presence. Unholy ones are never welcome in the Divine Presence, no.

This is a summary of all books that are asking people to come and surrender. If you do not surrender, you can't be a holy one. First, you must surrender your ego to a holy one's training.

[Parodies:] "Eh! We are the Liverpool *futbol* team!"[284]

I am asking, "How will you be first?"

"Because we have an *entreneur*—yes, a trainer. A trainer, first class! We learnt from him! Otherwise, we would be like people coming from the jungle—like this, like that, not knowing their right or left side."

---

[284]Tr., soccer.

If for *futbol*, about which all nations have lost their minds, you need a trainer, what about training for holiness? They never think about anything except being sportsmen; sportsmen, those people. Yes, and half the world is going to be inhabited by some *futbol* club, some others saying, "Yah, we must be here!"

That is people's whole effort now. They like to play. Those people will never reach any heavenly station—never! There should be a jungle for them, those people who have no other *hem*, no interest, concern, except *futbol*, changing them to be like people living in a jungle and leaving them there. Run and hunt each other, eat and run! That is your level because you have rejected the real level of humanity.

Humanity! You may be from mankind, but not everyone's level is the level of humanity. When you are going to be changed from the level of mankind by training under a trainer's commands, then you may reach the level of humanity. If not, your level is always going to be the level of jungle people, and they should be there, eating each other and dirtying each other, running after each other. That should be for them!

O people, O people! First you must teach your children on such a base that it is impossible for them to be moved from their true positions. That base is just put from Heavens. If you do not keep that, your life is going to be wasted, no meaning, because, if you do not keep that heavenly base, you are never going to change from the level of mankind to be on the level of humanity.

Everyone belongs to the big family of mankind, but very few people reach the level of humanity. Humanity gives honour to you, and you need a trainer to teach you. People have lost it. And now there are perhaps six or seven billion people living on earth, and all of them are just under the heading of "mankind". But there is another column where it is written, "This is for humanity."

Humanity gives honour. To be from mankind is no honour for them. Therefore, you must leave off being an ordinary one from mankind. You must train your ego under a trainer to complete it, and then you can become a member of humanity. Humanity—honour is for *humanity*, not for being from mankind.

Now mankind are doing some wild things that even the most terrible beasts do not do. How are you saying that that is an honour for them? No honour! Therefore, you must try to be a holy one. If you do not belong under the title of "holy one," you can't come under the title of "humanity". Yes!

I was passing through Switzerland, and there is Saint Nikolaus. He belonged to holy ones, but no one understands who he is or who he was, and during his entire life, no one or very few ones understood about that Saint Nikolaus. And sainthood means to be a holy one.

Not everyone is going to be a saint by a pope's signature, no. Those, all of them, are imitation saints. It is not acceptable to have your name written as a saint because the Pope or cardinals or patriarchs or bishops signed that he was a saint, no.

There is a saint here in the Turkish side of Cyprus, in Famagusta. He was among the disciples, Saint Barnabas. Saint Barnabas, God bless him, he was a disciple of Jesus Christ, peace be upon him, and now he is lying underground.

You must go down perhaps seven steps to look, and it is so humble, humble a grave. I was going, when my way was passing by there, and when I was saying, *"Fa'lam annahu la ilaha illa-Lah,"*[285] his tomb was shaking and his spirit was coming to say with us, *"La ilaha illa-Lah."*

Their sainthood is just signed and *musaddaq,* approved, by Heavens—real ones, that Saint Nikolaus, also. They think that he was as they are imagining. No! Therefore, when I was passing by, he was always calling me, "O Shaykh, come! Please visit me!" I went there and visited. He was very happy.

You were with me sometimes when I was coming from Switzerland to the Black Forest? I was once passing through and going out. After visiting him, he was so happy.

Then I saw a person coming on the stairs. I saw that his dress was not an ordinary dress, and I understood that he was a religious person of that monastery. He greeted me and I greeted him. And I asked, "Your Holiness is here doing your worshipping and looking after that Saint Nikolaus?"

He said, "I am sorry, I am not a holy one." He was such a humble person, saying, "I am not a holy one, O Shaykh."

And immediately it came to me to ask, "Even the Pope?"

He said, "Even the Pope, he is not a holy one," because everyone who is appointed on earth, holiness is something that no emperors or governors or bishops or cardinals can give. "O Shaykh, it is not something that, if cardinals are signing, a person is going to be a holy one. Even the Pope, he is not a holy one."

---

[285] *"Know that indeed there is no deity except Allah."* (47:19)

He was just speaking the truth. Holiness and being a holy one, that is from Heavens, not from people. If all people say, "This is a holy one," no value. If I say, "Dr. ____ is the Chancellor of Germany," would you accept it? No. They may say, perhaps, "He is a holy one in a mental house."

Yes. Therefore, that is our way. We must try to be holy ones for the holy presence of the Seal of Prophets, and he may take you to the Lord's Divine Presence, no one except him. Therefore, we must ask for real holy ones, to take from them the secret power of being holy ones. Otherwise, we are going to carry so many things, here and Hereafter.

O people, don't work for *dunya* but work to be a holy one. You may be a gardener and you may be a holy one; you may be a shepherd and you may be a holy one; you may be a carpenter and you may be a holy one. Doesn't matter, but you must put your ego under the feet of a holy one to kill it. Then you should reach real life here and Hereafter.

May Allah forgive us during these holy days. May Allah Almighty send us a holy *sultan* to take us and to train all nations, all mankind, to make them clean for the Day of Resurrection. For the honour of the most honoured one in the Divine Presence, Sayyidina Muhammad ﷺ—*Fateha!*

33

NOT TRUSTING IN YOUR EGO

As-salamu 'alaikum! Salam is from Heavens. Therefore, say it! As much you can say it, blessings are coming—don't worry!

May Allah forgive us! *A'udhu bil-Lahi min ash-Shaytani-r-rajim. Bismillahi-r-Rahmani-r-Rahim. Meded, ya Sultanu-l-Awliya! Meded, ya Rijal-Allah!*

There are now new machines. Whichever person you want to speak to, you press that button, quickly reaching. Yes? Understand or not? Therefore, we, also, we can say, "Oh, *destur, ya Sayyidi!*" so that I am reaching the heart of our Grandshaykh and I am saying, "O our master, we are waiting for something from the blessings of Allah, to make us closer to the Divine Presence. Help us!"

Whoever forgets, he is also forgotten. Therefore, the Prophet was saying, peace be upon him, *"Allahumma, la takilni ila nafsi tarfat 'ain.'"*[286] This is one meaning of this *hadith*.

Hadith Nabawi Sharif, the Prophet's holy words, came from Heavens, and every word, every speech of the Prophet's, peace be upon him, is like an ocean. This means that one of the meanings of *"Allahumma, la takilni ila nafsi"* is that if a person *yaktafi,* is sufficient

---

[286]"O our Lord, don't leave me with my ego for the blink of an eye. *(Hadith)*

for himself—that means without thinking, without asking for a connection with heavenly people—he is going to be left with his weakness and helplessness. Whoever says, "I know, I can speak, I can do," that person is left to himself. And we are such weak people. What can we do? If there is no heavenly support, we are so weak!

And this has a good meaning, that you must not trust in your ego, because ego says, "I am here! I don't like anyone with me! All power is in my hands!" It is the biggest liar! Out of pride, our ego never likes to say, "Help me! Help me, O heavenly beings!" not saying this, and that person is going to be *mahrum*, deprived, never reaching anything.

Therefore, we are saying, "O our master, please help us! We are running to you! You send us what we are going to say. *Destur!*"

"Destur" means, "I am asking humbly, O our *sultan*—help us, support us!" If not thinking about it and saying, "I know, I can do," you are going to be left only with your capacity or ability, and it is so small. Therefore, *"Himmatu rijal taqta'u-l-jibal"*[287]—the power of heavenly, holy ones may take even the Himalayan Mountains up, keeping them like this. And if he, the holy one, crushes it, he may make it sand.

Therefore, O people, don't trust in your capability, ability, capacity, your power. You are *nothing*! Say, "O my Lord, I am *nothing*! I am *nothing*. Help me!"

Therefore, Allah Almighty is sending chosen servants, who are holy ones that are followers of the steps of heavenly ones. If not, they are at zero point; they can't do anything. An ant can do *something*. That person can't do *anything*!

---

[287] The fervour of [holy] men will cut down mountains.

This is an important point that They are reminding us of: don't trust in your power! Today you may be at the point of power, tomorrow you may be under the feet of people. But now people, they are showing themselves and coming and saying, "I am this one! Like Dr. ____, I am this one! I am going to do this, I am going to make this, I am going to change this, I am going to bring this!"

How can you say this? You are only one person, even if people say, "You are the President" or "You are the Chancellor."

The Chancellor of Germany, that big-bodied person, Helmut Kohl—a good one, good one, but he fell. He was a good person; I was praising him. A good person, but he trusted in himself and fell down. There was not any heavenly connection to support him, finished.

And people now are mostly ignorant ones. They think that if they give a good speech to people, those people will look at them, at what they are saying. But people, they are in the worst position. *Dunya, dunya,* our world that we are living in, it is like a very old house. From every side, it is beginning to fall down. How can you bring such a power or *tadbir,* arrangement, to restore this house?

Those people who left and went out, they were also not able to do anything for it—so old, and it looks like, if you touch it, kicking it, oh-h, coming down. And you are saying, in the face of that, "I am that one who is coming to renew, restore, this building." It may fall on your head!

People are ignorant ones. Those who do not believe in God, they are such ignorant ones, understanding nothing, having learned nothing. And that is the situation on earth now. One side of that building, if coming down—*sher-r-r!*

People are astonished. Ten days ago, they said, "The U.S. is coming down." What happened? Because one side was suddenly— *hur-r-r!*—just falling down.

What is that? There was a bank that lost 700 billion. They were looking—ooh! They were running to East and West: "How can we stop this? If we can't stop it, the whole building will come down on us!"

That is what we are saying: if touching one point, the entire structure will come down. Where is your mind? Where is your knowledge? Where is your power to stop it?

Germans, they are more clever. The capital bank that the German economy is based on was also beginning to shake when seeing that shaking, and it was saying, "We are also shaking now! We are afraid of falling down! Oh-h-h! What am I doing? I was thinking that I was powerfulwith billions of euros but now I see that we are nothing! Billions of euros can't support us!" Yes.

Men are ignorant ones now, and this is the second Period of Ignorance.[288] At the time of the Seal of Prophets, there was Ignorance, but, as the Holy Qur'an is saying or indicating, there should be another period of Ignorance.

Now we are in it because people have forgotten their Lord. All of them, they are trusting in their power, in their minds, in their knowledge, in their intelligence, and those are going to be very, very, very weak things. They can't carry the world now. The whole world and all the world's wise men and expert ones, they are in *bahru-l-*

---

[288]*Jahiliyyah.* The first Period of Ignorance refers to the period of idolatry and unawareness of the divine guidance prior to Islam.

hayrah,[289] astonishment. They now understand that we know nothing, we know nothing.

America, which was claiming, "We are at the top point," is now wondering how it can save itself, and second, following them, the German people. The German government is saying, "We are strong ones, we are never going to fall!" while it is coming on them. Whoever claims that I am powerful, quickly he comes to the point of weakness, the point of zero.

You may go up, up, up—one, two, three, four, five, ten, twenty, fifty, hundred, thousands and millions, billions, trillions, quadrillions—but the scale that it reaches, you can't reach. Can you reach the point of trillions or quadrillions or pentillions or sextillions? You may put zero, but this is a limitless scale. You are always nothing, you are always at the point of zero. You must know this!

Now, before Jesus Christ comes, before Sayyidina Mehdi ﷺ comes, Allah Almighty wants to teach people. *Wake up, O people, wake up!* Try to understand who are you, who created you, and how He deals with His creatures. Wake up and look! But people are not yet opening their eyes. Allah Almighty wants to make them wake up but they are still sleeping.

This is too big, big a lesson, heavenly powers trying to make people wake up because the time of Sayyidina al-Mehdi and Jesus Christ is arriving. When their time arrives, that means the end of life on this planet. It will finish and the Day of Resurrection will come.

And Allah Almighty wants to wake up people, and because people do not believe in holy books, He is showing them something

---

[289]A sea of bewilderment.

that they may understand—that they may understand! *Amirna, ya ma'ashara-l-anbiya, an nukallimu-n-naas 'ala qadar 'uqulihim.*[290] You must speak, you must address people to the extent that their understanding reaches. Don't go higher. At their understanding level you must speak.

This is a heavenly declaration to all nations through the language of Heavens. O people, look! We are not making a heavenly address to you, but We are speaking to you in such a way that you may understand. You are learning but not understanding.

That is another sign that the Last Day is just at the door. O people, think about it and wake up!

And then, we are coming from that [to our original theme]. O our master, help us! *Destur, ya Sayyidi! Meded!* We are asking for heavenly support.

They are not understanding heavenly support, always denying it, but now they are beginning to understand what is heavenly support. And we hope that it will be the beginning of a new understanding. They must change their ways of understanding.

May Allah forgive us! We are in need to be forgiven, and forgiveness comes by the way of leaving forbidden things. If you do not leave forbidden things, never will there come heavenly forgiveness. Heavenly support never comes to people if they do not leave the forbidden. Leave the forbidden, and forgiveness will come from Heavens, and following forgiveness will come blessings. And you should be saved at that time.

---

[290]We have been ordered, O assembly of prophets, to speak to people according to the degree of their understanding.

May Allah forgive us! For the honour of most honoured one in His Divine Presence, Sayyidina Muhammad ﷺ—*Fateha!*

34

"PUT YOUR EGO UNDER YOUR FEET AND MAKE IT BE A SERVANT."

As-salamu 'alaikum! Welcome to you! Do you know for what you have come?

Destur, ya Sultanu-l-Awliya! Meded! Meded! O holy ones, we know nothing except what you are teaching us. We don't know what to say except what you are making us say. We are not listeners unless you make us be listeners because our egos are the worst, worst creatures in creation.

Destur, ya Rijal-Allah! Meded! A'udhu bil-Lahi min ash-Shaytani-r-rajim. Bismillahi-r-Rahmani-r-Rahim. O our Lord, don't leave us in the hands of our egos. And you are trying to *ikram*,[291] to give your best to your ego, but it never tries to give its best to you, always insisting on being at the top point of power and always insisting on making you its servant, never accepting that you can do a service for anyone else.

Your ego, our ego, is worse than Shaytan! Our egos are saying, "Don't work for anyone except Me! You must work for Me, you must try to make Me happy! I don't like that you are going to be for

---

[291]Honor, respect, i.e. pampering.

any one besides Me! I am your Lord, I am your king, and you must try only to make *Me* happy!"

And people now, they are trying to do that. Everyone wants to make himself happy and to be Number One everywhere, and everyone wants to be the most respected one. Our egos are never happy to make anyone else respected within themselves, saying, "Where are you going? You are going to do something by which you will try to give your full respect to another person, while *I* am here? Why you are going to the mosque—for what?" because praying is the utmost respect to our Lord. And it is saying, "Why are you going to the mosque? I like that I must be the only respected one, I don't like anyone else to be. You should be most respectful to Me, and I am also asking from all people that they should be most respectful to Me!" Everyone is trying to do that.

"Elementary school, you finished elementary? Eh, _____, you have a certificate from elementary school?"

"So many!"

And our ego is saying, "No, it is not enough to have an elementary school certificate. After elementary school, I must attend a secondary school to get a higher certificate!"[292]

When finishing, he is saying, "So many people have this. And they will not give me high respect if they have graduated from high school or college or a university or academy. Therefore, I must try to reach the top point of science and knowledge." He is saying, "I must try to bring a certificate!"

---

[292]This and other related comments about higher education must be understood in the context of Middle Eastern society where higher education is often a sign of status and a source of false pride.

And I am saying, "*Yahu*, there is no job for you."

"Doesn't matter! When I speak, I will carry my diploma so that people may know how they should address me—to say, 'O sir, O our master! Oh, you are a lecturer,' or 'You are a professor!' They must give respect to me!"

This is a secret, secret desire in the hearts of people who are under their egos' control. "For what am I studying? To be respected!"

So many girls are coming and saying, "Now we have finished secondary school and we want to go to university, to study."

I am saying, "For what? You must marry!"

"No, no, no! If I haven't any diploma or certificate, people they will think, 'That one is coming from the desert or from a village. She knows nothing!' They will not respect me. But when I study in high school and I make three copies, one copy I will put outside my door so that people who are coming and going will see it and say, 'Oh!' When they come to visit my family, my home, I will put that diploma high, high, high up."

I am asking, "Who is that in the photo?"

"Me, when I was young."

"Eh, you were young. This is you?"

"Yes, sir, yes, sir! I have a certificate from Oxford University or Sorbonne University or Toronto or Moronto, so that people must give their respect to me according to that."

"You are married?"

"Unmarried."

"Why?"

"Because I was trying to get that paper."

"And now?"

"Eh, I am waiting."

"Eh!"

Her mum is saying, "I am looking for a good one, a respected one, for my daughter." And I am asking if she can't find any suitable one, like ____.

"We are thinking of making our daughter into a pickle." They are buying a jar, to make her pickled in it. "But we are now thinking whether we should use an ordinary jar or a Phonecian jar. They are saying that you can find such a jar in Cyprus."

That is Shaytan's teaching to people. "You must try to be a V.I.P. person, to be respected!" Wrong, wrong, wrong, and they are mistaken! Respect is for those who are respected by Heavens, not with that paper. Yes, you may do so many copies, changing the name and putting there.

"How many years was she in university?"

"Eh, now she is thirty-three years old, and she was in university for eighteen years."

"Okay, masha'Allah! Capital for your daughter because she reached forty years and never found a suitable one!"

"No, no, no, sir! It is enough to have such a certificate! Marriage is not important. Important is that I must be respected everywhere because I graduated from Bonn University or Berlin University, or I am coming from Wien University."

"Or we are coming from Lefke European University."

They are saying, "We never saw this 'Lefke European Universi-ty.'" Therefore, I am sending ____ there. He can jump very well. When he walks, ten of these are running after him. Yes? Can you do that?

Yes, sir! *Bala'un 'adhim!*[293] This is a curse, people cursed through shaytanic ways. Everywhere, you should find in front of you one shaytan or one servant of Shaytan, to put mankind down, down, down, deep, deep, disappearing!

What are we saying? "We have a certificate from Cambridge!" For everything, our ego is saying, "I must be Number One! I never like to respect anyone else!" Ego is saying, and teaching foolish and ignorant people, "You must be a respected one! And you must re-spect Me more than anyone else!" Therefore, people are wholly un-der the command of their egos. They are not servants of the Lord. They have been thrown out and cursed, cursed!

What do they put on the necks of animals? Most people are us-ing that for their horses and donkeys, a different-coloured one. Their egos want to be with them in such a way. *Subhanallahu-l-'Aliyu-l-'Adhim!*

Therefore, I am afraid of falling into what they have fallen into. They are losing their *dunya* as well as their eternal life. If you want an eternal life of full pleasure, full love, full respect, full wisdoms, full powers, full beauty, you must follow the ways of heavenly people.

Now, no one is following a heavenly person. They are saying, "No, we are not in need. Rather, we are trying to follow anyone *ex-*

---

[293]The greatest misfortune, calamity, trial.

cept those holy ones. Leave those holy ones whose time is over! Finished; they have no value! We must look for another way."

This is their "other way," and Shaytan is making them be like himself, because he was always insisting and trying to be the Number One deputy of the Lord of Heavens. He was even asking further, to be one step from the Lord of Heavens. Therefore, when Allah Almighty ordered, "Fall into *sajdah* to Adam," Shaytan said, "No, I am not going to do that!" That means, "I will not listen to You. I will not make *sajdah* to You, also!" Therefore, he was kicked down!

O people, put your egos under your feet and make them be servants, to accept their Creator's and their Lord's command! You must try to do this so that the Lord of Heavens accepts you as His servant. If you do not do this, you are going to be slaves of your egos and Shaytan.

May Allah forgive us! For the honour of the most honoured one in His Divine Presence, Sayyidina Muhammad ﷺ—*Fateha!*

35

THE SEED OF LOVE IN OUR HEARTS

As-salamu 'alaikum! Welcome to you!

Allah Almighty, He likes His servants to work only for His pleasure. You are coming here for Allah, you are not coming here to enjoy yourself. It is not an enjoyment place. It is a place—what are you saying? *Bu şeylere cami değil ama halvethane eski zamanda.*[294] In olden times, people they were going, leaving *dunya*, leaving everything, and going to a *halvethane*, like a monastery. What do you say for 'monastery' in Arabic.[295]

This is a humble place, and people are coming here to learn something, to do some practicing. Therefore, we are saying, "Welcome! Welcome on behalf of the most beloved servant of Allah Almighty, Rasul-Allah ﷺ [Maulana stands up and gives *salam* to the Prophet], and we hope that it is going to be a pleasure for you because you are making Allah Almighty pleased with you.

Pleasure does not come from outside. Now people are trying to make themselves enjoy with so many things, but they never become

---

[294]These things are not a mosque but a place of *khalwah* [spiritual seclusion] in olden times.

[295]Here, the Shaykh adds, *"Ayet-i Kerime var hakkında.* There is a holy verse concerning it," referring to *"And if it were not that Allah checks people, some by means of others, there would surely have been destroyed monasteries [sawami'], churches, synagogue and mosques in which the name of Allah is much mentioned"* (22:40).

228

happy. They may go with pleasure but when they come back, they come sad. But in such a place that we can call a small place, if anyone comes sad, he or she is going to open, going to open. But whoever goes with pleasure, particularly nightlife people, who think that if tonight we go to this or that or that place, it should be a pleasure for us, it never happens. Coming back, and they are sad, not enjoying.

Such a meeting, such a place as here, those people are not interested in, particularly since most people now are depressed, depressed people. They want to get out of depression through night life, going to night clubs, casinos or cinemas or such places that are calling people, "Come and enjoy! Come and enjoy!" But it is the opposite. They go there to find pleasure with themselves but they come back, not enjoying, not enjoying!

A'udhu bil-Lahi min ash-Shaytani-r-rajim! We are running to Allah Almighty to save us from the cheating of Shaytan, because everything he shows us as a pleasure finally becomes not a pleasure or not a place of enjoyment.

Alhamdulillah! *"Al-hamdu lil-Lahi-l-ladhi hadana li-hadha.'*[296] We are thankful to our Lord, Allah Almighty, that we are coming here, and all the heaviness of our egos is leaving us and we are getting to be joyful, *khafif*, light. That heaviness leaves us. If not, I don't think that people would come here from far distances to stay longer.

Alhamdulillah, they are coming here. We are not using such things by which those casinos, night clubs and other places are calling people to enjoy themselves but finally they want to go back to their homes. Nothing is here except that we are trying to pray, we

---

[296] *"Praise be to Allah, who has guided us to this."* (7:43)

are trying to worship, we are asking to hear something that belongs to our spirituality. Even if no one is speaking here, the atmosphere that is in this place gives them rest and they are saying, "We would like to stay here more. O Shaykh, can you give us a chance to be here longer?" And most people, when they leave, they are saying, "O Shaykh, when may we come here again?" That means they are happy. And we are doing nothing here.

My level, I am not saying it is the same level as you. I am looking at my level as lower than your levels. But this atmosphere gives people something, some rest and pleasure in their hearts. That is the difference between this and their shaytanic places that are calling people, "Come and enjoy!" We are not saying, "Come and enjoy physically." We are saying something that belongs only to their spirituality, and spirituality is finding what it needs and asking to stay— not to go back, to be here. It is a good sign.

It is not a business, no. Now, so many places you can find and they are imitation spiritual centers—imitation, not real ones. Because if you want to go there, you must first send a letter, asking from its people, "O Center-Keeper, we want to come for a seminar."

_____ went. I was asking him some questions. They were saying, "Oh! We want to come and to be with you and to make a seminar." Yes!

"O my brother, I am interested in some spirituality. And I heard that in Switzerland, when winter comes, it should be good for us to visit in the snowy mountains and to enjoy, also, by skiing, coming like this, coming like that. And we will make a seminar."

The second one was saying, "I heard that there is a seminar in Cyprus."

"Seminar in Cyprus? We never heard! Maybe a coffee shop."

"It looks like a coffee shop. Very happy place!"

"I don't think so. They have skiing?"

"No, no, no! No skiing, but they are sitting in a place like a flock of sheep and never complaining. We are giving boiling water. Then putting in it dry bread, and they are saying, 'So, so, so, so tasteful soup!'" Only Green Shaykh is saying, "O Shaykh, every day water, dry bread! Let us slaughter a cow or an ox, that I may put it in that big pot. That is what I want, seeing every day soup from old vegetables, old aubergines—in the morning aubergines, at night potatoes, in the morning tomatoes! I am getting to be like this. What is this, O Shaykh? Let us bring an ox, slaughtering it and eating!"

[Shaykh Nazim:] "*Yahu*, I am cooking one ox for people throughout one year!"

[Green Shaykh:] "For what, one year? We may eat it from morning up to evening, finishing!"

Therefore, people are asking to go to seminars. I am asking, "What do they give?"

"Eh, seminar people, they are vegetarian."

"Huh? What is that 'vegetarian'?"

"Only giving us a quarter of an egg, two olives, one spoonful of *sebze*, vegetables, and bread. If you are doing this like this, you may put it all in your mouth at once, finishing. But I think it is good for us. We must go!"

And they are going. When they come back, I am asking, "How did you find that place?"

"Good, only we would have died if we had stayed there more than one month. We would go to the graveyard from not eating!"

"What about the seminar?"

"Seminar, we never understood it."

"You had dancing?"

"Eh, dancing—eh!"

"There was a piano?"

"Piano, yes."

"Oh-ho!"

"And I was interesting in the *kemençe,* violin."

"How much did you pay?"

"We only paid one hundred euros daily. For ten days, one thousand euros."

"It is not too much."

"Doesn't matter if it is too much, even, because we were changing our atmosphere there, looking at each other, seeing who may be for me, for you, who may be better for me."

"Don't speak! We are listening to the seminar! Don't look right or left! For what have you come?"

"We must look for someone, if it is . . . Because my wife left me two months ago, I am also looking for someone to be like my . . . I am looking."

"O my brother, you never understand anything!"

"Doesn't matter! I did not come to understand. I came to look, to be happy!"

"Yes, sir!"

Now everything, O our listeners, everything is imitation—imitation, no reality. Do you think that it is a medicine? Instead, it is going to be a poisoned syrup for you, to make you to sleep—upstairs and downstairs, also. And you are drinking it. And they are coming and saying, "O my brother, what are they eating? They are sleeping the whole night! We do not know who is sleeping with us. What is this?'

"This is the seminar of the coming twenty-fifth century. We are preparing people for those seminars." All drunk! All drunk!

Alhamdulillah, we are here a humble meeting, humble gathering (only *such* people, too much jumping). You know *hadra*, making *hadra?*[297] I am afraid that they may reach up and fall on people. If falling on me, it may harm my legs. Therefore I am escaping, *masha'Allah*, up, up, up! Without wings, asking to go up. Be a little bit patient!

Merhaban, welcome! Welcome to you! What shall we do? Eh, they may ask, "What is Shaykh saying?"

"Shaykh is saying that we never heard such a thing, making an analysis."

"He is an analyst?"

"Yes, a first class analyst, making an analysis of our characteristics, making a deep analysis of our souls, and we went away better than we came. When we went there, we saw that our feelings had changed, changed. We were happy! We didn't understand that happiness while we were there but when we were leaving, our feeling had changed and now we are enjoying! What he put into our hearts, that made us happy and joyful."

---

[297]An active form of *dhikr*, done while standing and often with movement, such as continuous bowing, rocking back and forth, and so forth.

"That is the meaning of *hibret*.[298] That is wisdom; giving to you wisdom."

"We do not understand wisdom. We only understand that his speech does something to our real being, to our spirituality. We are feeling and understanding and looking and seeing!"

May Allah forgive us! *Bismillahi-r-Rahmani-r-Rahim*. We are coming here in the Name of Allah Almighty. We are asking to be good servants to our Lord. We are coming to learn how we can be good servants because we are all occupied by slavery to Shaytan and to *dunya*. We are losing our precious lives for nonsense.

We are learning *something:* that we are servants of our Creator, and how we must deal with Him because He created us for His servanthood. Where? In His Divine Presence! And we are only beginners. We hope that that, like a small seed, you may plant it and finally it is going to be huge oak tree. And our feelings are on that way, that what Shaykh is giving us, even a very small seed in our hearts, that is the seed of love. And real love is for our Lord, real love is for His beloved ones, first of all for His most beloved servant, Sayyidina Muhammad ﷺ, and it is growing, growing.

It is not from eating and drinking and dressing. It is something that is granted from Heavens to people on earth because their real life is continuing only through love. If that love is finished, they are finishing! And this assembly, this meeting, gives power to our very small *bizr,* seed, of love!

---

[298]Ar., *khibrah, khubr:* experience, knowledge.

Only be with love because this universe is just created for love, the love of the Lord of Heavens to His most beloved servant, Sayyidina Muhammad 鐵. And we are asking for that.

May Allah forgive us! *As-salamu 'alaikum wa rahmatullahi wa barakatuhu. Fateha!*

36

MUSLIMS ARE THE MOST FORTUNATE PEOPLE

As-salamu 'alaikum. On this holy night of Shawwal Mu'adhdham, its second *laylatu-l-Juma*,[299] we are asking forgiveness from Allah Almighty. We are trying to be humble servants to Allah Almighty.

Don't think that His servants are a handful people. Countless universes, countless servants, angels, countless creatures that Allah Almighty created, they are glorifying Allah Almighty. This very, very, very, very humble and small meeting He granted us, during these holy months, to reach His endless Favour Oceans and Blessing Oceans.

He granted us a chance to follow His most beloved and glorified servant, Sayyidina Muhammad ﷺ. He is our honour, as well as the honour of all nations, as well as being the honour of all creation. All, everything that He created, was just created for the honour of the most honoured one in His Divine Presence, Sayyidina Muhammad ﷺ, and everything that comes into existence comes for his honour.[300]

---

[299]The second Thursday night of the month of Shawwal, "the Esteemed".

[300]Referring to a *hadith qudsi* (a *hadith* conveyed to the Prophet ﷺ by divine inspiration, its meaning being Allah's, while the words are Prophet Muhammad's), stating,
Footnote continued…

O people, you are fortunate! We are the most fortunate people that we are from his distinguished nation, from his most honoured *ummah*. And we have been granted that endless honour without our doing anything. Allah Almighty just granted it to us.

Be clever and think about it, and try to be a thankful servant of your Lord, Allah Almighty. Don't say, "I have something to do." Nothing can be more valuable than working for the honour of our most glorified Prophet ﷺ. What did he bring us from the Divine Presence? Countless honours!

O people try to reach that! Today we are here, tomorrow we are going. If not tomorrow, the next day. If not the next day, the next month; if not the next month, another year, another year, another year. But we must know that we are going to His Divine Presence because we have been invited.

The holy month [Shawwal] is also once again visiting and beginning to reach its end. Tonight is the second night of Shawwal al-Mu'adhdham. After four weeks, it will be gone. And our lives are running, running, and day by day our lives are going down and we are reaching our end. O people, think about that day when we are going to leave this life and we will jump to another line of life that should be glorified up to eternity. And eternity means never-ending!

May Allah forgive us! And we are trying, *insha'Allah*. We hope that we should be an accepted nation, for the honour of the Seal of the Prophets, may Allah bless him and grant to him more and more and more and more honour and glorifying. *Amin! Al-Fateha!*

"If it were not for you, [O Muhammad], I would not have created creation." (*Ihya* of Imam Ghazali; it was considered *da'if* by Imam Suyuti, but its meaning was affirmed, even by Ibn Taymiyah)

37

ONLY TITLES GIVEN BY HEAVENS ARE IMPORTANT

As-salamu 'alaikum! A'udhu bil-Lahi min ash Shaytani-r-rajim. Bismillahi-r- Rahmani-r-Rahim.

The worst and most dangerous enemy of mankind, of the children of Adam, is Satan. You must teach that first to your descendants, after teaching them to say "Allah Allah Allah." That is going to be their first word, the Holy Name of Allah, and we hope that, at the end of their lives, the last word coming from their lips will be "Allah Allah Allah."

38

KEEPING TO THE LEVEL OF SERVANTHOOD

(This *sohbet* took place after a lengthy break in *sohbets* due to Maulana Shaykh Nazim being ill.)

O people, we are saying, *"A'udhu bil-Lahi min ash-Shaytani-ash-rajim. Bismillahi-r-Rahmani-r-Rahim."*

Allah Almighty *sharafana,* gives honour, endless honour to us and grants from His endless Mercy Oceans because He granted us to say, *"La ilaha illa-Lah, Sayyiduna Muhammadun Rasul-Allah ﷺ,"* and He is granting us to be able to say, *"Bismillahi-r-Rahmani-r-Rahim."*

"Bismillahi-r-Rahmani-r-Rahim"—that is the key of all Mercy Oceans, to say *"Bismillahi-r-Rahmani-r-Rahim." "Bismillahi-r-Rahmani-r-Rahim"* opens all Mercy Oceans, and then there are running on us divine blessings.

We are asking forgiveness during these holy days, during this holy month of Dhu-l-Hijjah,[301] asking from our Lord to grant us to be visitors to the House of the Lord, *Bait-Ullah.* To be there for a

---

[301]The twelfth month of the Islamic calendar, the month of *Hajj,* the annual pilgrimage to Mecca.

visit, even once during our life, that is the key of Paradise. Whoever may visit that holy House, the House of the Lord, finally he must reach to Allah Almighty's blessings in the eternal life.

O people, *dunya* is nothing! Try to be honoured, here and Hereafter. Don't leave your Lord's blessings for *dunya*. *Dunya* is nothing! It is not our final goal, no.

O people, I am sorry to say that now all nations, all mankind, are running after *dunya*, asking to reach more of *dunya*. That is very sad for mankind, and we are seeing that mankind are doing their worst. Instead of doing their best, men are trying to do their worst for everyone.

Allah Almighty, He created mankind to be obedient servants to Him, not to leave His divine servanthood and run after Shaytan. It is so simple, in all divine Messages. All messengers came only to teach mankind what is their mission during this life, what they must do, how they must live.

Two things. First, Allah Almighty is asking from you, O mankind, to keep our promise that we would be His servants, that we would try to keep His servanthood.[302] Before everything, you must think about this first goal: to be His servants, to keep His servanthood. Before everything else, you must first try to fulfill His servanthood.

And then, the second order concerning your mission that has reached mankind through all messages, through all messengers: The first is to be obedient servants to their Lord, and the second is to do their best in everything, firstly for mankind.

---

[302]On the Day of Promises; see 7:172.

You must try to do your best for everyone, particularly for man. Then, because Allah Almighty created countless creatures, we have also been ordered to safeguard all creatures, not to make them restless or to do a bad action. Allah created them and He knows for what He created them. Nothing is created without a wisdom. Everything is created for some reason and everything is created to do its best for mankind, so that men have been ordered to do their best for every creature.

O people, it is so easy, what heavenly messages are giving to all mankind. Names are not important. To say, "I am Muslim" or "Christian" or "Catholic" or "Protestant" or "Orthodox" or "Jewish"—that title is not important. All of us are from Adam and Eve, and everyone must keep their honour as a man, as caliphs, deputies, of the Lord of Heavens. The highest honour has been granted to you, and you must try to keep that honour with you till you reach the Divine Presence of your Lord, the Creator, the Lord of Heavens.

So simple, but people are doing so many things and they do not understand what they are doing, and mostly they are trying to follow Shaytan and shaytanic ways. Otherwise, it is so easy, our creation, for what we have been created—to be servants and to do good to every creature in creation.

O people, that is *ta'lim*, heavenly teaching, through prophets, to everyone living who is going on the wrong way. Whoever is going the wrong way must be punished.

O people, try to keep your honour here and Hereafter. You should be honoured. Try to do the most meaningful, most glorified works, so that you should be a glorified servant in the Divine Presence. Don't forget your servanthood! If you do not forget your servanthood, you must also try to know the Lord Almighty's Lordship. He is the Lord and you are a servant. Don't try to pass in front of that limit. That is your limit, to stay on the level of servant-hood. Don't try to claim that I am something; no! Lordship is only for Allah and servanthood is for you.

Don't claim anything with such *uyuduruk*, imitation, titles. Don't think that imitation titles will make you go up to the level of lordship. *Hasha, astaghfirullah!* Lordship is only for One! No one, not even prophets, said, "I have reached the level of Lordship." No, you can't say that. You are only a servant. Lordship is only for One. *"Qul: Huwa-Lahu Ahad,"*[303] no second one. Not understanding that makes people lose their ways, lose their goals, lose their honours.

Try to understand! This is not my speech, but it is from heavenly support, making a weak servant address all nations that have lost their ways. They have lost the understanding that they are only serv-ants. A servant may be in the presence of a king or *sultan* or emper-or, he may be close to the *sultan,* but he is never going to be a *sultan* himself. Understand?

This is a *tabligh,* declaration, a divine declaration to save people from coming terrible, terrible events. Whoever wants to be saved during dangerous and very terrible events, whoever wants to be shel-tered here and Hereafter, he must try to leave imitation titles, and he must try to know that he is only a simple servant and that servant-hood never brings a person to Lordship. Lordsip is only for Allah.

O our Lord, send us someone who can teach us who we are and for what we have been brought into existence, and how we may be sheltered, here and Hereafter. For the honour of the most hon-oured servant in Your Divine Presence, Sayyidina Muhammad ﷺ.

---

[303] *"Say, [O Muhammad]: 'He is Allah, One.'"* (112:1)

Allahumma, salli 'ala Sayyidina Muhammadin, Nabiyi-l-Ummiyyi, wa 'ala ahlihi wa sahbihi wa sallim.[304] Don't try to rise up to Lordship. Just keep down! Whoever does not keep his station should be kicked down, like Shaytan. Try to be like the Seal of Prophets, Sayyidina Muhammad ﷺ. That Shaytan wants you to be like himself, and he fell down. No honour for him, here and Hereafter!

May Allah forgive us and shelter us, here and Hereafter. For the honour of the most honoured one in His Divine Presence, Sayyidina Muhammad—*Fateha!*

---

[304]Our Lord, bless and grant peace and blessings to our master Muhammad, the Unlettered Prophet, and to his family and Companions.

39

THE POWER OF ISLAM

As-salamu 'alaikum! 'Eid mubarak! Ashhadu an la ilaha illa-Lah wa ashhadu anna Sayyiduna Muhammadun 'abduhu wa habibuhu wa rasul-Allah.[305]

O people, we are saying, *"A'udhu bil-Lahi min ash-Shaytani-r-rajim. Bismillahi-r-Rahmani-r-Rahim. La haula wa la quwwata illa bi-Lahi-l-'Aliyi-l-'Adhim.*

I was not thinking that I would be able to come for 'Eid prayer,[306] I was feeling that I am weak. But for the honour of that holy day on which Allah Almighty grants His forgiveness and blessings to *ummati Muhammad*,[307] particularly to those who are on 'Arafat and going from Muzdalifah to Mina,[308] He is giving to me, also. From Allah Almighty, blessings are coming and I am feeling better. There-

---

[305]Peace be upon you! A blessed 'Eid! I bear witness that there is no deity except Allah and I bear witness that Muhammad is His slave and His beloved and the Messenger of Allah.

[306]The prayer of 'Eid al-Adha, the Festival of Sacrifice at the time of the *Hajj*, about which the Shaykh is speaking here.

[307]The nation or community of Muhammad.

[308]'Arafat is the huge plain eighteen miles outside Mecca where all the pilgrims spend the afternoon of the ninth of Dhu-l-Hijjah up to sunset engaged in supplication. From there, they travel the few miles to Muzdalifah, a barren, rocky tract, where they gather pebbles for the stoning of the three pillars representing Satan while encamped at Mina during the following two or three days.

fore, I am only making a reminder of something that is granted to me tonight to say to you.

O people in the East and West, from the North to the South! The live religion, living religion, is only Islam! I was looking at television last night and seeing people, how they are moving from 'Arafat to Muzdalifah, saying, "*Labbayk, Allahumma, labbayk! Labbayka, la sharika Laka, labbayk. Inna-l-hamda wa ni'mata Laka wa-l-mulk. La sharika Laka!*"[309] They were moving like rivers! They were saying that there were three million people, coming and moving.

I was thinking about these three million who are able to come and visit the holy sites. And then I was told that, if there were a chance for thirty million, what about that? Thirty million would also be running! What about if there could be granted a chance to three hundred million Muslims to come to that holy place—what do you think? They would run, also, full of respect and love, three hundred million Muslims, running! What about if it was going to be three billion people, Muslims, granted a chance to come to 'Arafat, and 'Arafat was so big and the road so wide? What do you think? Three billion people, they would ask to go there and to run!

What about you? Is anyone given a chance to go to *Hajj* and stays here? No, *subhanallah!* Therefore, when I was looking last night—*subhanallahu-l-'Aliyu-l-'Adhim!*—it was an ocean of people, moving rivers. Those moving rivers were never tiring. They were saying, "*Labbayk, Allahumma, labbayk,*" those words.

---

[309]The repeated call of the *Hajj* pilgrims, meaning, "Here I am, O Lord, here I am! Here I am! No partner have You [in divinity]. Here I am! Indeed, the praise and the favor is Yours, and the dominion. No partner have You!"

O people, mankind must think about it! What must they think about? Which engine *muharrik*, can move them or which one is able to make millions of people move from East to West, from West to East, from North to South, from South to North? For what do people come? Does someone pay them to come and visit that place and move through deserts?

Yahu! People, the twenty-first century's people, they have lost their minds! They have lost thinking about it. They are drunk people. Think about it! You should find that Islam, it is a living religion, supported by Heavens. Heavenly power is making all those people move. But such people do not think.

That Pope, why does he not think? That Patriarch, why does he not think? That Haham Başı, Chief Rabbi, why does he not think? Where is their power? Christians, where is their power? O Jewish people, where is your power? O millions of Hindus, where are your powers? We are here! Where is your power? Show it!

"Islam is coming! We are afraid that Islam is coming to Europe!" *Raghman 'ala anfihim*—in spite of themselves, against their will, Islam is coming, coming and covering from East to West, from North to South, over oceans, on continents! Even though they are not happy about it, Islam is coming. *Alhamdulillah!* That is the biggest reward, biggest honour, biggest glory for a Muslim, who can say, "I am Muslim. I like being a Muslim!"

O people, hear, listen, and come and obey the holy command of Heavens! May Allah bless us in this holy month, this holy day!

Allahu Akbar, Allahu Akbar; la ilaha illa-Lah.

Allahu Akbar, Allahu Akbar, wa lil-Lahi-l-hamd.

Allahu Akbar, Allahu Akbar, la ilaha illa-Lah;

Allahu Akbar, Allahu Akbar, wa lil-Lahi-l-hamd.

Allahu Akbar, Allahu Akbar, la ilaha illa-Lah;

Allahu Akbar, Allahu Akbar, wa lil-Lahi-l-hamd.[310]

We hope that there should be a change, a grant, power coming, more power for the Muslim world, for Muslims, and that the satanic sultanate is going to be under my feet! *Fateha!*

Allahu Akbar, Allahu Akbar, la ilaha illa-Lah.

Allahu Akbar, Allahu Akbar, wa lil-Lahi-l-hamd.

---

[310]The chant of Muslims worldwide on the way to 'Eid prayers: "Allah is Most Great, Allah is Most Great. There is no deity except Allah. Allah is Most Great, Allah is Most Great, and all praise is for Him," repeated three times.

40

FOLLOW THE PATH OF *AHL AS-SUNNAH WA'L-JAMA'AH*

As-salamu 'alaikum! May Allah forgive us! This is like our Shaykh Hisham Efendi, giving a *khutbah*, sermon.

Dhu-l qima, valuable. If anyone asks to know his way, he must follow the way of Heavens. If we leave the way of Heavens, we will go to *hawiyah*. That means *daru-l-jahim*, that means *jahannam*, Hells. And we are running to the Prophet, peace be upon him, asking for his *shafa'ah*, intercession. Whoever gives his high respect to the Seal of Prophets should reach the intercession of the most beloved one, most glorified one in the Divine Presence. Follow him! As much as possible, give your high respect and glory to that one for whom all creation was created, as Allah Almighty says, "I created everything for your honor, O My beloved servant!"[311]

Beyond that belief, no way to reach honour from Allah Almighty. Allah Almighty never accepts anyone to leave respect for His most respected servant, never accepting anything else. Therefore, O people, now Shaytan is trying to destroy our beliefs that we have been with for fifteen centuries. Some no-mind people, they are asking to make another way, leaving out the Prophet and asking to reach Allah. If a person leaves the bridge, he can't step from one

---

[311]See footnote 300.

side to the other side. And Rasul-Allah, Sayyidina Muhammad ﷺ, he is the main door for all nations, for all creations, to reach Allah Almighty's glory and His blessings.

O people, keep your stand on the way of *Ahl as-Sunnah wa 'l-Jama'ah*.[312] Now, *shirzimatun qalila,* a small group, they are trying to change our beliefs and to make us followers of an unknown person, no value for him.[313] May Allah forgive us!

Pray for me! I have, by Allah Almighty's blessings, reached this old age and I am asking forgiveness from my Lord. I don't know how long I am going to be with you. Everyone should pass from here to Allah Almighty's Divine Presence. May Allah make our faces shine, shine with heavenly *nur,* to be glorified in the Divine Presence and acceptable.

O people, no work or *mashgala,* occupation, can be more valuable than Allah Almighty's worship. Leave everything and run to Allah Almighty's worship. That is the highest honour for you. If anyone leaves that and runs after *dunya,* no value for him.

O people, try to make Allah Almighty's obedience first! Then anything may be easy for you. May Allah protect you and shelter you. For the honour of the most honoured and beloved one, respected one, glorified one in His Divine Presence, Sayyidina Muhammad ﷺ—*Fateha!*

---

[312]People of the Prophet's *Sunnah* [Practice] and Congregation, i.e., Sunni Muslims, following the traditions of the Prophet and his noble Companions.

[313]A reference to the Wahabi/Salafi group, and its found Muhammad ibn 'Abdul-Wahhab.

GLOSSARY

Adab—good manners.

Aferin—bravo.

Alhamdulillah—Praise be to Allah. *Al-hamdu lil-Lahi Rabbi-l-'Alamin*—"All praise is for Allah, Lord of the worlds," the opening words of the Qur'an.

'Alim (pl., *'ulema*)—scholar.

Allahu Akbar—Allah is Most Great.

Aman—safety, security.

Akhirah—the Hereafter, the eternal life.

Allah Jalla Jalalahu—Allah, may His Glory be exalted.

Allahu Akbar—Allah is Most Great.

Amin—amen.

Ashadu an la ilaha illa-Lah wa ashadu anna Sayyidina Muhammadan 'abduhu wa rasuluhu—I bear witness that there is no deity except Allah and I bear witness that Muhammad is His slave and messenger.

As-salamu 'alaikum—Peace be upon you; *As-salamu 'alaikum wa rahmat-Allahi wa barakatuhu*—Peace be upon you and Allah's mercy and blessings.

Astaghfirullah—I seek Allah's forgiveness.

A'udhu bil-Lahi min ash-Shaytani-r-Rajim—I seek refuge with Allah from Satan the accursed.

Awliya (sing., *wali*)—Islamic saints, holy ones.

Ayah—Qur'anic verse, sign; *Ayat ul-karima*—noble verse.

Barakat/barakah—blessings.

Batil—falsehood.

Bismillahi-r-Rahmani-r-Rahim—In the name of Allah, the Beneficent, the Merciful.

Dajjal— the Anti-Christ, the arch-deceiver foretold by the Prophet for the End-Time of this world;

Destur, ya Sayyidi—Permission, O my master!

Din—religion.

Dunya—this world; the planet Earth.

Efendi—mister, sir.

'Eid—festival.

'Eid ul-Adha—the festival marking the *Hajj* observances.

'Eid al-Fitr—the festival marking the end of Ramadan.

Fateha—the opening verses of the Holy Qur'an.

Grandshaykh—Shaykh 'Abdullah ad-Daghestani, Shaykh Nazim's shaykh and immediate predecessor.

Hadith (pl., *ahadith*)—a verbatim, eye-witness report of the Prophet's words or actions.

Hajj—the pilgrimage to Mecca.

Haqq—Truth, Reality.

Haqqani—truthful, defemders of truth.

Haram—prohibited, forbidden.

Hasha!—never, God forbid!

Hazretleri—Turkish title of respect for *awliya*.

Hijri—the Islamic calendar, beginning with the *Hijrah*, the emigration of the Prophet from Mecca to Medina in the year 622 C.E.

Ikram—grant.

Imam—leader of prayers.

Insha'Allah—if Allah wills, God willing.

'Isa—Jesus.

Jalla Jallahu—May His glory be exalted!

Jama'at—congregation.

Khalifa—calih, vicegerent, deputy.

Kufr—unbelief, denial of truth.

La haula wa la quwwata illa bil-Lahi-l-'Aliyi-l-'Adhim—There is no power nor might except with Allah, the Most High, the Almighty.

Mahdi—the divinely-appointed leader whose coming at the end-time of this world is mentioned in several *ahadith*.

Malhamatu-l-Kubra—the Greatest Battle/Massacre/Slaughter, i.e., Armageddon.

Makkah—Mecca; *Makkatu-l-Mukarramah*—Mecca the Honoured.

Masha'Allah—as Allah willed.

Maulana (Tr., *Mevlana*)—our master.

Meded, ya Sultanu-l-Awliya—Support, king of the saints; *Meded, ya Rijal-Allah*—Support, O men of Allah.

Me'raj—the miraculous ascension of the Prophet to the Heavens and Allah's Divine Presence.

Mubarak—blessed.

Muharram—the first month of the Islamic *(Hijri)* calendar.

Mu'min—believer.

Murid—disciples or follower.

Nasihah—advice, counsel.

Rak'at—a unit or cycle of the prescribed Islamic prayer.

Rasul-Allah—the Messenger of Allah.

Sadanas—Satan.

Sahabah—the Prophet's Companions, the first Muslims.

Sajdah—prostration.

Salam—the Islamic greeting, *"Assalamu 'alaikum."*

Sayyidi—my master; *Sayyidina*—our master; *Sayyidatina*—our lady.

Shamu-sh-Sharif—Syria, often used specifically for Damascus.

Shari'at/Shari'ah—the divine legislation of Islam, based primarily on the teachings of the Holy Qur'an and the Prophet's *sunnah.*

Sohbet (Ar., *suhbah*)—discourse.

Subhanallah—glory be to Allah.

Sultan—ruler; *Sultanu-l-Awliya*—sultan of the saints.

Sunnah—the Prophet's practice; also, practices that are non-obligatory but were done regularly by the Prophet.

Tauba—repentance; *Tauba, astaghfirullah*—repentance; I seek Allah's forgiveness.

Ummah—nation, faith community.

Wahhabi—a strict group of Muslims emphasizing outward actions and literalist interpretations. They reject the concept of saints in Islam and accuse traditional Muslims of being polytheists.

Wali (pl., *awliya*)—holy one, saint.

Wird—daily Sufi devotions.

Ya Allah—O Allah!

Ya Rabbi—O my Lord!

The Path to Spiritual Excellence

By Shaykh Muhammad Nazim Adil al-Haqqani
ISBN 1-930409-18-4, Paperback. 180 pp.

This compact volume provides practical steps to purify the heart and overcome the destructive characteristics that deprive us of peace and inner satisfaction. On this amazing journey doubt, fear, and other negative influences that plague our lives - and which we often pass on to our children - can be forever put aside. Simply by introducing in our daily lives those positive thought patterns and actions that attract divine support, we can reach spiritual levels that were previously inaccessible.

In the Mystic Footsteps of Saints

By Shaykh Muhammad Nazim Adil al-Haqqani
Volume 1 - ISBN 1-930409-05-2
Volume 2 - ISBN 1-930409-09-5
Volume 3 - ISBN 1-930409-13-3, Paperback. Ave. length 200 pp.

Narrated in a charming, old-world storytelling style, this highly spiritual series offers several volumes of practical guidance on how to establish serenity and peace in daily life, heal emotional and spiritual scars, and discover the role we are each destined to play in the universal scheme.

Classical Islam and the Naqshbandi Sufi Tradition
By Shaykh Muhammad Hisham Kabbani
ISBN 1-930409-23-0, Hardback. 950 pp.
ISBN 1-930409-10-9, Paperback. 744 pp.

This esteemed work includes an unprecedented historical narrative of the forty saints of the renowned Naqshbandi Golden Chain, dating back to Prophet Muhammad in the early seventh century. With close personal ties to the most recent saints, the author has painstakingly compiled rare accounts of their miracles, disciplines, and how they have lent spiritual support throughout the world for fifteen centuries. Traditional Islam and the Naqshbandi Sufi Tradition is a shining tribute to developing human relations at the highest level, and the power of spirituality to uplift humanity from its lower nature to that of spiritual triumph.

The Naqshbandi Sufi Tradition
Guidebook of Daily Practices and Devotions
By Shaykh Muhammad Hisham Kabbani
ISBN 1-930409-22-2, Paperback. 352 pp.

This book details the spiritual practices which have enabled devout seekers to awaken certainty of belief and to attain stations of nearness to the Divine Presence. The Naqshbandi Devotions are a source of light and energy, an oasis in a worldly desert. Through the manifestations of Divine Blessings bestowed on the practitioners of these magnificent rites, they will be granted the power of magnanimous healing, by which they seek to cure the hearts of mankind darkened by the gloom of spiritual poverty and materialism.

This detailed compilation, in English, Arabic and transliteration, includes the daily personal dhikr as well as the rites performed with every obligatory prayer, rites for holy days and details of the pilgrimage to Makkah and the visit of Prophet Muhammad in Madinah.

Naqshbandi Awrad
of Mawlana Shaykh Muhammad Nazim Adil al-Haqqani
Compiled by Shaykh Muhammad Hisham Kabbani
ISBN 1-930409-06-0, Paperback. 104 pp.

This book presents in detail, in both English, Arabic and trans-literation, the daily, weekly and date-specific devotional rites of Naqshbandi practitioners, as prescribed by the world guide of the Naqshbandi-Haqqani Sufi Order, Mawlana Shaykh Muhammad Nazim Adil al-Haqqani.

Pearls and Coral, I & II
By Shaykh Muhammad Hisham Kabbani
ISBN 1-930409-07-9, Paperback. 220 pp.
ISBN 1-930409-08-7, Paperback. 220 pp.

A series of lectures on the unique teachings of the Naqshbandi Order, originating in the Near East and Central Asia, which has been highly influential in determining the course of human history in these regions. Always pushing aspirants on the path of Gnosis to seek higher stations of nearness to the God, the Naqshbandi Masters of Wisdom melded practical methods with deep spiritual wisdom to build an unequalled methodology of ascension to the Divine Presence.

The Sufi Science of Self-Realization
A Guide to the Seventeen Ruinous Traits, the Ten Steps to Discipleship and the Six Realities of the Heart
By Shaykh Muhammad Hisham Kabbani
ISBN 1-930409-29-X, Paperback. 244 pp.

The path from submersion in the negative traits to the unveiling of these six powers is known as migration to Perfected Character. Through a ten-step program, the author--a master of the Naqshbandi Sufi Path--describes the science of eliminating the seventeen ruinous characteristics of the tyrannical ego, to achieve purification of the soul. The sincere seeker who follows these steps, with devotion and discipline, will acheive an unveiling of the six powers which lie dormant within every human heart.

Encyclopedia of Islamic Doctrine
Shaykh Muhammad Hisham Kabbani
ISBN: 1-871031-86-9, Paperback, Vol. 1-7.

The most comprehensive treatise on Islamic belief in the English language. The only work of its kind in English, Shaykh Hisham Kabbani's seven volume Encyclopedia of Islamic Doctrine is a monumental work covering in great detail the subtle points of Islamic belief and practice. Based on the four canonical schools of thought, this is an excellent and vital resource to anyone seriously interested in spirituality. There is no doubt that in retrospect, this will be the most significant work of this age.

The Approach of Armageddon?
An Islamic Perspective
by Shaykh Muhammad Hisham Kabbani
ISBN 1-930409-20-6, Paperback 292 pp.

This unprecedented work is a "must read" for religious scholars and laypersons interested in broadening their understanding of centuries-old religious traditions pertaining to the Last Days. This book chronicles scientific breakthroughs and world events of the Last Days as foretold by Prophet Muhammad. Also included are often concealed ancient predictions of Islam regarding the appearance of the anti-Christ, Armageddon, the leadership of believers by Mahdi ("the Savior"), the second coming of Jesus Christ, and the tribulations preceding the Day of Judgment. We are given final hope of a time on earth filled with peace, reconciliation, and prosperity; an age in which enmity and wars will end, while wealth is overflowing. No person shall be in need and the entire focus of life will be spirituality."

Keys to the Divine Kingdom
By Shaykh Muhammad Hisham Kabbani
ISBN 1-930409-28-1, Paperback. 140 pp.

God said, "We have created everything in pairs." This has to do with reality versus imitation. Our physical form here in this earthly life is only a reflection of our heavenly form. Like plastic fruit and real fruit, one is real, while the other is an imitation. This book looks at the nature of the physical world, the laws governing the universe and from this starting point, jumps into the realm of spiritual knowledge - Sufi teachings which must be "tasted" as opposed to read or spoken. It will serve to open up to the reader the mystical path of saints which takes human beings from the world of forms and senses to the world within the heart, the world of gnosis and spirituality - a world filled with wonders and blessings.

My Little Lore of Light
By Hajjah Amina Adil
ISBN 1-930409-35-4, Paperback, 204 pp.

A children's version of Hajjah Amina Adil's four volume work, *Lore Of Light*, this books relates the stories of God's prophets, from Adam to Muhammad, upon whom be peace, drawn from traditional Ottoman sources. This book is intended to be read aloud to young children and to be read by older children for themselves. The stories are shortened and simplified but not changed. The intention is to introduce young children to their prophets and to encourage thought and discussion in the family about the eternal wisdom these stories embody.

Muhammad: The Messenger of Islam
His Life and Prophecy
By Hajjah Amina Adil
ISBN 1-930409-11-7, Paperback. 608 pp.

Since the 7th century, the sacred biography of Islam's Prophet Muhammad has shaped the perception of the religion and its place in world history. This book skilfully etches the personal portrait of a man of incomparable moral and spiritual stature, as seen through the eyes of Muslims around the world. Compiled from classical Ottoman Turkish sources and translated into English, this comprehensive biography is deeply rooted in the life example of its prophet.

Lightning Source UK Ltd.
Milton Keynes UK
UKOW041211070613

211914UK00002B/48/P